Rave Reviews for SMOKESTACK LIGHTNING:

A passionate paean to the elusive art of barbecue and the culture that surrounds it.

—FLORENCE FABRICANT, *The New York Times*

A book that every barbecue fanatic from the Eastern Seaboard to the Near West will love to read.

—JOHN EGERTON, author of *Southern Food*

Smokestack Lightning proves that smoked butt can inspire fine literature.

—*Time Out New York*

Of the three topics closest to every Southerner's heart—religion, politics, and barbecue—barbecue is unquestionably the most important. In *Smokestack Lightning*, Lolis Elie and Frank Stewart introduce us to the people and places that have immortalized Southern barbecue. This wonderful book evokes the familiar smell of hickory smoke and the mouth-watering taste every Southerner has known and loved since childhood.

—WILLIAM FERRIS, Director, Center for the Study of Southern Culture
University of Mississippi

One of the freshest, best-written recent books about food . . . sophisticated and funny.

—ED BEHR, *The Art of Eating*

Smokestack Lightning is slathered with great photographs, stories, savory recipes, and slabs of babyback-ribbing humor. A fiery, finger-licking, mouth-smearing classic.

—VERTAMAE GROSVENOR, NPR Cultural Correspondent and host of "Seasonings"

A wonderful journey . . . with history and insight into a food that is more American than apple pie.

—SUSAN TUCKER, *Louisiana Endowment for the Humanities*

Smokestack Lightning—it makes you hungry. Elie and Stewart's road trip makes you want to take one of your own.

—DWIGHT GARNER, *Newsday*

A thoughtful and absorbing study of national identity. Buy this book and, after devouring its contents . . . keep it on your coffee table for guests to peruse during your next *salon de littéraire*—over paper plates heaping with baked beans, coleslaw, and thinly sliced brisket.

—JEFF TURRENTINE, *The Dallas Morning News*

If you've ever wondered about the nuances of barbecue, this is the book to buy.

—HEATHER MCPHERSON, *The Orlando Sentinel*

A book that will set your brain to thinking while your stomach is growling.

—ED WARD, *The Austin Chronicle*

An insightful, humorous, and definitely unique book.

—SUE PUTMAN, *The Memphis Flyer*

A must-read for the barbecue aficionado, and a thoughtful, lively, and entertaining introduction to the world of barbecue for those who may wonder what all the fuss is about.

—MICHAEL SWINDLE, *St. Petersburg Times*

Smokestack Lightning

Adventures in the Heart of Barbecue Country

Lolis Eric Elie

Photographs by

FRANK STEWART

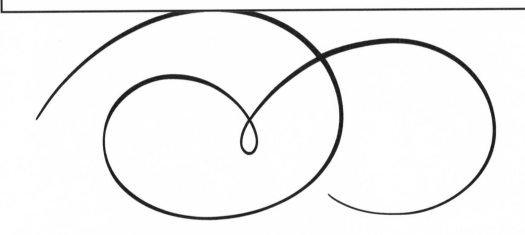

TEN SPEED PRESS
Berkeley | Toronto

To Gerri, Migel, Lolis Edward, and, of course, Grammy (1913–2002).
L.E.E.

To the men in my life: Frank Stewart, Sr., Charles K. Johnson, and Roy
DeCarava; and in memory of Romare Bearden, Adolf Caesar, and Phineas
Newborn. If they had not been the men that they were, I could not have
become the man that I am.
F.S.

Ten Speed Press
Box 7123
Berkeley, California 94707
www.tenspeed.com

Distributed in Australia by Simon and Schus-
ter Australia, in Canada by Ten Speed Press
Canada, in New Zealand by Southern Publish-
ers Group, in South Africa by Real Books, and
in the United Kingdom and Europe by Airlift
Book Company.

Cover design by Ed Anderson/Skout
Interior design by Concrete, Chicago

Library of Congress Cataloging-in-
Publication Data on file with the publisher.
ISBN 1-58008-660-8

Printed in Canada
First published in 1996 by Farrar, Straus and
Giroux.
First printing this edition, 2005

1 2 3 4 5 6 7 8 9 10 — 09 08 07 06 05

In Appreciation

Toni Yvonne Joseph
(September 8, 1961 ~ July 26, 1993)

Toni and Garvey DALLAS, TEXAS

When I told Miss Joseph about this book she probably laughed like everyone else, but she also took me and the book seriously enough to look up some old news stories on the subject. For a long time those clips made up my entire library of barbecue-related material.

Later I told her that Frank and I would be in Dallas, and she insisted that we stay with her and Garvey, who she assured us was the world's smartest dog. When we arrived she had a list of restaurants for us to visit and people for us to talk to (she was the one who told us about Mexia and barbacoa). She also had a bottle of cold champagne and one of those cheesecakes of hers, the only ones I've ever really liked.

Much of this and so much else is owed to her. At its best it echoes the champagne and cheesecake and laughter of those nights in Dallas with Toni and Garvey.

Contents

Preface

So, how's the cookbook coming?

That's a humbling question when you've chosen to see yourself as the Edward Gibbon of barbecue, the man self-anointed to chronicle decline and fall of a great American food tradition in a one-volume masterpiece. Besides, I was planning to go Gibbon one better. I had Frank Stewart, a photographer skilled in making the wry crack and capturing the decisive moment. But this question of the cookbook popped up throughout the preparation of this book. The question came from friends, family, and casual acquaintances. No one, it seems, could conceive of a barbecue book that was anything other than an anthology of recipes. It didn't matter that I had crafted a ready answer explaining the complexity of my subject matter and the brilliance of my approach to it. Even people who had endured my explanation would see me months later and ask the same question.

So, how's the cookbook coming?

I'll admit it was disheartening when I sometimes got the same reaction from the subjects of my book, the men and women whose talents I hoped to celebrate, analyze, and chronicle. Didn't they know that we were making history together? I still remember that day in Blue Goose, Tennessee, when the pit master Billy Anderson tired of our questions. "You fellers gon' through a lot of trouble just to write a book, ain't you?," he asked.

A lot of trouble indeed . . .

Our thesis was this. Barbecue reflects and embodies all the important themes in American history and culture—region, race, migration, immigration, religion, politics. Yet this art, so vital to our national identity was dying or at least endangered.

We were half right.

Many of the old people and places that we came to love and admire are dead.

We arrived in Kansas City just in time to tap Anthony Riecke's incredible memories of the good days when ribs were about ten or eleven cents a pound and the bad days when World War II–era rations meant you could hardly get meat at all. We were able to capture the indomitable spirit of Otis P. Boyd. The genius pit master never got his due or his coveted spot on *Oprah*, but even after all these years, his sauce is, without doubt, the best I ever tasted. A world away in San Antonio, we encountered Boyd's unwitting alter ego, Bob Wells, the cancer survivor who, like Boyd, served a subtly mild sauce and deliciously smoked lamb breast.

Years later, when we returned to many of these old places with David Bransten and Scott Stohler to make a documentary film, *Smokestack Lightning: A Day in the Life of Barbecue*, we were able to put the Memphis Masters Raymond Robinson, J.C. Hardaway, and the doyen of Hell's Half Acre, Mrs. Lerline Scott on film. Raymond, who had provided us with some many insights on this food and this life, would be dead before the film was completed. J.C. Hardaway and Mrs. Scott saw the film before they died, but neither is still with us. J.C.'s Kraft barbecue–sauce based recipe is in these pages, but Mrs. Scott was not nearly so public with her knowledge.

If we were half right in our prediction of barbecue's decline and fall, we were also half wrong. Any comparisons we might have liked to draw between ourselves and Gibbon were thankfully premature.

We still continue to lose many of the old places and some of the old traditions. But what we failed to adequately predict was the strongly nostalgic trend in the country these days, a longing for the old ways. A longing so strong that it has brought real barbecue to relative prominence in places where it was previously little more than a novelty. Danny Meyer and David Swinghamer, two of New York's most prominent fine dining restaurateurs, took a Southern turn in creating their restaurant venture, Blue Smoke, an upscale barbecue joint. And Las Vegas, famous for its fascination with the new, is the latest outpost for Mike Mills's baby back ribs. And how were we to know that Ed Mitchell, a North Carolinian who had long ago left his family's grocery store to work at Ford Motor Company would return to his whole-hog roots and open a barbecue restaurant and catering outfit? In California, where the great black migration brought barbecue to Oakland and Watts, a half century later the great migration of Brooklyn Jews, (a much smaller and less celebrated event) brought Bob Kantor and his brisket and homemade pies to the Haight in San Francisco. And, despite the uncharitable comment we made about allowing sons-in-law into the barbecue business, at Big Bob Gibson's in Decatur, Alabama, Chris Lilly married the founder's great granddaughter and seems to be that rare in-law who hasn't ruined a great barbecue tradition.

Now, nearly a decade after the first edition of this book was published, there are details that are no longer exactly as they were. There are places that have since closed; there are other places that deserve to be included, but that we didn't discover until far too late.

So this book is not a state of barbecue today. It's an outlining of those basic issues of tradition and transition that remain important to any discussion of this food. And, despite the few recipes in the last pages of this book, it's still not a cookbook.

The Offerings POLITICAL FUNDRAISER **EAST ST. LOUIS, ILLINOIS**

By Way of Introduction

This thing started over a plate of barbecue in Wilson, North Carolina. Barbecue there is different from the national norm. They don't use sweet, tomato-based sauces, and they mostly barbecue whole hogs, not ribs.

At the time of that eating I was employed as the road manager for the Wynton Marsalis Septet, and that fact also has a lot to do with how this came to be. I was getting paid to travel around the world and listen to great music but also to perform menial tasks that became more burdensome and less glamorous with each performance. So I was looking for some other way to earn my living, preferably one that required no résumé, no job application, and no regular hours.

Frank was also working with the band at the time, traveling with us and collaborating on a book with Wynton called *Sweet Swing Blues on the Road*. Every time we went somewhere that was supposed to have good barbecue, he'd ask the promoter where he could get some, and then, by way of warning, he'd say that he grew up in Chicago and Memphis and did not suffer mediocrity in barbecue lightly.

That one meal in North Carolina stayed with us, conjuring memories of barbecue in other places, cooked in different ways, finished with different sauces. We decided then that we would travel the country studying the various conceptions of barbecue and write a book.

We've learned a lot since then. We know that barbecue is a metaphor for American culture in a broad sense, and that it is a more appropriate metaphor than any other American food. Barbecue alone encompasses the high- and lowbrows, the sacred and the profane, the urban and the rural, the learned and the unlettered, the blacks, the browns, the yellows, the reds, and the whites. Barbecue, then, is a fitting barometer for the changes, good and bad, that have taken place in the country, and this book, ostensibly about that food, is really about the people and places and consistencies and changes that produce it.

With the generally reliable assistance of the 1981 Volvo that came to earn the nickname the Living Legend, we learned just how large barbecue country is. There was the quick stop for gas in Houston that lasted four days. ("What you have there is an exotic," the mechanic told us.

Lolis, Frank, and the Legend HAWKINS GRILL **MEMPHIS, TENNESSEE**

"All them cars—your Porsches, your Ferraris, your Volvos—you cain't just git parts for those cars too easy.") There were those six days in Fayetteville, North Carolina, when we bought our second alternator in as many weeks, and there's that funny groan that began outside Memphis and still persists when the car gets tired. But all in all we spent more time moving on the road than stopped alongside it. Packed in the back seat were a small ice chest and the small library of books and tapes that we came to rely on for sanity, especially the song that became both our title and our theme, Howlin' Wolf's "Smokestack Lightning" ("Who been here, baby, since I been gone?").

We started our tour in Memphis because it was familiar ground to Frank. From there our itinerary was dictated mostly by the barbecue-related events and competitions that happen around this country from spring to fall, from Memphis in May to the Big Pig Jig, but also by the legends of people and places and tastes that our various guides pointed us in the direction of.

On most days we stopped at three or four places, on some days six or eight. On good days we camped in one place and observed and engaged in the luxury of eating only the choicest morsels. To be sure, most of the barbecue we ate was bad. When you spend all of every day critiquing just one small genre of culinary art you get sharp; barbecue is no longer exciting simply because of the Fourth of July rarity of it or the great outdoors freshness of it. If it is to stand out it must truly be good, and just as in all disciplines, there are—in ascending order of rarity—the amateurs, the experts, and the geniuses.

We missed a few places. There's the red oak Santa Maria, California, barbecue with its own special beans, and the Sonoma County barbecue of that California region. And there are all the uncles and aunts and husbands who we were told had the best barbecue in the world, if only we could make it out to Rosebud or Bangor to get some. But we couldn't, and for that we apologize.

So this thing is not encyclopedic or exhaustive. And despite all that we did to avoid false judgments, maybe some of the chefs have been praised for food cooked on their absolute best days while others have been damned for the fault of being in less than top form on the one day in the last thousand that we came by. And by the time this thing is finally printed and bound, some of these people will have retired or sold out or allowed their recipe to be changed just slightly and just tragically on the advice of that son-in-law with the tongue of iron and the mail-order degree in keypunch technology. So it goes.

These things notwithstanding, what we do have is one long summer of the people and the tastes and the places of barbecue that could have been arrived at by no other route.

J.C. Serving It Up HAWKINS GRILL **MEMPHIS, TENNESSEE.**

Of Blues and Barbecue: Memphis and Environs

The shoulder sandwich is to west Tennessee barbecue what the second hump is to the Bactrian camel—a distinguishing if not unique feature. Ribs and brisket, the first humps of barbecue in some other cities, are also available here, but you have to ask for them by name. By contrast, just four words, "Give me a barbecue," are usually sufficient to procure the local staple, though you still have to say whether you want it hot or mild, chopped or sliced.

Frank, who has more than one home town, grew up here. He equates this experience with majoring in barbecue at a small liberal arts college. (He received his advanced barbecue training later in his other home town, Chicago.) We enter Memphis on this Sunday night nearly twelve hours after our leisurely departure from New Orleans, but Frank insists that before we bathe or sleep I must be properly introduced to Memphis barbecue. Said introduction, in Frank's book, can take place only over a shoulder sandwich at Hawkins Grill. Frank's favorite uncle, Suicide Red, used to work at Hawkins, and this establishment is the source of some of Frank's earliest experience with the smoked ambrosia that is the object of his current addiction. For Frank the attraction to this place is at once sentimental and gastronomical.

Despite what Frank may think, I've come to this sojourn at least somewhat prepared. First of all, I grew up in New Orleans, a city that, while not known for its barbecue, requires no introduction to good food. I've also been reading the recent barbecue literature. The authors of these books agree on a few rules of thumb in the search for good "'que." First, the place must be small and out of the way; the silverware must be made of plastic, the china of cardboard, and the fine wine of barley and hops. The clientele must be pure and bucolic and have been coming to the place for years, and the proprietor must be old and innocently amused that outsiders find his food so exceptional. Second, such places no longer exist, because if they did, the world would have heard about them long ago and be clamoring to get inside. Such, we are told, is the nature of world demand for good barbecue. If you encounter a small place with no line, even if there is sawdust on the floor and a spittoon by the bar, you should dine with caution. Its small size, rather than being a credit to its quaintness, doubtless reflects the fact that its revenues are too small to support a more expansive location.

Hawkins has no line.

As we open the glass door and the burglar bars rattle slightly, Al Green is singing "How Can You Mend a Broken Heart," and I'm hit by a familiar feeling. Late on Christmas nights, when a lot of the family had left and my aunt Anna was washing the dishes and smoking Kool menthol cigarettes, she would play Al Green because he was her favorite and his songs, whether slow or uptempo, were good to wind down to. It is this feeling of the dying embers of a once-blazing party that you get on a Sunday night at Hawkins—this feeling except also with it the feeling that the party probably last blazed many years ago.

Hawkins is a small place and feels old. The sounds of the jukebox and of the people talking loudly over its music make it seem even smaller. Add dim lighting, dark brown wood paneling—it gets smaller still. The room is cut nearly in half lengthwise by the bar. On one side, covered by a large range hood, is the grill. On the other side are barstools and four booths. The grill, of course, is not for barbecuing. It's for frying hamburgers, grilling hot dogs, and toasting buns. The pit in which the pork shoulders are cooked is built into the wall and is hidden by a black metal door.

J.C. Hardaway has worked here more than half a century, first as delivery boy, then as weekend waiter/cook, now as sole employee. He is a reddish brown man, the color of burnt sienna, and has a small gray mustache on his upper lip in a style made sinister by its association with Adolf Hitler. J.C., who is anything but sinister, alternates strangely from carefully enunciating his words through his sharp Tennessee twang to mumbling and chewing the edges of them. Whatever word his sentences end on is dragged out just a little.

"What can I get for you boys-z?"

"Two shoulder sandwiches and a quart of beer," Frank says.

"You want hot or mild sauce on those-z?"

"Hot."

From the cooler underneath the bar, J.C. pulls out two chilled highball glasses, sticking a napkin into them as he puts them on the bar. Next the quart bottle of beer, which is at precisely the correct serving temperature—cold, very cold. J.C. then puts two hamburger buns on the grill. He unwraps a piece of tin foil to expose a barbecued pork shoulder. He slices off some meat and puts it on a small chopping block to the left of the grill. There is a slow deliberation about J.C. during this whole process except at two points, when he quickens from his characteristic andante to a lively allegretto. First, cleaver in hand, he chops the meat. Short strokes. Cleaver up; cleaver down. This done, he smoothly scoops up the meat and places it on the bottom of one partially toasted bun. The bun serves to measure the portion. When it is sufficiently covered, the meat is taken back off and put on the grill.

"Hot, did you say-y?"

The hot sauce is in an old Palmolive dish detergent bottle. It is orange, unlike the mild sauce, which is maroon and kept in an old salad dressing bottle. As J.C. squirts the sauce onto the meat, the smell of vinegar rises up from it and burns the nose. Then he scoops up a sandwich worth of meat with a metal spatula and puts it on the bun again. Coleslaw is standard on a Memphis shoulder sandwich. J.C. spoons on a generous amount, retrieves the top bun from the grill, puts the whole thing on a plain white plate, sticks a toothpick in, and serves.

It is the soft outer side of the bun that first makes contact with your teeth; then they continue through the toasted crispness beneath and finally land in a bed of smoke and barbecue sauce and meat. J.C.'s hot sauce is hot, but there is flavor beneath the pepper and the overall experience brings a smile to the tongue. It is the sort of sandwich that makes you begin debating, halfway through it, whether you should order a second immediately so that it will be ready the moment you finish the first.

If you're serious about it, good food, especially when discovered in a new city, does not induce sleep. Rather, it inspires you to think of all the other equivalent if not superior meals that this one taste of ecstasy portends. After a shoulder sandwich at Hawkins we are more interested in seeing what other offerings Memphis has, either culinary or otherwise cultural, than we are in sleeping. And where else should a portentous Sunday night in Memphis be spent but on its famous Beale Street?

Smoke and the Lovers HAWKINS GRILL **MEMPHIS, TENNESSEE**

Beale Street by Night

∽

Halvern Johnson, a boyhood friend of Frank's, agrees to take us down to the new Beale Street. But he takes one look at our car and decides that he'll drive his own. "I know that thing is a living legend," he says, "but it looks like it needs a rest." And he repeats the phrase a few times, "a living legend," until the car and the name become fused in our minds.

We have hardly taken a step on Beale Street when we encounter Ray Robinson, Jr., an acquaintance of Halvern's whose father, we are told, owns a barbecue restaurant. He hands us his card—Cozy Corner Restaurant: The Bar-B-Q Place. We ask him if it's any good. Although Ray has sufficient girth to be the son of a great barbecue artist, he lacks the degree of volume and braggadocio that is generally characteristic of those with great confidence in their food. "We think we can hold our own with just about anybody," he says. We interpret this to mean that Cozy Corner serves some of the best average barbecue one is apt to find. But as average barbecue is not the grail for which we quest, we politely pocket his card and vaguely promise to put it to use.

B.B. King's, which is co-owned by the blues singer, is a fairly large club and restaurant with a huge stage and a second-floor viewing area. In a case on the wall is one of the many "Lucilles" King has played throughout his career. Posters advertising old concerts for various blues artists hang on other walls, and street signs suspended from the ceiling bear names like Albert King Avenue and Stevie Ray Vaughn Memorial Boulevard.

The crowd is small tonight. Just as well. The trio performing is bad in about every way it can be. They've mistaken their three-chord rock 'n' roll for blues and are imposing this ignorance loudly on the rest of us. Unlike blues musicians, for whom communication with the audience is a definitive part of the performance, these men play as if the audience were irrelevant. The audience, in turn, applauds as if the music were irrelevant. Our time at the club is about to be as brief as it is pointless. Then Halvern spots Ms. Ruby Wilson.

Ruby is the house singer at B.B. King's, performing three nights one week and five nights the next. Halvern and Frank had hung out with Ruby one night a couple of years ago, but she doesn't remember. So we buy her a drink and invite her to our table in hopes that the combination of alcohol and conversation might help jar her memory. It works. Soon the conversation is rolling along nicely. Ruby is telling us all about her upcoming trip to Paris and the busloads of people who pack in here on the nights when she is performing. We exchange business cards. Hers says:

MS. RUBY WILSON
Queen

AMBASSADOR OF BEALE STREET

"The Quain," Frank says as he reads the card. "We here with the Quain."

Just as Beale Street is no usual kingdom, it has spawned no usual queen. The old Beale Street, made famous in part by W.C. "Father of the Blues" Handy, was a commercial center complete with a variety of stores and restaurants. Little remains of that era now but a hardware store, A.S. Schwab, est. 1876. Though they are located in the exact same place, the old Beale Street would have difficulty recognizing its progeny. The street is now alive with neon lights and clubs with names like Mr. Handy's Blues Hall Juke Joint, the Band Box, and B.B. King's, each of which promises blues music.

The Queen, draped in a black shawl trimmed with gold, holds forth with us at a table near the entrance, occasionally interrupting the conversation to greet fans or to make a call on the cellular phone she keeps in her purse. Figuring that no one would know better where to find good barbecue in Memphis than its queen, we begin ticking off a list of barbecue places we've heard of. As we go along, Ruby makes noncommittal comments for the most part—"I've heard that one's pretty good," or "They supposed to have good barbecue there." Then we get to Cozy Corner, Ray Robinson's father's place, and she awards it about the highest compliment a barbecue place can ever hope to receive: "Now, they can sweat you some meat over there!"

I have not heard the Queen sing, but like so many great blues singers, she has a body that seems designed for maximum projection. My hope is that I can convince her to take over the stage and bring some music to the chaos we are hearing. Unfortunately, no amount of coaxing will get her to sing this night; she's not here to work. But there is a party at an after-hours club, she tells us. There'll be some music there, and we are welcome to come along if we'd like. We accept.

Club Unique

When I was growing up in the New Orleans of the 1970s I used to get my hair cut at Afro House, a barbershop near the corner of St. Bernard and Claiborne avenues. Afro House was the international repository of hip. They had African carvings on the wall, and William Gant, my barber, had an oil-on-black-velvet replica of Miles Davis' *Bitches' Brew* album cover behind his chair. Though I hadn't yet heard of Jimi Hendrix, I realize now that it was "Who Knows" from his *Band of Gypsies* album that so often accompanied the rhythmic snapping of scissors. It was of course fitting for the capital of cool to be housed in a barbershop because in the 1970s your cool received its most articulate expression through your coiffure. Thus coiffeurs were all but holy men, and a trip to the barbershop was a doubly important step in the ever-important journey toward getting your head together. Owing to my mother's intervention, William always cut my own cultural statements more brief than I would have liked. This fueled my enthusiasm for growing older and one day being able to grow my hair as long as that of the other customers at Afro House. Little did I know that by the time I reached majority, the majority

of people would, like me, be cutting their statements almost to the scalp. I often wondered where these people of my youth had gone and whether they took their hair and flamboyant clothes with them.

Now I know. They are at Club Unique in Memphis, Tennessee, hair a little shorter and accents a bit more Southern and less New Orleanian, but believe me, these are the same people. I'd know them anywhere.

On this night they are packed in as tight as large items in a small suitcase. The woman who owns the club seems a bit harried when she greets us at the door. The imagination need not be stretched far to envision the range of potentially combustive problems that can arise when people and liquor are packed so closely together. Added to that source of anxiety is the fact that Ruby, whom she is expecting, has arrived with three unexpected guests of her own—us. At this point I begin to get some idea of the proportions of Ruby Wilson's celebrity. Unlike most local entertainers who are hardly known, let alone celebrated, outside their clique of fans, Ruby's status is like that of a local television news anchor. Everyone recognizes "the Quain" and is at least a little honored by her presence. A place has been reserved for Ruby near the front. We, on the other hand, are politely asked to wait in the hope that three seats can be found.

There is a band from Chicago on stage playing R&B and some old Motown songs. Our big chance to get seats comes when they take a break and it is announced that

refreshments are being served in the small area that serves as a dance floor in front of the stage. A line quickly forms leading up to a table. Most of the food is the usual fare—pickles, olives, potato chips, deviled eggs. But at the very end of the table is a smoked turkey. I put a few slices on my plate, assuming that if it is good I can come back and get more. It is exceptionally good, so I go back when I notice that the food line has thinned. Too late. A pack of wolves could not have made shorter work of a turkey. But we are finally able to join Ruby at her recently vacated table. A bottle of complimentary champagne soon arrives. Frank yells, almost above the sounds of the disc jockey, "The Quain! We here with the Quain!"

The crowd varies in age from about thirty to sixty. "They got all kinds in here tonight," Ruby says. "You name it—pimps, prostitutes, dope pushers." But Ruby's description fails to capture the true range. There may be criminals here, but they are probably outnumbered by just plain people out to have a good time. The women at the table next to us, for example, are hairdressers in their mid-thirties.

The patrons are dressed in a variety of custom-made enclosures—outfits designed if not to complement then certainly to plainly outline the figures they cover. There is everything from a black leotard with a hole around the navel, to a white shimmy dress like the ones Ma Rainey once wore, to jeans so tight that one especially steatopygous woman must have used a large shoe horn and duck fat to get into hers. Hovering near the turkey tray is a

The *"Quain"* MS. RUBY WILSON **MEMPHIS, TENNESSEE**

Dip My Dipper CICERO BLAKE **MEMPHIS, TENNESSEE**

man in what looks like a grand boubou, the traditional dress of much of west Africa. But when I look more closely I realize that it is a brown leather maxicoat that covers him from neck to near ankle. Frank is impressed.

"These people musta auditioned to get in here!"

The highlight of tonight's show is a surprise performance by Cicero Blake, a Chicago-based blues singer. Cicero is in Memphis to play a gala at B.B. King's the next night. One look at him makes clear that he is every inch a blues singer. First of all, he has the eyes for it—piercing, handsome eyes that can look out and communicate to each person in an audience that, never mind what the words of the songs say, he is singing about you. And he has the clothes for it—a brown tuxedo-style jacket that stops abruptly at the waist, where it is met by matching slacks. Hanging from his neck and over his tan silk shirt is a small gold chain from which the word "Cicero" is suspended.

I have no idea how many songs Mr. Blake has recorded, but his reputation rests largely and grandly on one in particular, "Dip My Dipper." The themes of the blues, like the themes of life itself, are eternal. It is the duty of each generation of artists to contribute fresh metaphors for these old concerns, metaphors that are both timeless and contemporary. Four decades ago Dinah Washington, in "New Blow Top Blues," sang about feeling so good that she took her man "right to his wife's front door." (The woman turned out to be "a .45-packing mama," and Dinah sang, "I ain't gon' do that no more!") "Dip My Dipper" is Mr. Blake's own variation on the stolen-water-is-sweet theme, but with a twist. Rather than being the bad guy in all of this, a carnal opportunist, Mr. Blake paints himself as a comforter and counselor:

> *The fella who lives down the street*
> *All he wants to do is fuss and fight*
> *Says his woman's always wrong*
> *She can't do nothing right.*
> *When she needs a little comforting*
> *A man to understand*
> *You know she dials my number*
> *'Cause I'm an understanding man …*

When the verses culminate in the refrain of Cicero's heartfelt admission, the crowd goes wild. He looks out into the audience with those eyes as if seeking forgiveness for a sin he fully hopes to commit again in the next verse, and confesses,

> *I like to dip my dipper*
> *In someone else's dippings*
> *Because the dipping is a little bit neater*
> *And the sugar's a little bit sweeter*
> *When you dip your dipper*
> *In someone else's dippings.*

At this point the voice of the most animated of the hairdressers climbs above the other sounds of the room and beseeches him, "Dip it over heyah, Cicerowl! Dip it over heyah!"

But Cicero is cool.

He shakes his head guiltily and just keeps on singing as if to make plain that his intention was not to flirt but merely to confess the weakness of his flesh. Yet the more he sings, the louder the women get.

After he's whipped the crowd up into a nice lather, Cicero closes his set with "She's Cheatin' on You," in which he tells an unfortunate husband the news that a man least likes to hear about his wife. "She's just like a hit record," Cicero sings to him, "they singing her name all over town."

But the bard is obviously hurt by all this infidelity. By the end of the song, during the improvised coda, he's joined on stage briefly by another singer. Cicero playfully accuses the man of having been less than faithful himself. Then he tries to enlist him in a tuneful pact not to cheat anymore. And by the end of it all we are left as convinced of Cicero's capacity for repentance as we were of his lust for sin.

Memphis Before May

When you ask people in Memphis how the city came to be so famous for its barbecue, the first thing they tell you about is the barbecue competition during the Memphis in May festival. This raises a classic chicken-and-egg question: Which came first, Memphis barbecue or Memphis in May? Though Memphis in May, which attracts barbecue competitors from as far away as Europe, has certainly raised the city's profile as a smoked meat center, the festival is less than twenty years old, and Memphis has a substantive history of good barbecue on which its new reputation is based. As far back as the 1930s Johnny Mills had a barbecue joint on 4th Street. Local legend has it that Bing Crosby and other stars used to have ribs from Johnny Mills flown out to them in Hollywood. Culpepper's, Jeff's, Joe's After Hours, and Jim's Rib Shack on Thomas Street are all remembered as having good food. "Where can you get good barbecue now?" I ask one of the old-timers. She thinks a minute and shrugs her shoulders.

History does not record how or when barbecue first arrived in western Tennessee, but there are many factors that help to explain why this place is a natural barbecue center. Whenever pork and people come together, it's a safe assumption that the rich people will end up with the hams and chops and the poor people will end up with the ribs, lips, foots, and chitterlings. Barbecue is largely the art of turning the bony, less desirable portions of the pig into something worth chewing the gristle for. Thus it was almost certainly developed by poor people, a disproportionate number of whom tend to be of African descent.

In Memphis, particularly in the black sections of the city, barbecue pits are more common than lawn furniture. Many stores also have an oil drum smoker chained to a telephone pole out front to advertise that in addition to grits and groceries, they sell barbecue. But no corner says more about the history and culture of barbecue in Memphis than the corner of Bellevue and MacLemore. Hawkins Grill, which is a half block from this corner, is popular among its local clientele and a few connoisseurs, but it is perhaps best known as the place around the corner from the place that was,

until its recent demise and relocation, the most famous barbecue spot in Memphis. That place is Leonard's Pit Barbecue.

Leonard's hails from the 1940s, when drive-in restaurants were common and a plate of "bar-beerQue" was only ten cents. Leonard's had so many pits that they had to be housed in a separate building behind the restaurant. There was space for more than 150 cars in Leonard's drive-up, which suggests something about the pace of business in the restaurant's heyday.

The old Leonard's stretches for two thirds of a city block in one direction and half a block in another, but these days it looks like a ghost town in miniature. The awnings that once covered the three parking areas now cover more weeds than cars. The neon pig with its top hat and twirling cane, the sign once synonymous with this place, no longer lights up. Another of the many signs on this sprawling shell of a restaurant proclaims LEONARD'S: WE'RE GLAD YOU'RE HERE, but no one is.

Like so much of urban America, the neighborhood around Leonard's has changed. For most of its history Leonard's was a white-owned and white-patronized anomaly in a predominantly black neighborhood. But the black people here now are poorer than their parents and grandparents were. To accommodate the neighborhood's diminished buying power there are a couple of new discount stores on this corner. In the past few years, as if to make life even harder for Hawkins and Leonard's, several fast-food restaurants opened within a few blocks. This combination of factors ultimately led Leonard's to close its Bellevue

Street restaurant and move to the outskirts of town.

The new Leonard's looks much like the fast-food restaurants it's competing with. As you walk in, there is a counter where you place your order. The menu is posted on a board directly behind it. To the left of the counter is a large dining area where you can eat.

It is always difficult to judge the validity of statements about how good a restaurant used to be. Have tastes changed? Has the quality of the food gone down? Has the ownership changed? Was it ever any good? The legendary jazz trumpeter Miles Davis was once asked why he sounded so mediocre on his early recordings with the great Charlie Parker. "You should have heard that shit in 1946!" he shot back, as if to suggest that the difference between mediocrity and greatness is context.

We eat part of the shoulder sandwich we order from Leonard's, and it is not very good. But neither is it 1946.

Corky's
∽

Corky's Bar-B-Q has now replaced Leonard's as the most famous barbecue spot in Memphis. When locals are asked for a list of barbecue places worth visiting, it is the place most frequently mentioned. This fact is as loud on the subject of name recognition as it is silent on the matter of food quality. As we arrive in the parking lot near nine o'clock one night, the security guard, a native of Canada, is busy chomping on a shoulder sandwich. He says that since moving to Memphis three years ago, he has become a barbecue fanatic, eating it several times a week. Corky's, he proclaims, has the best barbecue in Memphis.

Corky's is the kind of place that old-line barbecue enthusiasts cite as evidence of the crumbling of barbecue civilization. It wouldn't take much to turn this place into a TGI Friday's or a Houston's or any one of a number of the chain restaurants that now dominate the moderate-price segment of the restaurant market. Like them, Corky's is replete with ceiling fans and brass railings and carpeting and a greeter at the front. The crowd here reflects this image. Corky's patrons tend to be a bit younger than those at a place like Hawkins. Many of the people here are tourists who've heard that this is the place for "real Memphis barbecue." A lot of them wear the coat-and-tie or blue-dress-and-pumps uniform of junior executives.

It is immediately apparent that Corky's has a very different mission from the traditional barbecue joint. It is not after truck-drivers and tour buses; it is catering to a distinctly middle-class, relatively sophisticated customer who, were he to tire of the long wait for a table that is the norm here, would probably not go to another barbecue restaurant.

I try for several days to interview either Dan Pelts, the owner of Corky's, or his son. Both are extremely busy preparing for the opening of new Corky's "stores" in New Orleans, Nashville, and Orlando. A bushy-tailed young manager, whose prior experience includes working for an insurance company in Atlanta, is dispatched to talk to the press. "I think the main difference here is our management style," he says. "Our number-one priority is customer satisfaction. Every single item that goes out of our kitchen is viewed by our manager." The same is true at Hawkins, I think to myself, though arguably for different reasons.

In Corky's the traditional definition of a barbecue place is put to the test. Are barbecue restaurants defined only by the food they serve, or are mediocre service and drab decor part and parcel of the barbecue experience? More to the point, can a place like Corky's, with its 120 employees, really barbecue? What is clear is that this is a decent restaurant. The service is good and the food better than adequate. But there's an antiseptic quality to both. The service is cordial, though not personal. The food is tasty; it's consistent; it's professional. But all the quality controls that mitigate against a substandard plate exiting the kitchen also insure that nothing stellar will emerge.

Dateline Blue Goose, TN

In the late 1980s Greg Johnson and Vince Staten set out to find the best barbecue restaurants in America for their book *Real Barbecue*. One of their favorites was B.E. Scott's Bar-B-Q near Lexington, Tennessee, where cooking demanded all-night vigilance. B.E. slept with his meat, setting his alarm clock to wake him up at regular intervals so that he could tend to it with the care good food demands. His barbecue got the highest rating Johnson and Staten allowed: "as good as we've ever had." If Johnson and Staten are right, B.E. Scott's is not to be missed.

So early this Wednesday morning we set out from Memphis hoping to find Mr. Scott *in medias res*. The Living Legend is running out of gas as we approach Lexington, and we decide to stop at a BP station along Highway 20 to fill up. As Frank pumps the gas, I go inside the combination gas station and general store and begin talking to the woman who owns the place, Mrs. Anderson. The subject turns to barbecue. They sell it right beside the gas station, she tells me; in fact, her husband is outside cooking it now. By this time Frank is rushing into the store, camera in hand, yelling "Eureka! Eureka!" He has gotten Mr. Anderson's permission to take pictures and is ready to go to work. Our plans have changed.

Next to the gas station is a small building, the front porch of which is screened in and furnished with chairs and picnic tables. Inside the building Mr. Anderson has a large piece of barbecue machinery. At the base is a pit approximately six feet by three feet of cinderblock construction. There are two iron doors in the side where the coals are put in. The pit is covered with chain-link fencing onto which whole hogs are laid out. Covering the whole outfit and keeping the smoke in with the meat are several metal doors. Above all this is a large range hood with two lights. Anderson says that when this grill as well as a similar one right outside this room are going, he can cook nine hogs at a time.

Chinaman Hutch CHINAMAN HUTCH'S BAR-B-Q **CEDAR GROVE, TENNESSEE**

Billy Anderson ANDERSON'S BAR-B-QUE AND GROCERY **LEXINGTON, TENNESSEE**

In the cities most people barbecue over charcoal briquets; a few use hardwood. Mr. Anderson barbecues the hard way, by burning the wood down to the coals and cooking the meat on this glowing, distilled essence of hickory. Among the weeds and debris outside is a pile of sawmill slabs of hickory wood; right behind these is a trash barrel in which several slabs are burning. As slabs burn, the embers collect at the bottom of the barrel. Anderson shovels these up and walks to the shed in which the meat is cooking.

The smoke is so thick inside that it is hard to breathe. Anderson is used to it. Undaunted, he places the embers under the meat. At sixty-two he is not a young man. On the rare occasions when he takes off his baseball cap to scratch his head, you can see that his gray hair is thinning. But his body is neither thin nor frail. He's a little more than six feet tall and weighs about two hundred pounds. After he has completed the process of putting the embers under the meat, he sits on a bench outside the smoke shed, arms folded, looking at the highway, waiting until it is time to repeat the process. It is clearly hard, hot, tedious work interrupted only occasionally and briefly by rests—which is why I am a bit surprised when he responds to one of my questions by saying coldly, "You fellers gon' through a lot of trouble just to write a book, ain't you?"

It is clear by this time that Billy Anderson is not thrilled to see us. As he realizes that we intend to stay long enough to really observe the process, he becomes even less happy. Does he not cotton to having company so early in the morning, or does he, a white Tennessean, not cotton to having colored company? Hard to say. What is obvious, though, is that he is not given to in-depth conversation on this particular morning. So I go back to the store vaguely mumbling something about wanting some orange juice, hoping that perhaps Mrs. Anderson will be more talkative.

There are a bench and several milk crates covered with cushions in the store. When business is slow, Mrs. Anderson, her mother-in-law, and sometimes her thirty-odd-year-old son Randy sit and talk. Mr. and Mrs. Anderson have been up since four-thirty. "Us Tennesseans have to start early," she says. "We have to make a leavin'."

The Andersons opened their store twenty years ago, Mrs. Anderson explains, but the barbecue stand is a recent addition. Back then, Billy Anderson used to raise hogs. But as meat prices dropped, it didn't pay to sell them, so he started barbecuing. Now he buys his hogs live and takes them to a slaughterhouse where he pays sixteen dollars a head to have them slaughtered and dressed. The hogs start off weighing a little more than two hundred pounds. They lose fifty pounds of that once they are slaughtered and another twenty to thirty pounds in the cooking. What remains, Anderson sells by the sandwich or by the pound at six dollars per.

The elder Mrs. Anderson recalls the days when "we woun'n kill hogs till it was blue cold anyway." But much has changed. Hogs are being killed year-round, and chit-terlings, which she still has a weakness for, smell too bad for her family's liking, so she no longer eats them.

"I still say your older black people have the best barbecue I've ever seen," Randy contributes. "We picked up a lot of history from them. A lot of younger black people are cooking it now. I don't know what the difference is, but the majority of times I say your older black people cook the best barbecue."

Frank has been known to engage even deaf-mutes in conversation. Something about him convinces people that they want to talk to him, and somehow Billy Anderson has warmed up to him. By the time I go back outside, the two of them are tighter than God and Gabriel. "It's just hard work and paying attention," Anderson is explaining to him. "They ain't nothing to do but just pay attention. You put too much fire, you burn it. Don't put enough, you spoil it. Me, I cook by smell; I used to cook by sight. By the smell of the grease you can tell when it's cooking fresh or when it's burning. A lot of people use thermometers, but I don't."

I tell him about some of the mediocre barbecue we've endured in Memphis, meat with all the flavor of boiled cotton. He's not surprised. "They say they have barbecue, but they don't have a thing in the world but baked meat with barbecue sauce on it," he says. I mention a man named Hardy, one of the old black people who Randy said was one of the masters of barbecue in the area. "Uncle Hardy was good," Anderson says, "but Tom Gardner's 'one learned me how to cook." He doesn't know where Uncle Hardy can be found. Tom Gardner is in a retirement home in Jackson, Tennessee, we're told. Anderson visited him once or twice, he says, but they've lost touch.

We choose this time to explain what has brought us here. Blue Goose was not on our original itinerary, we tell Anderson, and probably not on our map. We were on our way to B.E. Scott's and just happened to luck up on his place. We show him what Johnson and Staten have written about his neighbor up the road. Disappointment flashes in his light brown eyes, the disappointment of knowing that he breaks his back barbecuing his meat for twelve hours and leaves it on the dying embers for another twelve, much as Smith is reputed to do, only it seems that Smith gets all the recognition. In fact, he tells us, Smith has been written up in some other publications as well.

"I don't do no advertising," he says. "I admit it. I let the people who eat it talk about it. If it ain't worth talking about, it ain't worth having. I don't spend my money for it."

Suddenly he seems genuinely glad that we stopped by. We talk for a few more minutes, and he invites Randy to come and have a look at what Staten and Johnson have written about B.E. Scott. We tell him that we still have to go and check out Scott's place, but we promise to return the next day, by which time the first meat of this week's batch should be done. There's another man not too far from here who also barbecues in this style, he and Randy tell us, a man named Chinaman Hutch. They give us directions.

"You know what's funny?" Anderson calls to us as we are leaving. "Me and Scott have the same initials, B.E."

∽

Unlike B.E. Anderson's, B.E. Scott's is set up like a small restaurant. You order at a glass-enclosed formica counter and eat your food in the adjoining dining area. It is not crowded, but each time a pickup truck pulls away, another drives up. This place is on a busier part of the highway than Anderson's. It's across the road from Adams Furniture and down the street from a car wash. It's easy to see why it would be a convenient place to stop for lunch. As it turns out, B.E. Scott no longer owns the place. The new owner is fairly young, mid to late thirties, and friendly. He knows many of his customers by name and greets them as they order and thanks them warmly for stopping in.

"Two regulars," a woman in front of us says, "one plain and one with a lot of fat on it."

We order a shoulder sandwich and a fried peach pie. Of the two, the pie is much better. The meat is bland and uneventful and is done a sizable disservice by the cold bun it is served on. The sauce is vinegar-based and thinner than the tomato-based sauces we had in Memphis. It's tangy but does little to improve the taste of the sandwich. Though we saw a stack of hickory wood in the yard where Scott's barbecues its meat, we had heard disturbing rumors from a couple of people in the Jackson area

that the meat here is no longer barbecued the old way. The rumors taste true.

Chinaman Hutch

The path to Hutch's place passes a church and its graveyard, a shop selling handmade quilts, and several Bar B Que signs, one of which is so far away from Hutch's place that you wonder if it is his sign or that of a competitor. In the front yard of a white mobile home is a hand-painted piece of plywood with Hutch's name. There are also a pickup truck with a monogrammed license plate, two goats, and a dog, all of which help to convince us that we are in the right place.

When we pull into the driveway, the "Chinaman" is sitting in a lawn chair outside the building that serves as his smokehouse and restaurant. Hutch, who holds up his blue jeans with both belt and suspenders, wears a baseball cap. He is the same color brown as a red fox stole. Large, fleshy jaws frame his mouth and mustache in a diamond. But even on the darkest of nights he could not be mistaken for Chinese. A Native American perhaps. He has the long, broad nose so common to the profile of our nation's first inhabitants, but little on his face would suggest the name Chinaman.

"A white feller name me that," he tells us. "He just said I favored a Chinaman. A lot of people don't know my name. Theet's all they ever knowed was Chinaman." His given name is Alma.

Hutch, like Anderson, cooks all day Wednesday and sells the meat Thursday,

Friday, and Saturday. So there's little to do today but sit, wait, and talk. We get two metal lawn chairs from the picnic tables in the front of the yard and bring them back to where Hutch is sitting. He's an extremely friendly man, happy to have someone to talk to whether the subject is "politee-shuns," women, or barbecue.

"Thees run in the Hutches," he says, "and I still cook mine the old way. I burn the wood out thar and put the coals up un'er it. If you let it cool first it gets ribbery and it never gets right after that. In cooking hogs you have to be more careful with them than with shoulders cause thar's more fat."

The items in the yard, the bottles, the old cans, could easily be mistaken for a pile of debris, but at least some of it plays an integral role in Hutch's culinary science. There is a pile of wood bordered on two sides by pieces of sheet metal and on another by the tub of an old wheelbarrow. This is where the wood burns down to coals. You can tell when it's time to add more coals, he says, because the fat from the meat will quit dripping.

"It's a worrisome job," Hutch tells us as he puts his shovel into the burning wood pile to withdraw the orange, black, and white coals. "But it's just a certain amount of heat you got to put under thar, I don't care if it's a elayphunt." He then adds wood to the fire, taking about five trips, carrying three boards each time. The new wood has a sweet smell to it; as it burns it loses this, along with most of its volume. Cooking with embers instead of wood or charcoal is clearly an expensive, inefficient process.

Hutch explains to us that his business is now closely regulated. It is illegal for him to butcher and sell his own hogs as he used to do years ago. When he, like Anderson, goes to Lexington and pays his sixteen dollars for each hog to be slaughtered, the head and vital organs are examined and kept by the slaughterhouse. If there are any irregularities, which thus far there have not been, they keep the meat as well. Regulation at its best serves the consumer well, insuring that all meat sold commercially is fit to eat. At its worst it has the potential to do just the opposite.

"You see, we got a lot of inspectors and things—and I know that inspector's daddy; I don't know the inspector well. He told me what I don't sell I have to put in the deep freeze immediyut. I say, 'You'll keell everybody take a bite, you do that. You let it cool, then put it in the freeze.'" Once the inspector was corrected, Hutch continued leaving his meat on the grill overnight. "There's no way it'll spoil. It just ain't gon' spoil. What spoils meat is being half done. If it' cooked good, done to the bone, it won't spoil."

Somebody Done Finked on Us

In Blue Goose, Tennessee, the seasons pass more quickly than in most other parts of the world. On our first visit, in a span of less than an hour, we were able to witness the thawing of winter's coldness and the rising warmth of summer's sun. By eight the next morning, the hour at which Mr. Anderson told us he would commence barbecuing

Thursday's hog, winter has returned with much vengeance.

As we drive up, Anderson and an assistant are pulling the carcass of a newly butchered hog from the back of a pickup truck. "Could you hold it a minute, just a minute?" Frank says as he runs back to the car to get the appropriate cameras. But Anderson's ears have deafened to our voices. The hog is put on a table beside the smokehouse with no regard for Frank's request. There Anderson cuts off its ankles and feet and throws them in a metal basin. With a knife he digs deep gashes at the joints of each of the hog's two front legs. Into these gashes he pours what appears to be half a cup of salt directly from the box. The pig is then lifted from the table and put on a grill inside. Once this has been completed, Anderson and Joseph Parker, his twenty-six-year-old assistant, sit down on the bench and talk as if we aren't there.

"Big crop of apples this year?" Anderson asks.

"Ain't many. Ain't many a-t'all. I ain't saw a' apple this year. Blueberries everywhere."

"Big crop of them, wa'nt there."

"Sho' was."

Anderson's assistant takes the basin of feet and drives off. I walk back to the store again. The two Mrs. Andersons, Billy Anderson's wife and his mother, are sitting in their usual spot, as friendly as they were yesterday. "I make the slaw and the hot sauce," says the younger Mrs. Anderson. "I usually make baked beans, but they haven't been going too good these last couple of weeks so I'm not making any this week."

On a Mission THE BAR-B-QUE BUS **MEMPHIS, TENNESSEE**

The pleasant banter doesn't last. Mr. Anderson walks into the store to get a few bags of hamburger buns. The temperature drops then and silence descends.

The flashing red light on the screened porch of the smokehouse has been turned on, which means that Anderson's Bar B Q is open for business. We order a couple of sandwiches and Frank prepares to take pictures of Anderson, tongs in hand, pulling the meat from the carcass of the pig. We walk into the smokehouse, with its Dr. Pepper cooler full of sodas and its tray of small plastic containers full of sauce. Anderson pulls back the metal door under which the pig still rests and prepares to pull the meat. At that point Frank begins to focus his camera.

"I prefer you not to take no more pictures in here," Anderson says without warmth.

The bun is also cold, and by the time Frank has set the sandwiches outside on the picnic table and taken pictures of them, the meat is cold as well. But it yields easily to the teeth, falling tenderly on the tongue. It's a bit salty, though, and I wonder whether Anderson has managed to salt the whole pig through a massive infusion in its front legs or if we have been served from the saltiest portion of the carcass.

"Tender as a mother's love," Frank says to Anderson, who has not asked us our opinion.

"Mother's love ain't always so tender," Anderson says, again without warmth. This we take to be an exit cue. We promise to send him a picture or two, but he is unmoved. Our goodbye is met by silence.

There is silence, too, in the car as we drive away. Anderson is an important part of the culture of barbecue. He cooks his meat in a way that is all but unheard of in Memphis, a barbecue capital not far away. For that alone he is interesting. Moreover, Anderson, a white man taught to prepare this food by black men during the pre-integration era, could be an important source of information on the tangled racial recipe that has gone into making barbecue the peculiarly American food that it has become. But, at least on this morning, these are not issues he chooses to discuss.

Though it is on both our minds, I am the one who asks the obvious question. "You think somebody told him we was black?"

"Yes," says Frank, his voice heavy with dejection. "I reckon somebody done finked on us."

∽

Chinaman Hutch has been "thowed late" this morning because he had to drive his girlfriend to Jackson, Tennessee. We are already waiting when his pickup drives into the yard. Arthur Gray, Hutch's eighteen-year-old grand-nephew, is here to help him—at least until the new McDonald's in Jackson opens. He intends to start working there as soon as it does.

"That woman tickled the hell out of me talkin' 'bout yaw'll last night," Hutch says as he gets out. "'Wonder what them men is, reckon they some kinda spies?'"

We follow him into the building where his grills are kept. This is the fourth such structure, he tells us. One by one, the other three burned down. He picks up the four quarters of the pig, wipes the ashes off them with a dish towel, and wraps them in aluminum foil. "How yaw'll want it?" he asks, "about medium hot?" He pulls some meat from one of the quarters and places it on a small wooden stand, sprinkles a little salt on it, a little thin, red sauce, and begins to chop the meat with a cleaver.

The meat tastes very different from Anderson's, though they use the same process. It's not as salty, but it does have a kick owing partly to the sauce. What is most interesting is that neither Anderson's barbecue nor Hutch's has a strong smoke flavor. One would think that after twelve hours over the flame and another twelve hours over the dying embers the smoke would be running out of it. But much of the smoke, of course, was burned off as the wood was burned down to the embers, leaving the meat with a mellow taste.

Barbecue sauces are generally divided into three types: tomato-based, mustard-based, and vinegar-based. Mustard-based sauces are foreign to Tennessee. Here the other two conceptions rule. Most vinegar-based sauces are red and obviously contain some ketchup or tomato sauce, and tomato-based sauce usually contains some vinegar. But whereas typical store-bought barbecue sauce is thick and sweet like ketchup, the restaurant sauce in Memphis barbecue places is closer to the consistency of evaporated milk. In the rural areas the consistency is more like low-fat milk. There is also much less sugar in these rural sauces. In fact, the people here don't usually call it barbecue sauce at all; they refer to it as hot sauce, even when it is not especially spicy. Just fifty miles outside Memphis, barbecue is clearly very different.

"That sauce thar," Hutch explains, "a lot of sauces you go in these places it's vinegar standing on it and you have to shake it e'up. It'll be no vinegar thar. It'll be like it is an' I'll have people carrying it back to Chicago and have it for a year and they'll be no vinegar. I had a li'l white gal go to school at Jackson. She used one of these small bottles every week. She put in on her aigs, sausage, breakfast, and everything."

Faux Folk
∞

The waiter and the security guard at Corky's agree that their employer sells the best barbecue in Memphis, but they differ on the question of which barbecue restaurant has the best atmosphere. The security guard likes the Germantown Commissary, a place on the outskirts of Memphis. The waiter says that the atmosphere at Charlie Vergos' Rendezvous "kicks ass." Rib joint atmosphere is of course an oxymoron. But just as barbecue itself is a process by which lowly cuts of meat are made not only edible but desirable, classic barbecue restaurants transform the vice of their inelegant surroundings into rustic virtue. This issue of atmosphere and barbecue has become increasingly significant in recent years as

barbecue restaurants like Corky's have gone upscale. Separating the flavor of the food from the flavor of the place is often difficult for old-line barbecue enthusiasts.

The Commissary features "Epicurean BBQ & Ribs in Old Germantown by the R.R. Tracks," its menu tells us. It is unclear what "epicurean" means in the context of barbecue. There is nothing radically different about the preparation of the Commissary's food, at least nothing that could be discerned by the tongue. In fact it is average at best. But in fairness, it was not the food for which the restaurant was recommended. Strewn about the walls are dozens of pieces of Depression-era memorabilia like old soft-drink signs, some old Gulf gas station signs, and advertisements for elixirs. None of the products are associated with barbecue per se. Rather, they are relevant to some bygone era assumed to be related in some vague way to an old style of cooking.

The Rendezvous is underground and has exposed brick walls that give it a cave-like atmosphere. A fire here five years ago almost gutted the place; now the charred, exposed beams contribute to the overall effect. But at both the Commissary and the Rendezvous what is at work is a kind of faux folk effect, sort of like television's most famous junk men, Sanford and Son, moving uptown.

I first encountered faux folk at Houlihan's, a restaurant on Bourbon Street in New Orleans. Among other curiosities, it featured an antique tricycle suspended from the ceiling. I remember being amazed

that a restaurant had been able to amass what appeared to my young eyes to be a priceless collection of antique memorabilia. It was a mild shock to learn that Houlihan's was in fact a chain of restaurants and that antique tricycles were not uncommon. That was when I first began to suspect that the production of antiques may now be a bigger business than it ever was in antiquity.

Beale Street Talking
∞

During our earlier visit to Beale Street we missed the Center for Southern Culture in the glare of nightclub neon. By day the Center is worth a trip. Its current exhibit is about WDIA, the radio station that is largely responsible for Memphis' reputation as a center for popular music. WDIA ("Making Black Waves") started off in 1947 as an all-white "good music" station at a time when there were no black disc jockeys in the South. But "good music" wasn't cutting it, so in 1948 Tan Town Jamboree, a black music program, was given twenty minutes of air time per day. A year later Bert Ferguson and John Pepper, the station's founders, expanded the black music format to all day. Riley "Beale Street Blues Boy" King was an early disc jockey. So was Rufus "Can Your Monkey Do the Dog?" Thomas. Among the memorabilia is an advertisement featuring Mrs. Hattie H. Culpepper, manager of Culpepper's Chicken Shack, specializing in fried chicken and "Bbecue" ribs and shoulders.

The Blues Museum, a couple of blocks away, is a well-conceived tour of blues history. Enclosed in glass are photographs, album covers, autographed guitars, and other memorabilia tracing the development of this music from the work of traditional blues legends like Robert Johnson and Son House to electric blues practitioners like Albert King and Muddy Waters. Telephones hanging on the outside of the glass panels make it possible to hear the music of the performers featured in the exhibit. Listening to these phones in historical sequence, while not aurally satisfying, is a clear lesson in how the blues changed from rural to urban, from acoustic to electric, and from folk art of the highest order to pop music for the masses. Gone is the intricate guitar work, the expansive range of vocal techniques, the often joyous expression of a full range of human experience. Gone, in short, is the essence of the blues. In its place is an entire room dedicated to the irrelevant gyrations of Memphis' favorite adopted son, Elvis.

That's the complicated thing, of course—maintaining the essence. The early blues can never mean to us what it meant to its earlier hearers because it can never be tied to any current, personal reference points like 1920s Saturday nights or juke joints in which we have ourselves danced to it. But there are things about it that are still fresh and relevant today. Things related to well-turned phrases, instrumental mastery, and the blues as existential confrontation with the hardness and sadness that characterize life for each of us at one point or another. The trio that first night at B.B.

King's didn't understand this, didn't even try to. Consequently there was nothing of the sharing or celebration in their music that is at the heart of such Robert Johnson performances as "Preaching Blues." You can't imagine a beautician in the trio's audience yelling "Dip it over heyah!" and you can't imagine the trio realizing that this statement is not so much an invitation to intimacy as the acceptance of an invitation to be an intimate part of the performance. The venues of Beale Street operate at a great disadvantage: so many of their patrons are tourists that the clubs have no real hope of establishing a groove based on the presence of a core group of regulars whose personalities combine to create the personality of the place. Perhaps they do the best they can with their nostalgic decors and tributes to the legends of the blues. Which is why Club Unique remains unique.

Barbecue, now that its appeal has broadened so widely, is in a similar position. Form and function are no longer so neatly tied together. One imagines barbecue beginning as a technique for cooking meat in celebration of a successful hunt. As hunting gives way to domestication of animals, barbecue becomes the technique for cooking in celebration of the slaughter of the fatted sow. As home slaughter gives way to grocery shopping, barbecue becomes the slow-roasting technique that allows families and friends to talk and visit for hours in anticipation of the payoff. Finally, in the early stages of commercial barbecue, the main thing that remains is the technique of cooking the meat slowly

and with smoke. This is of course a slow, expensive, and labor-intensive process, and it ultimately gives way to a concept of barbecue that puts a premium not on the smoking of the meat but on the flavor of the sauce, which, in the absence of any real meat flavor, must alone communicate to the tongue that this is barbecue. Many, if not most, of the newer barbecue restaurants eschew the slow smoking process of J.C. Hardaway, let alone that of Billy Anderson or Chinaman Hutch. So while barbecue itself may be more popular than ever, much of it is less and less like real barbecue. "What we have here," Frank says while working through one of the many bad shoulder sandwiches Memphis has to offer, "is food for the masses."

They Can Sweat You Some Meat

It is a truism that you find what you seek in the last place you look. With the exception of a nightcap at Hawkins, Cozy Corner will be the last restaurant we visit on this trip.

It seems promising because we can hear the sound of Hank Crawford's saxophone over the restaurant noises. If there's good jazz playing, we figure, the place can't be all bad. Still, we are cautious. We are careful not to attract the attention of Ray Robinson, Jr., whom we met on our first night in Memphis. If this is just another average restaurant, we don't want to be forced to speak untruths about the food for the sake of civility.

We order modestly, a plate of rib tips. Then, with the synchronization of aqua bal-

Ray Robinson and Son COZY CORNER **MEMPHIS, TENNESSEE**

lerinas, Frank and I take one bite, look across the table at each other, and break into the smile that comes from having tasted truth. This is barbecue of the first order. Then, even though it's not really within our purview, we order one of the barbecued Cornish game hens, because imagining so delicate a bird bathed in the smoke and goodness of this cozy corner leaves us no alternative. We have imagined accurately. There's enough smoke on the inside to make you bite into these birds with relish, and there're enough herbs and spices coating the crisp skin to justify the shameless licking of fingers. We take a few more bites of the rib tips just to check ourselves, but it isn't necessary.

"Who would have thought that in Memphis, Tennessee, we would have discovered the Art Tatum of the Cornish game hen?" Frank says.

From his chosen table in the front of Cozy Corner, Ray Robinson, Sr. (no relation to Sugar), can see the parking lot where his customers drive up, the counter where they place their orders, the kitchen where their orders are prepared, and the dining room where many of their orders are consumed. He claims to be in semi-retirement, allowing his son, Ray Jr., to handle most of the business operations. But little escapes his notice, and the quality of the food here reflects that. Since meeting the younger Robinson we've consulted the barbecue authorities as well as average Memphians for recommendations on barbecue restaurants to visit in and around the city. Occasionally Cozy Corner makes their lists, but not often. The reputations of the oft-lauded places that do make these lists often evaporate with the first bite of their food. So much for critics, amateur or professional.

Robinson Sr. and his wife, Desiree, join us at our table and begin to tell us how their interest in barbecue went from hobby to obsession. Robinson, an electrician by trade, was working in Denver, Colorado. In the early 70s, he says, there were no good barbecue restaurants in Denver. Having grown up in Memphis, Robinson began to crave the smoked meat that was a staple of his home town. With no place to turn, Robinson began barbecuing for himself.

"It'd be snowing outside. And I had a patio with a little thirty-gallon barrel," he recalls. "I'd have it in the door and the screen door open, and every once in a while I'd come out and turn it and go back in."

"It really was not an obsession," Desiree insists, as if we might be tempted to conclude that it was. "Both of us are food enthusiasts. Where we were living at that time we couldn't find any good barbecue. Had we been unable to find good pizza, we might be doing pizza now."

Robinson approached the study of good barbecue cooking with almost scientific discipline. It was slow going at first, more false starts than true. But he speaks of the various barbecue techniques people use with the authority of a man who has truly honed his craft.

"The mistake I made was basting," he says. "I used to take an onion, garlic, vinegar, and water baste and mop this stuff on, and it was running right there in the pit. Marinating for barbecue doesn't work. So I started using a dry sauce. Just lightly sprinkle it on the meat. See, that way your sauce is cooked into the meat, I don't care what you put on it or don't put on it 'cause the meat is cooked right. Every time you use a sauce you're trying to cover something up. When you done messed up the fried chicken and you make gravy—hell, it's right then. Then, too, a lot of people boil their meat. Once water hits the meat, the meat ain't no good no more; you need to take it, throw it away, and cook some greens in that water.

"And listen," he tells us. "If you're gonna write a book, do me one damn favor. Explain to people that barbecue is a way of cooking. So don't walk into a place and say, 'Give me a barbecue.' Give me a barbecue what? It's like walking into a place and saying, 'Give me a fried.' A fried what? That's very important to help barbecue along."

Pit Boss Howard NEW ZION MISSIONARY BAPTIST CHURCH HUNTSVILLE, TEXAS

Toward a History of Barbecue

The first time Frank and I were confronted head-on with the issue of where barbecue comes from was in Nashville, Tennessee, a city that is justifiably absent from maps of great barbecue capitals. Led by John Baeder, the artist whose paintings of diners and other vanishing icons of Americana have helped revive interest in them, we had scoured the city. Despite his best efforts, we found little of culinary note. Later, as we were on our way back to our hotel, some young men leaning on a car told us we could find good barbecue at a place called Lit'l Hoggy's. They knew the food was good there; they had built the pit. Sure enough, the barbecue there was the best we'd had in Nashville, even though it was a bit on the salty side. We struck up a conversation with the pit-master, Bill Kuntz, and he made an interesting observation. Many of the early Texans hailed from Tennessee. As evidence, he noted that most of the people who died at the Alamo were from Tennessee. Texas barbecue, he claimed, was really an attempt by transplanted Tennesseans to recapture the flavor of their native state. Texans barbecue beef rather than pork, he said, but that's a reflection of the fact that Texans tend to raise beef and not pork.

In San Antonio, at the Alamo Museum, they list the home states of the various fighters killed in the famous standoff. Thirty-three of those killed were Tennesseans, including James Bowie and Davy Crockett. Virginians numbered a distant second, with thirteen dead.

The connection between Tennessee and Texas barbecue hit home later on. By then we had seen Chinaman Hutch and Billy Anderson cook barbecue in rural western Tennessee. We had watched them burn wood down to embers and place these embers directly under the meat with a shovel. In Texas, almost everyone we encountered burned the wood at one end of the pit and let the smoke travel to the meat; the meat was cooked indirectly, not over the coals. But at Cooper's Old Time Pit Bar-B-Que, in Llano, Texas, they don't cook indirectly. They cook like Billy Anderson and Chinaman Hutch, only faster.

"This is hill country cooking," explained Terry Wooten, the owner of Cooper's. "We don't claim to smoke meat, we cook meat. German-type cooking is smoking; this is the cowboy way. When the juices fall off and hit the fire, that's when it starts to smoking and you get the flavor."

Again the meat was good, but it was salty like Kuntz's and very much like the barbecue at two places we tried in Fredericksburg, Texas: Pardi's at Birck's and Ken Hall's Texas Barbecue. Whether we ate goat or pork or beef, a coating of salt and spices interfered with our enjoyment of what was otherwise excellent barbecue. This distaste for salt seemed to mark us as outsiders as surely as our Louisiana license plate.

Often in our travels we encountered restaurateurs who had studied barbecue and chosen a style not reflective of their region. But such a similarity between two relatively isolated places—Blue Goose, Tennessee, and Llano, Texas—seemed more than coincidental and less than academic, and offers some credence to the transplanted-Tennessean theory.

If you trace it back and further back, where does barbecue really come from? Theories on its origin abound.

The word "barbecue" is generally thought to have evolved from "barbacoa," which first appeared in Gonzalo Fernandez de Oviedo's 1526 book *De la HistoriaGeneral y Natural de las Indias*. Oviedo, who explored the Caribbean, wrote that the Indians of Tierra Firme roasted meats on sticks and then placed them in the ground, "like a grating or trivet, over a pit." But though "barbacoa" was the word he used, it may not have been the word that the cooks themselves used to describe the proceedings.

Another theory claims that barbecue is derived from the French phrase "de barbe à queue," which translates as "from beard to tail" and basically describes the technique of roasting a whole animal. The *Oxford English Dictionary* discounts this theory, however, claiming that "the alleged French barbe à queue 'beard to tail' is absurd conjecture suggested merely by the sound of the word."

The word "barbacoa" has survived intact and is still used in Mexico and southern Texas to mean meat, generally cow, lamb, or goat heads, buried in a pit and cooked over coals. Mario Montaño, a professor of folklore who has done an extensive study of barbacoa and Mexican food ways, discovered several references to meat cooked underground in the writings of early Spanish explorers. Among the references he cites is one found in the writings of Father Bernardino Sahagun, Hernán Cortés' chronicler. In his description of the foods available in the Aztec capital Tenochtitlán (now Mexico City), he wrote, "And other things they do are delicious stews; they also, as their trade, sell roasted meats and meats roasted under the ground." Since the Spaniards are generally credited with bringing domesticated cows and pigs to Mexico, it is unclear what kind of meat was being cooked.

"Barbecue" itself has at least three meanings. It is a verb meaning to cook meat over a wood or charcoal fire and/or with the smoke from wood or charcoal. It is a noun meaning meat cooked by one of the many barbecue methods, and it is also a noun meaning the gathering at which this type of cooking takes place.

This range of complementary definitions for the word dates back at least to American colonial times. Two postcolonial examples from the historical files of the Colonial Williamsburg Foundation perhaps best illustrate the point:

His house was the seat of plenty and plainness, mirth and good-humor and genuine hospitality without ostentation ... here I found a large table loaded with fat roasted turkies, geese and ducks, boiled fowls, large hams, hung-beef, barbecued pig, &c. enough for five and twenty men. [J.F.D. Smythe, *A Tour of the United States of America*, I, 1784, p. 104, CWF Research Files b]

The people in this part of the country, bordering upon James River, are extremely fond of an entertainment which they call a barbacue. It consists in a large party meeting together, either under some trees, or in a house, to partake of a sturgeon or pig roasted in the open air, on a sort of hurdle, over a slow fire; this however, is an entertainment chiefly confined to the lower ranks, and, like most others of the same nature, it generally ends in intoxication. [Isaac Weld, *Travels Through North America During the Years 1795, 1796, and 1797*, p. 107, CWF Research Files b]

But even these three meanings have a range of meanings. In the Southeast, barbecue refers almost exclusively to pork; in the Southwest, almost exclusively to beef; and in the Midwest (specifically Kansas City), generally to both. The Midwest is easily explained; it's a merger. But the distinction between east and west leads you to wonder whether the two conceptions evolved from the same source or whether the two coasts began with distinct traditions that much later evolved toward similar recipes.

A parallel discussion among geographers and folklorists on the origin of American cattle-ranching techniques sheds light on the question of where barbecue originated and how it spread. Terry G. Jordan, in his book *Trails to Texas*, explores several theories. Admittedly, the connection between the production of food and the preparation of it is not always direct. It is conceivable that in our own time one could be a great chef while laboring under the delusion that milk is raised in cartons. All the same, it seems logical to look at developments in the raising and marketing of meat for some clues as to developments in the preparation of it.

The first theory that Jordan reports holds that cattle ranching in America simply evolved from European roots. In colonial America livestock roamed freely and found their own food until they were herded up and driven to market. Ranchers accumulated larger herds than those common in Great Britain; they identified them with brands, and they used hired hands or enslaved laborers to tend them. These techniques were logical adaptations to the American environment. Similarly, British colonists faced with the challenge of developing cooking techniques appropriate to their new home could simply have adapted British roasting techniques. In her essay "Early Fair Foods and Barbecuing" Rosemary Brandau notes that the barbecue event was much like an English fair and pig roast.

But there were outside influences, perhaps chief among them Americans of African descent. Even if one sets aside the revisionist histories of Ivan van Sertima and Cheikh anta Diop, the fact is that Africans predated the British on the shores of South Carolina as part of a 1526 Spanish expedition from the West Indies. In his book *Black Majority: Negroes in Colonial South Carolina from 1670 Through the Stono Rebellion*, Peter H. Wood suggests that open grazing was common in the Senegambia region of west Africa and that South Carolina slave dealers "expressed a steady preference" for Africans from that region.

Many of the Africans who arrived in colonial South Carolina arrived from the West Indies, the place where linguistic evidence suggests barbecue originated. This may not be mere coincidence as it relates to the history of barbecue; enslaved Africans may have learned some culinary techniques from West Indian natives. The African influence on American cuisine, though often downplayed, is undeniable. Barbecue, more than most American foods, has come to be inextricably tied to African-American culture. "Almost all barbecuing was done by Negroes in past years, and much of it still is," wrote Rufus Jarman in "Dixie's Most Disputed Dish," his 1954 article in the *Saturday Evening Post*.

Long before cattle raising became synonymous with the western plains, it was widespread along the eastern seaboard, specifically in South Carolina. Charles Kovacik, a University of South Carolina geography professor, posits a South Carolinian origin for barbecue and contends that the food spread west. He notes that Charleston was founded early among colonial cities, in 1670, and that by the end of the American Revolution it was the only sizable city south of Philadelphia. Because it was large and a port city, Charleston was an influential cultural center. Additionally, South Carolina is the only state in which all three of the dominant types of barbecue sauce can be found: vinegar-, tomato-, and mustard-based.

A third theory examined by Jordan contends that the development of ranching can be traced to the Hispanic influence on American culture. Specifically, cattle ranching in the western United States was developed under the influence of people from across the Mexican border. Jordan notes that as Anglo-Americans moved into Texas, they simply adopted the Hispanic cattle tradition they found there. Buttressing this theory is the linguistic evidence that such quintessential cowboy words as "ranch," "lariat," "lasso," "bronc," "dally roping," and "corral" seem to be corrupted versions of Spanish words.

Given the enduring use of the word "barbacoa" and the technique that accompanied it among Spanish-speaking Americans, the notion of a Hispanic origin for barbecue is defensible. Yet there is no evidence that any Carolina barbecues were held up while the cooks awaited recipes from Texas.

Of course the major distinction between eastern and western barbecue is that in the east barbecue is synonymous with pork and in the west it is synonymous with beef. In smaller restaurants in both regions these distinctions are very much intact, but large restaurants in Texas almost invariably have pork ribs on the menu, and often, though not always, large restaurants in Georgia and Tennessee will carry brisket or beef ribs.

These regional menu preferences appear related to ranching patterns.

According to Jordan, ranchers in South Carolina generally kept pigs and cows on the same ranch. Since much of the area on which the animals roamed was forest, both pigs and cows were able to find their preferred foods. Cows could graze; pigs could forage. In eastern Texas, the practice of raising both types of stock persisted. As ranching moved westward into the plains, however, pig raising decreased substantially. In fact, pigs were penned up at the ranch rather than left out on the range, and they were generally kept in numbers large enough only for the consumption of the rancher and his family. So although pork was not scarce in Texas, beef came to dominate the state's economy and its menu.

Ultimately Jordan contends that African-Americans and Anglo-Americans evolved a system of open-range cattle herding that diffused westward, taking roots in eastern Texas. There, contact with a Hispanic ranching tradition produced a hybrid ranching technique that spread through much of the Great Plains.

In my view, barbecue is also the product of the blending of techniques. It is clear that barbecue existed and flourished in the American colonies long before the word "barbacoa" or the associated technique could have traveled eastward from Texas and played any significant role. In the eastern colonies the mingling of Native, Anglo, and African cultures produced a hybrid culture that included, among other things, barbecue. Yet the technique of Texas barbecue is no mere replica of an eastern tradition but rather a stylization of it. That stylization, it appears, owes its development to a combination of eastern and Hispanic roots and Texas ingenuity.

Mr. Vera VERA'S BACKYARD BAR-B-QUE **BROWNSVILLE, TEXAS**

Texas

We had a nice plan for the conquest of Texas. We would start in Brownsville in early June, work our way up to middle Texas by Juneteenth, and be out of the state by July. That was long before we came to understand how large Texas is and how much good barbecue it contains. Everyone we talked to made a compelling case for why their favorite barbecue place could not be missed.

In Dallas we met Donald Payton from the Dallas Historical Society, a garrulous and knowledgeable tour guide who took off the afternoon to sample barbecue with us. Throughout the tour Payton told us about his family, who in 1847 became the first African-Americans to arrive in Dallas. They were among the many other "belongings" of William Bob Miller. Even now Payton never fails to refer to Miller as "Moss Billy," as a token of disrespect.

Our tour started at Two Podner's with stacked plates of good barbecue but not such good side orders. Fred Conwright, one of the owners, told us much about the business of barbecue and the business of redlining, which he fears may play a large role in hindering his efforts to franchise. Among the other important things Conwright told us was that we should see his pit manufacturer, A.N. Bewley. And Bewley told us to check out Bodacious Bar-B-Q in Longview, and it was great advice.

Southwest of Dallas, in Glen Rose, we stopped at Maurice Pylant's Western Kitchen (Real Pit Barbecue, Hickory Smoked), where we watched Maurice fry huge steaks as he explained to us that in order to arrive at the appropriate richness of flavor in his briskets he cooks them for twenty-five or thirty hours. "Hell no, we don't put any seasoning on them," he told us. "Hell no!"

Further east we toured Lockhart and Luling, which I still think of as a unit like Minneapolis–St. Paul, though the Texas cities are a couple of dozen miles apart. Lockhart barbecue is well known. In Luling there's Luling Bar-B-Q and Luling City Market. Both serve barbecue the excellence of which can scarcely be overstated.

In the end, it was made deliciously clear that, whether your taste be for barbacoa, brisket, or ribs, you'll find no better quality and variety than that in Texas.

Barbecue on the Border: Brownsville

Mando said to be here Saturday morning about nine so that we could see the whole thing take place. We are here, but it has already started. The wood—small trunks and large branches of trees—is burning in the pit. Mr. Vera says it has been burning since eight o'clock. By two, he says, it should be ready.

Florenzio, who says nothing, is draped in a garbage bag. Florenzio with his brown skin and slight, boyish frame. Florenzio with his gray hairs among the black. His pants are rolled up and he's not wearing socks.

It is cool in the small tin building that is connected by a doorway to the hot yellow building where the fire is burning.

Florenzio's morning job is to clean the cows' heads. He walks into the freezer of the cool building and picks up two or three by their clear plastic enclosures, then sets them on the counter near the sink. There is already a line of cleaned heads on the counter, stacked two high. The heads arrive from the slaughterhouse skinless. Their teeth show as if clamped in a grimace. Once Florenzio has taken six or eight heads out of the freezer, he begins to clean them.

Mr. Vera pronounces "cow" with a second, whispered syllable. Cow-oo. "Sometimes when they keell the cow-oo it will throw up," he says, "so you have to clean the heads." There is also the blood and also the mucus, he tells us. "Sometimes when they keell the cow-oo it will have a cold, so there will be mucus in the cow-oo's head."

Florenzio takes a long cow's tongue in his hand and sprays it with a concentrated stream of water from the nozzle of the hose. The tongue has a United States Department of Agriculture brand on it. It is connected only by a small piece of skin at the back of the head, so it is easily turned over and around and cleaned from every angle. The tongue clean, Florenzio begins to shoot water full force into each of the openings in the cow's head. There are the nostrils, the openings at the back of the head, and one small hole in the front of the head. You can tell the ones that are cleaned already because Florenzio has put the tongues back into the mouths.

"Way back you keell the cow-oo with a sledgehammer. Then you keell them with a gun," Mr. Vera explains. "Now you keell them with a gun, but it doesn't have a real bullet. It goes in and out, so you can use the bullet again."

As Florenzio shoots the water, a small pool of slime and blood forms and floats in the water on the counter. More water splashes all around and onto his garbage bag. The smell of blood and raw meat arrives at your nose with the cool mist.

Mando has arrived. Mr. Vera is his father and Mr. Vera started the business, but Mando is in charge now.

Mando adds his silence to Florenzio's. One by one he wraps the clean heads in aluminum foil. No salt, no pepper. They work with the wordless synchronization of neighboring machines on an assembly line. Wrap this way. Wrap that way. Turn the head. Wrap this way. Done. Tongue out. Splash. Tongue in. Splash. Spray in the front. Splash. Spray in the back. Splash. Wrap. Splash.

It is becoming crowded in the small room. Frank and I walk next door with Mr. Vera into the small yellow building with the high ceiling and the pit dug in the middle of its dirt floor. The pit is deep enough for a man to stand in up to his chest. It is walled with bricks and framed by a metal band. Outside this smokeroom at eleven o'clock it is already near 100 degrees. Inside, it feels hot enough to melt dirt. Limbs and branches are burning in the pit. Some long ones stick out. "We use mesquite and ebony," Mr. Vera tells us.

Vera's Backyard Bar-B-Que is at the corner of 26th and Southmost. Southmost is a commercial street while 26th is residential. I walk with Mr. Vera a few doors down on 26th Street and he shows me ebony trees and mesquite trees. Both have pods of beans or seeds growing on them. Those of the ebony tree are hard. But mesquite beans, he tells us, are sweet and taste good. People eat them and sometimes feed them to their cattle.

Once all the heads are cleaned, Florenzio begins to take the ones Mando has already wrapped and stack them in the smokehouse. Mr. Vera starts to remove the wood from the pit. The ends of most of the branches are not burned, only the parts in the pit. Some of the smaller branches can easily be picked up by hand. Mr. Vera drags them outside to the parking lot, where he hoses them down to stop the burning.

Soon Mando and Florenzio join him. Using a sharp-ended metal pole, they maneuver each big limb into position so that they can get a chain around it and drag it out of the pit and onto the concrete outside. Mr. Vera's job is to hose off the wood they bring out to him.

Mando checks the temperature of the pit with his hand, waiting until the flames have died down so that he can put the wrapped heads in. The heads range from eighteen to thirty-five pounds. Florenzio throws them to Mando; they drip water as they fly through the air. Then Mando places them into the pit, moving around so he can stack them properly. A few of the heads, those of goats, are wrapped in burlap pinto-bean sacks.

Coco, one of Mando's older brothers, has arrived and begins to help. Like Mando, he is wearing a white uniform work shirt with his name monogrammed on it. Once all the heads are in place, wet burlap sacks are put on top. Then a metal cover goes over the pit.

Now Manuel, the third Vera brother, arrives. After Coco has hosed down the metal top, Manuel begins to shovel dirt onto it. The dirt is spread evenly around and then wetted so that no smoke can escape. By the time we walk back outside the smokeroom, Mr. Vera has finished cleaning up. All that remains visible of the charred wood and the soot is the water that was used to rinse off the street.

❧

Mr. Vera's first name is Alberto. His gray hair has retreated, leaving a bronze, bald field at the top of his head. His fingers are gnarled, working fingers. As he speaks, they hold his Winston cigarette. He was born here in Brownsville, he tells us. After serving in the army for three years during World War II, he returned here and began doing a variety of jobs.

"For a year I would buy soap in Brownsville and sell it across the border in Mexico. After that my brother started a slaughterhouse, and I worked for him at the slaughterhouse for about four years. Then I went with another man and worked for him for about two years. Then I went back with my brother for about two years."

During this time a man from Mexico came up to Brownsville and showed Mr. Vera and his brother how to make barbacoa. They would make it and sell it as a sideline to the slaughterhouse business. Then in the mid-1950s Mr. Vera decided to strike out on his own, selling barbacoa full time at a place across the street from the current location.

"I started with one head, then two, then up to 120," he says. "Each time I'd have to dig a bigger and bigger pit. When it got to where it was too big, I put the bricks in.

"When it started, it was a very cheap meat," he continues. "Now they sell the brain, the tongue, and they put the rest in bologna and things like that. But before, when I started, I used to buy them for fifty cents and sell the whole head for three dollars and still make money. I guess we were selling a pound of barbecue for about fifty cents per pound. I still was making four or five dollars for them when I was selling them by the pound. And that was a lot of money. In that time a dollar was a dollar. But now what can you buy with a dollar?"

When Mr. Vera and his sons speak of the food they prepare, they call it barbecue. Sometimes they distinguish between "American barbecue" and "barbacoa" if they are talking about both in the same sentence. But generally, barbecue for them means cows' heads.

I ask him about the various preparation methods I've heard about, like wrapping heads in burlap sacks and banana leaves. "The idea was that burlap would give you a flavor, but it's not true, and it's messy. Even if it's wrapped with aluminum foil, the flavor will get in there some kind of way, through a crack or something. They also claim that in Mexico they use cactus leaves, but I've never done it."

Vera's is the only place in Brownsville that is allowed to sell barbacoa cooked in the ground, Mr. Vera tells us. Although there are probably a dozen places that advertise it, they make it in the oven. "As far as I know, nobody can open a place like this because it's under a grandfather clause. Even us, if we closed, we won't be able to open it again.

"This is the only place that's cooking over wood," he says. "[Oven barbacoa] doesn't have the same taste. Some people don't know the difference, I guess. People drink beer and they just buy the cheapest beer and they don't know the difference. People who don't know the difference, they buy anything. If they sell it cheaper, we don't care. We have our customers that know the difference."

It takes about eight hours to cook barbacoa. What makes it especially difficult, Mr. Vera says, is that once you close the pit you can't make any adjustments. So you have to know exactly when it is right. "We don't have any gauges," he says. "If it's too hot, it'll dry it out and you'll have too much shrinkage and you lose money. If it's not hot enough, it won't be quite done. If you know it's not hot enough when you put it in, you can leave it in another hour."

☙

As you walk and drive around downtown Brownsville, most of the signs you see are in Spanish. And although the outskirts of Brownsville look very much like any other suburban area in the country, which is to say there are several fast-food restaurants, shopping malls, and a highway, downtown Brownsville seems stagnant and unchanging. Most of the stores there are discount stores. There's a Woolworth's, a 50% Off Annex, a place where you can buy watches for $1.00, $2.00, or $3.99, and two Payless shoe stores a pair of blocks apart.

Ultimately, it is neither barbacoa nor border-town status for which Brownsville is best known. The city's unfortunate claim to infamy rests on the fact that it was the scene of the so-called Brownsville raid. The city is still touchy about it and seems to have a bit of trouble keeping its story straight. Everyone agrees that in May of 1906 it was announced that the white troops at Fort Brown would be replaced with black soldiers. Racial tensions grew once the troops arrived, culminating in a gun battle on August 13, 1906, during which shots were fired in the vicinity of the army garrison. One Brownsville resident was killed in the incident. The soldiers, who had served their country in Cuba and the Philippines, were blamed for the incident, discharged, and denied their army benefits.

In the Brownsville Museum, among several pieces of period furniture and clothing and displays depicting the city's more shining moments, is a display dedicated to the raid. In one place the museum takes a fairly neutral position, noting that some people believe that the troops maintained "a strict 'code of silence'" to conceal the fact that they had attacked the townspeople. It goes on to note that other people, "such as John Weaver, believe the raid was staged by townspeople. His book—*The Brownsville Raid*—is angrily dismissed by many south Texas residents." Yet a few inches from this balanced presentation of history the museum's signwriter tips the scales, concluding that "black troops rushed out of Fort Brown and fired into various homes and businesses." The display also includes personal effects and a baby picture of Fred Tate, a customs officer who admits to having pistol-whipped one of the black soldiers in the days leading up to the raid. The soldier's offense: he had failed to show proper deference to the white women with whom Tate was walking down the street.

People often have difficulty agreeing on the facts of a racially charged history. But I am a bit surprised that a museum would have such difficulty agreeing with itself. I telephone Bruce Aiken, the executive director of the museum, about the incident and Weaver's book on it. He, like the second page in his exhibit, is ultimately clear on how it happened.

"He white-washed it," Aiken says of Weaver. "He would infer that there were no black soldiers involved, which is totally

Heads Raw, Heads Wrapped VERA'S BACKYARD BAR-B-QUE **BROWNSVILLE, TEXAS**

contrary to what the old-timers saw with their own eyes." Having lived in Brownsville all his life, Aiken notes that it is impossible to keep a secret there. Had white citizens been involved, everyone would have known sooner or later. Since black troops were responsible, secrecy was somehow maintained.

∽

Mando said to be here about midnight. We could see them open the pit and remove the cows' heads then. It is eleven forty-five. Light flows from inside the smokehouse onto the warm darkness of the parking lot. The little yellow smokehouse and the adjoining preparation building are a lighted stitch of activity on the sleeping pattern of the street. Inside the smokehouse the pit is already open and several heads have been removed.

On the window sill is a small radio. It plays mariachi music and lyrical waltzes, music for lovers and others not working at midnight on Saturday.

Silently, at one end of the four-foot counter, Florenzio separates meat from bone. The jaw bones work out cleanly with no meat attached. His fingers inside the skull, Florenzio pokes out the eyes. He separates the meat into various trays.

Silently, at the other end of the counter, Mando does the tedious work of scraping the waste parts from the meat. He further separates it into the cheek meat, the tongue, the eyes, the palate, the sweetbreads. The room smells thickly of roasted meat and dripping fat.

Both of Mando's brothers grew up in the barbacoa business. But Mando is the youngest and was the last to get married, so he has inherited the major responsibility for the work. "I've been doing it twenty years," he says, "since the age of twelve." Although he is sitting out this semester, he's in college studying finance. "Hopefully, once I get an education, I'll do something else. After twenty years, you get tired of it. If I could find the people to work, I'd probably keep it. But it's hard to find the people to work. The only ones that'll work are the illegal aliens and you can't have them."

Once enough meat has been separated, Mando takes the various trays and dumps their contents into an electric roasting pan. The meat will stay moist and warm in these pans until it is sold five or six hours from now.

As the bones collect, they are taken outside by Florenzio. A garbage can on the curb is already full of bones and teeth. Next to it is a large garbage bin, into which Florenzio throws the heads and bones one by one.

As one o'clock approaches, there are still nearly a dozen heads in the pit. Along the wall there are several more. It has been and will continue to be a long night.

"I got up yesterday at six in the morning," Mando says. "I usually go home at four-thirty a.m. and sleep half an hour or an hour. That's one of the things I like besides eating—sleeping. Hopefully, if I start doing a little better, I can hire someone to help."

During the week Mando works on remodeling the three buildings that make up Vera's Backyard Bar-B-Que—the smokehouse, the preparation room, and the restaurant itself. The plan is to begin selling "American barbecue" (brisket) in the fall.

After cleaning and separating each set of heads, Mando and Florenzio hose down the counter and scrape the soiled water into a floor drain. Mando stops working after one of these cleaning breaks. He takes a twenty-ounce soda for himself and hands one to Florenzio. "I'm a tired man," he says, leaning on the counter.

I check my watch; less than a minute later, the break is over.

∽

Before dawn on Sunday morning, the pink and green building at 26th and Southmost is the place to be. Barbacoa is the traditional Sunday breakfast in this part of the country.

Vera's, with its antiseptic cleanliness and unscuffed tile floors, looks as if it has recently been renovated. To your left as you walk in, chairs and tables have been crowded together and in some cases stacked on top of one another as if there are plans to begin sit-down service. On the other end is the cafeteria-style counter. Mando's wife and brothers stand ready to take the orders and work the cash register.

By seven o'clock there is a line of customers waiting to get up to the counter and order. In front of them is the menu.

Frank and I sit with Mr. Vera and watch the customers come and go. "When I first started, the same person would be here every Sunday," Mr. Vera says. "Somebody will ask, 'Have you seen such and such?' 'No,' I said, 'but if he's not sick or out of town, he'll be here Sunday.'"

Mr. Vera asks us if we intend to try the barbacoa. By ten o'clock it's usually sold out, so if we want some, he tells us, we should get it now. We stand in line and order a pound of cheek meat and some corn tortillas and salsa. Although the meat is not fat, it is very rich, like brisket and other well-marbled cuts of meat, only more so. It's extremely tender. Mando has told us that the eyeballs are the favorite delicacy of the older people. "It's like butter on a tortilla," he said. But we don't try it this time.

We had tasted oven barbacoa at a couple of other restaurants. There was something missing in it, though. It had a little flavor and was tender, but it lacked the fullness of true barbacoa. Mr. Vera is glad to hear that, glad to know we can taste the difference.

"Life is getting too fast," he says. "No time to cook or nothing. You just get a hamburger. I even do it myself. I don't like to, but I do it. Life is getting too fast."

Juneteenth '93 19TH OF JUNE CELEBRATION **MEXIA, TEXAS**

Juneteenth: Homecoming and Reunion

Juneteenth Jamboree
I want to tell you a story from way back
Jump on down and dig me Jack
In eighteen hundred and sixty-five
A hip cat started some jive
He said come on kids jump with me
At the Juneteenth Jamboree

The rhythm was swinging at the picnic grounds
Fried chicken floating all around
Everybody there was full of glee
At the Juneteenth Jamboree

Trumpets flaring in the air
Mellow barbecue everywhere
Clarinets moaning in the hall
All the gates were having a ball

They didn't know how to cut no rugs
All the cats had a gallon jug
Everybody happy as they could be
At the Juneteenth Jamboree

Juneteenth Jamboree
As performed by Louis Jordan, 1940

By the June 19 on which Major General Gordon Granger made his announcement in Galveston, the Civil War had been over for two months and President Lincoln's Emancipation Proclamation was more than two years old. With a war on and communications cut off, and with Texas temporarily no longer in the Union—besides which somebody had to plant the crops and get them out of the fields to support the war effort—no one had gotten a chance to tell black Texans that the legal distinction between humanity and property had been extended to them. Granger's proclamation was news then. And born with the delayed emancipation it heralded was the ever-lingering suspicion that the new era was no more to be trusted than the antebellum period.

Juneteenth, as the day has come to be known, is now an official state holiday in Texas, accompanied by the closing of banks and the shutting down of state offices. But long before that it was the big picnic day when families got together over barbecue and baskets of fried chicken to celebrate and commemorate. In their book *Eats: A Folk History of Texas Foods*, Ernestine Sewell Linck and Joyce Gibson Roach quote an 1892 article from the *Austin Daily Statesman* that describes an early Juneteenth celebration:

> The festivities of the day were started by a grand street parade ... After leaving the Capitol the crowd repaired to Wheelers Grove in every conceivable style of conveyance. Oxcarts, country wagons, buses, carts, buggies and hacks were all brought into play, and during the remainder of the evening the vehicles were constantly on the go, carrying eager picnickers to the grove, and bringing those who were tired out back to their homes.

> The commemoration service reminded the community of the significance of emancipation ... Prayers sought the blessing of God

for the living and the recently dead. The songs of jubilee, "Free at Last" and "In That Great Gettin' Up Morning," re-created the joy of attaining freedom. Patriotic songs, "The Star Spangled Banner," for instance, were also sung, affirming newly won citizenship.

A minister's sermon or a speech by a community leader recognized Lincoln's contribution, praised the Union, or advocated a community project. It was customary to publicly read General Granger's declaration of freedom. But the highlight of the service came in testimonials by former captives about their life under bondage and their deliverance.

Recreation time generally featured competitive baseball games, horse racing, stunt riding, and sometimes rodeos...But the preparation and sharing of food was the main attraction. In keeping with convention men barbecued the meat, and women prepared the remainder of the food. Usually meeting several nights before the picnic, the men inventoried their resources—meat, wood, personnel—and established a work schedule. Pits were dug; wood was cut and hauled; and the cooking was monitored...Women prepared fried chicken, potato salad, greens, sweet potato pie, and peach cobbler. Homemade ice cream, "glassade" (a blend of shaved ice, sugar and fruit syrup), and red and orange soda were also served. While the meat was communally shared, other food was shared by relatives and close family friends.

On the Stroud Plantation, around Mexia (pronounced meh-HAY-ah), Texas, the celebration was shortly followed by sober and forward-thinking action. John Henderson and representatives from about twenty other families decided that land should be purchased so there would be a place where each year former slaves and their descendants could gather and commemorate emancipation. It took three years for them to pay for it, but by the early 1900s they had thirty acres of land. Emancipation has been celebrated there every year since. Thus Mexia's Juneteenth celebration has come to have a history and significance far larger than the size of this small town of seven thousand residents, and many of the Mexians who have since moved to other parts of the country make Juneteenth their annual homecoming.

We have been warned in Dallas that crowds will begin arriving in Mexia on Thursday, June 17, so we rush to get there that afternoon. We drive a few miles outside town to the picnic grounds and park beside the asphalt road that leads from the highway to the grounds. In front of us is an expanse of grass and a merry-go-round leading to the lake. Behind us, across the road, are restrooms on which the cryptic message "KKK is Hear" has been spray-painted.

Given that this celebration is supposed to draw a few thousand people, the place looks pretty dead. It doesn't help that it's a bit overcast. Most of the action is in setting up the various concession stands. Grouped in three different places on the grounds are small tin-roofed, wooden stands selling bar-

becue, fried fish, cakes and pies, potato chips and other snack foods, T-shirts, and liquor.

Louis Echols sits by the fish stand that his younger relatives are running. There's a minor crisis because the propane burner won't light. But Echols, an aged, dark-skinned man, meticulous in his straw hat, well-worn short-sleeved green shirt, and white patent leather shoes, is cool, dignified, and eager to talk about the Nineteenth of June celebration, as he calls it. Although I've heard the word "Juneteenth" for years in places as far away as New Orleans and New York, Mr. Echols and other people of his generation refer to it most often as the Nineteenth of June, with the same ease of phrasing you hear in the words "Fourth of July." In fact, the organization that administers the grounds and the celebration is the Nineteenth of June Organization of Limestone County, Texas.

Mr. Echols' father, born two years after emancipation, has told him the old stories of this place, about how before it came to be known as Booker T. Washington Park it was known as Indian Path or Comanche Crossing or just Comanche (not to be confused with the Texas town of the same name). It's a tale in the Thanksgiving mode about Comanche Indians traveling in the area and running out of food. "That was 1886, I believe," Mr. Echols says. The local farmers brought them a sack of corn. Years later the Indians returned, this time with plenty of corn and a "beef," which they dressed and barbecued. "It was so good, my daddy said you had to put brakes on your teeth to keep from biting your tongue!"

And there is the story that he personally remembers of the only year when they failed to have the Nineteenth of June celebration. Commemorations in other cities died during the Great Depression, he says. Although black cultural nationalism has helped bring them back in recent years, the folks at Comanche remain proud of the fact that the only time their celebration failed to be held was the year when John Hill was running for governor and the rains were so bad that the event had to be celebrated on the second, third, and fourth of July. ("But don't think the Fourth of July ever get in the way of this!" he cautions.) And there is the story of the best Nineteenth of June he ever had, when that pretty girl with the long hair came from Italy, Texas, and Mr. Echols, who remembers his young self as having been "one of the best-dressed guys of that day," was her escort. "She was my company and my girlfriend," he says with a sweet, faded innocence. "We walked from the spring to the tabernacle and the school and the ice cream parlor. Christinna Herron was her name. She's alone now and a widow like I am. But for years she would write and I would write and I would send her the Nineteenth of June programs."

Things are different now. Of course much has changed merely with the passage of time. But there are other things, sinister things. In April of 1987 the tabernacle burned down, and a year and a half later with similar mystery the dance hall was torched as well. Neither was a grand building; the sketches we are shown testify to that. But there is majesty in the story of former slaves and their descendants building these structures as monuments to freedom. That's the real loss. "I have my reservations about how they came to burn," Mr. Echols tells us with calculated directness. "The whites have always wanted the ground. They've tried to buy it."

And there was the drowning.

In the old days you wouldn't see any police out here, the people tell us. But then they started coming, and trouble was their accompaniment. In 1981 three young men were arrested for suspected drug-related offenses. The officers decided it would be easier to transport the suspects across the lake by boat than to walk them through the thick Juneteenth crowd. But the boat capsized. The policemen were able to escape, but the boys were handcuffed and so they drowned. Like the clouds, these events, the burnings and the drownings, hover, drifting in and out of conversations, shading the mood here.

The tradition at the Comanche Juneteenth Commemoration is to bid the various concessions out. The highest bidder wins the right to sell a particular type of food; no two concessionaires are allowed to sell the same thing. This constraint on competition may also be a de facto constraint on quality. At the barbecue concession there is a large and impressive grill, but the food is not good. It tastes as if it was cooked a day or two ago and warmed over. The actual food almost erases the flavors I imagined as I read the *Austin Daily Statesman* account. There are five or six pits dug into the grounds, one old-timer tells us. They used to be used for barbecuing and building fires for other cooking, like frying fish. But they have fallen into disuse now. The man who is selling snack foods says that he was going to buy frozen pies to cook and sell, but he feared people wouldn't want to pay the higher price for them. So he sells pies prepackaged in cellophane like the ones available at the gas stations along the highway.

As night falls, the crowd begins arriving. On the road leading to the grounds the traffic is steady. The lights have been turned on in the park. They illuminate much bear-hugging and cheek-kissing, the greetings of people who probably haven't seen one another since last year this time. Many are gathered around the fish stand and the liquor and barbecue concessions on either side of it. There's more drinking and talking than eating. "That's why the Nineteenth of June is so precious to us," Mr. Echols tells us. "People come from New York, Florida, California, all over, 'cause they have roots here."

For the adults there is no planned activity during the evenings, and there doesn't need to be—the reunion is enough. For kids, meaning anyone from preteen to early twenties, there is a disco tent.

On Friday night the tent's speakers, straining, blare rattling bass sounds onto the grounds. Around midnight the deejay announces that there will be a dance contest. Several contestants make their way to the front of the tent. For the first few rounds they compete to see who can move the best and the fastest to the music being played. After a while a couple of contestants begin to realize how difficult it is to distinguish themselves by mere dancing in a crowd full of good dancers. A few girls take their shirts off; one dances bare-breasted. The boys strip down to their underwear. The deejay announces that the finals of the dance competition will be held the next night, and the bare-breasted dancer, determined to spare no modesty in the pursuit of victory, promises to take off the rest of her clothes.

For Frank, this mass of gesturing hips and arms is the stuff of great photography. At two a.m. I leave him there and return to the Living Legend to get some rest. As I close my eyes, I hear people walking to their cars and saying farewell or promising to see each other tomorrow. One mother calls to her children, telling them to hurry up.

It almost isn't real then, this argument that emerges out of the darkness perhaps fifty feet behind me. "Was that your whore? Was that your bitch?" someone yells. Then I hear onlookers begin to separate whoever is arguing. But as they say the things you say to stop a fight from starting, I hear another voice say, "I'm from Sunnyside. That nigger don't scare me."

With that I decide to get out of the car and see what's going on. As I'm sitting up I see a man with a shotgun aiming in the direction of the argument and using my car as a shield. All I can think of is him shooting over and around my car to get to his targets and those targets returning fire. To get

to him, a volley of bullets would pretty much have to go through me.

Not being from Sunnyside, I'm scared. So I ease out of the car slowly, then dart past the marksman in front of my car, startling him in the process. He turns his shotgun on me briefly as I run away from him, then returns to his marksman's crouch. Far from the line of fire I find Frank, watching the whole thing unfold, laughing at my clumsy escape.

By then it's all over except for a few more choruses of "I'm from Sunnyside. That nigger don't scare me."

⌒

We get up early Saturday morning. The annual worship service is going to be held at eleven o'clock, and the only hotel we could find is a good thirty miles away. We expect parking to be at a premium, as it was last night, but when we arrive, shortly before ten, the Juneteenth grounds are nearly empty. The few people who are here are cleaning up their concessions to get ready for another day's business.

So when Luther Wade arrives, we notice him. He looks like the spectators you see in those pictures of baseball games from the 1950s, when men wore coats and ties for occasions that now strike us as informal. He is dressed as if he is going somewhere, which makes him look, like Mr. Echols yesterday, a little out of place on the picnic grounds. His brown shoes are shined, his pants are deeply pleated and held in place by a pair of suspenders, his hat is of stylish, summertime straw.

We talk, Frank and me leaning on the Legend, Mr. Wade standing in the damp breeze. He grew up in Mexia, he tells us, and has been coming to Juneteenth celebrations since the 1920s. He lives in Dallas now, though. When he got out of the army, there was no work to be found in Mexia, so he had to leave. But he comes back for Juneteenth. His daughter, who lives in Dallas, might come out today. His son may or may not come. His wife, who was Mr. Echols' daughter, is deceased. "It's coming to ten years and I still miss her," he says with a change of mood. "I miss her hard sometimes."

We ask him about the celebration here and whether it has changed over the years. "When they burned the tabernacle down, it just haven't been the Juneteenth that it was," he says. "I remember, by this time on the last day, it'd just be so many people you wouldn't believe. I really believe that the white people want this park, and they felt if they could burn this down the people wouldn't rebuild. But they trying to just carry on a tradition that they don't want to forget. To let the younger ones keep in mind the freeing of the colored people from slavery."

By eleven, the time when the service is supposed to start, it is clear that these younger people, so present in the disco tent last night, will be absent this morning. The average age in here must be seventy. The tabernacle is an open-sided yellow and white tent with folding chairs. The choir and the master of ceremonies sit in the

One of the Briscoes 19TH OF JUNE CELEBRATION **MEXIA, TEXAS**

front, behind a lectern, looking at the thirty or so members of the congregation. Other than Frank and me, everyone is dressed up.

"Today is one of those days when all your planning fails," the master of ceremonies sighs. His granddaughter, he says, was supposed to participate in the service, but something came up and she can't attend. The Sandy Grove choir—he gestures toward them with his left hand—is replacing another choir that had to cancel at the last minute. And the Reverend T.W. Medlock from Sandy Grove Primitive Baptist Church, who was scheduled to deliver the message, has yet to arrive.

Fifteen or twenty uncomfortable minutes pass before the reverend does arrive. He has been delayed by a train crossing or a flat tire or something, but it doesn't matter. He arrives ready to preach. "We are here despite the looks of rain," he says in that old Negro preacher cadence, "but when we were praying to God to save us from sin, we didn't say we'd praise Him only if it didn't rain."

Predictably, his sermon links the Old Testament freeing of the captives to the emancipation of enslaved Africans in the United States. "Let us now talk about our exodus," he says. "The Israelites had to leave Egypt, but God has made an exodus for us in our own land. And let me say to you, the Emancipation Proclamation won't do everything. There are some things we must do. You can have the Voter League, you can have the NAACP, but without God you can't be free. Only two of the old ones in the Bible saw the promised land. New generations came up. Those that would obey, they made it. What are you trying to say, Brother Medlock? I'm trying to say you can't make it unless you do what God say!"

Inside this tent where older women in white hats and dresses fan themselves, it feels like church. But this little gathering, though the focal point of the morning schedule, is really at odds with the basic thrust here. During the sermon, some children begin laughing and playing on a merry-go-round outside the tent. Their mother is asked to keep them quiet until after the service. Not long after that a young man rides a horse near the tent. The master of ceremonies again gets up and, in order not to disturb the sermon, gestures in animated silence with a manila folder, waving the horseman away from the tent. Oblivious, the young man rides on. Involuntarily the eyes of the congregation follow him and his horse as they pass directly behind the speaker.

Inside the tent, everyone is concentrating that much harder on what is being said. The City Commission of Mexia has donated $5,000 to help restore the tabernacle and the grounds, we are told. Part of it came from the hotel and motel tourism tax. The city of Groesbeck has pledged $2,000, though the money hasn't come yet. The tabernacle, when it is rebuilt, will be sixty-two by forty feet, and similar to its predecessor in design. But more funds must still be raised.

An uncomfortable silence about the merry-go-round and the horse and the smallness of the gathering might have been maintained but for Mr. Echols. At a point in the service members of the congregation are asked to contribute any reflections they have. He stands, and like a kettle unable to contain its steam, he fumes up to the lectern. There are problems adjusting the microphone. Then Mr. Echols' words erupt, with more force than organization. He pauses between sentences as if collecting his thoughts, and it is difficult to follow his logic. The path of his emotional trajectory, however, is clear.

"I want to tell you for sure, I'm hot under the collar!" he explodes. "With me there's no Juneteenth celebration." Nodding his head to emphasize key syllables, he says, "It's the Nineteenth of June celebration and it last three official days. And it's been horses here ever since I knowed about the Nineteenth celebration. They strung 'em up and down these fences. And they had a time to carry 'em down to get water.

"I got up this morning and my niece asked me, 'Where you going?' Where am I going? Where I'm going at eleven o'clock on the nineteenth day of June? That's the reason this thing is where it is, because of these prayer services at eleven. We've had some tragedies, but we're still here. This is holy ground here. Let these people know that this is holy ground!"

There is silence then, not even whispered commentary.

From the cool reaction Mr. Echols' remarks receive, it seems that these people, many of them octogenarians, have resigned themselves to living in this world in which so much of what they think and feel is now irrelevant. The service recovers from the outburst. The congregation joins the choir in a rendition of "Lift Every Voice and Sing," and Frank and I are asked to introduce ourselves and say a few words about our book. Soon it is all over except more hugging and kissing and shaking of hands. But long after I leave the shadow of the tent, Mr. Echols' words stay with me.

I think of them in every conversation I have that day because no one mentions the worship service or emancipation. I think of them as Frank points out the old drunk with yellowed eyes as he stumbles around. In his hand is an unopened bottle of fortified wine. ("The liquor companies are in big trouble," Frank says. "This boy has figured out how to get drunk without opening the bottle.") And I think of them that night at the dance contest. Even though the stripper fails to show up as promised, there is a huge crowd, and a few contestants again strip to their underwear. And although the music from the tent is loud enough to be heard all over Comanche Crossing, two young men still drive their car onto the grounds, park next to the tent, and blare their stereo to compete with the sounds of the disco.

We have come here expecting that this event, like any great Southern celebration held during the summer, will be accompanied by barbecue. Everyone we've talked to has told us as much. Linwood Reed, a Mexian living in Dallas now, has staked out a spot between the main grounds and the restrooms. His sons and friends are gathered there. He and his barbecue pit, which he has named George, are preparing ribs and turkey legs and brisket. He places some brisket between two slices of bread and shoves it at us almost as a challenge; it is very good. But I'm still surprised and disappointed that so few people are out here barbecuing and that the barbecue available for sale is not better.

In their book *The Taste of America*, John L. and Karen Hess admirably chronicle this decline. Americans, they note, are becoming conditioned to processed, artificial, tasteless nourishment. "A New England church we know of," they write, "abandoned its cake sales when it found that all the cakes were now either store-bought or made from mixes; it asked the women to donate cash instead." Although there is a booth where good homemade chess pie and poundcake are being sold, the snack-food concessionaire with his cellophane-wrapped pies is one errant step ahead of the national trend toward convenience food.

I can remember countless discussions I've had with African-Americans the general drift of which was that white folks can't cook and that the simplest soul-food dishes are infinitely better than anything you're apt to get at white folks' table, except of course when black hands stir the pots. ("Whenever the white people invite me to dinner, I don't take any chances," one friend says. "I always eat before I go.") It doesn't matter whether these statements are true. What matters is that the pride evidenced by the statements is fast being lost.

If the decline were limited to the domain of culinary culture, it would matter only to those of us for whom the palate is important. But the sad truth is that the same sense of loss and decline is felt everywhere in this Juneteenth celebration.

Juneteenth could not be expected to remain the same. But certainly essential elements of this celebration should be expected to be maintained. These elements—the spiritual dimension, the respect for tradition, the reverence for the occasion, and of course the barbecue—are now in gross disrepair. They are pining away, unmourned and largely unmissed.

Americans have never been known for their sense of history. Though this is most painfully obvious in the case of African-Americans, it is true of almost all of us that we have forgotten all but the most basic elements of our Old World cultures. This both forces and allows us to invent ourselves. But these days, in our efforts to reinvent, we are all too often discarding some of the most valuable parts of our former selves.

As if to confirm all that I am thinking, Robert Briscoe invites us to his home after the church service. He was born in Limestone County eighty-four years ago and has some Juneteenth memorabilia that he thinks might interest us for our book. Among the items he shows us is an old program from the 1980 celebration:

DATE 6-17   8:00 p.m. camping out activities,
                   exhibits, gospel singing,
                   games—baseball, etc.

      6-18 11:00 a.m. cookout, art exhibit,
                   sporting activities
             7:00 Miss Juneteenth Beauty pageant

      6-19   7:00 sunrise prayer service
             8:30 breakfast
             11:00 a.m. Annual Juneteenth
                   Memorial Service
                   speaker J.H. Hardin, Jasper TX
             12:00 lunch
              4:00 educational program
              5:00 Juneteenth Parade
              8:00 p.m. worship service

This is the sort of occasion that I came expecting to witness and chronicle. I also expect Mr. Briscoe to side with me and to point out how far the Nineteenth of June celebration has fallen. Rather, he gives me a sobering essay on change and its necessity, though not its price.

"You couldn't expect things to be like they were seventy-five years ago," Mr. Briscoe says. "They're not. First thing, they weren't even going to school together. And you. You don't know nothing about no outhouses. How could it be the same? It ain't never gonna be like it was before. And we don't want it that way. That wasn't what we worked and strived for. Slave people wanted their children to do more."

Cryptic Regards 19TH OF JUNE GROUNDS **MEXIA, TEXAS**

The Barbecue Belt: Middle Texas

These attractions along highways—these restaurants that have their own special biscuits with almost too much butter melted on top, or the places that know how to make a good fried pie with fruit or sweet potatoes like the ones you have imagined after tasting the fast-food versions; these waitresses whose cool wit or even whose comic slow-footed dullness is genuine and endearing; these road-side grocery stores whose HOME MADE PEACH ICE CREAM signs get you off the highway and out of the air-conditioned car but whose proprietors always want to sell you the latest gadget like the bandanna that "with just a little water" will keep your neck cool all day; these gardens or lakes or parks, crafts bazaars or Tee Pee Motels or drive-in movie theaters or abandoned architectural curiosities; these things and places and people that maybe are not worth setting out for but that are worth stopping at en route or even altering your course for—it is these things along with the cattle ranches and post oak trees that you see driving through Middle Texas.

And it is these places, small little places along roadsides and bayous, that are supposed to have the best barbecue. Everywhere we go, people envy us the luxury of being able to drive slowly along the back roads to discover the out-of-the-way barbecue restaurants that they have imagined to be God's own smokehouses. And (fools that we are!) we listen to them—our own schedule be damned—and stop at each place with a sign featuring barbecue in any of its spelling variations. The dirtier the place, the more illiterate the sign, the better.

We couldn't find even one good place along the Arkansas highways we traveled. Tennessee was a bit better, Georgia and the Carolinas somewhere in between. But Texas!

A barbecue belt runs through central Texas. Along the highways and through the towns of the region is a series of restaurants that, almost without exception, serve some of the best barbecue in the country. At first glance it seems surprising that these barbecue places, often several hundred miles apart, could be so similar to one another and so different from restaurants in the city. But perhaps it shouldn't be surprising. Ted Morgan, a naturalized citizen, noted in his book *On Becoming American* that the interstate highway system is a community unto itself. "Unbeknownst to the nation at large," he writes, "the interstate has become the 51st state—the state of mobility. It is self-sustaining, has its own economy and culture, and everything a person might need, from a hospital to be born in to a funeral parlor to die in."

James W. Latimer prefers to call the area enclosed by the barbecue belt Middle Texas, and he has drawn its boundaries in a guidebook, *The Pits of Middle Texas*. Bordered by several highways (I-10, Texas 46 to the south, US 87 and others to the west, 36 to the north, and US 77 to the east) and crisscrossed by several others (I-35, US 190, US 183), it includes cities and towns mostly unfamiliar to people outside Texas—Llano, Leander, Wimberly, Cyclone, Coleman, Abilene.

Latimer attributes much of the region's barbecue culture to its central European roots. In the classic story of American immigration (Europe–Ellis Island–New York and points west), the word "Texas" never appears. But in the mid-1800s, long before television shows and oil revenues made Texas a stylish place to be, central Europeans, specifically Germans, Poles, and Czechs, had set their eyes on this southwestern territory as their country away from country.

Cooper's **LLANO, TEXAS**

In *The First Polish Americans*, T. Lindsay Baker asserts that the Polish colony in Texas was the first of its kind in the United States. Harsh conditions in Poland, a desire to avoid army conscription, and glowing letters from Texas led many Poles to America.

The German presence in Texas was a far more ambitious and organized endeavor. Similarly repressive conditions in Germany led many German intellectuals to envision a homeland in the new world. Giessemer Gesellschaft wrote in 1830, "The foundation of a new and free Germany in the great North American Republic shall be laid by us; we must therefore gather people about us when we emigrate, and we must, at the same time, make the necessary arrangements providing for a large body of immigrants to follow us annually, and thus we may be able, at best in one of the American territories, to establish an essentially German state." But as conditions stabilized in Europe, specifically as German unification took place in 1871 under Bismarck, the stream of German immigration slowed.

Some of the German, Polish, and Czechoslovakian immigrants opened butcher shops, and some of the butcher shops evolved into barbecue places. Latimer claims that "Middle Texas barbecue is influenced by traditional German and Czech meat-smoking methods." In *We're Czechs*, a story about a Czech community in this region, much is said about butchering animals and preparing sausages. But there's not much in that book or half a dozen others like it that speaks directly to the issue of barbecue—which is to say mostly that the connection between central European immigration and Texas barbecue seems more circumstantial than causal.

The one tasty and undeniable vestige of central European culture on this region's barbecue is the smoked sausage. In most areas of the country, barbecue restaurants buy their smoked sausage from commercial producers. But most of the barbecue places in Middle Texas make their own sausage, sausage that tastes more European than American.

In Fredericksburg, the spiritual capital of German Texas, there is a palpable consciousness of the town's German roots. I attribute this to both pride in heritage and a tourism trade based far more on the town's cultural identity than on such modern attractions as the Admiral Nimitz Museum. Founded in 1846 by a group of immigrant families, Fredericksburg is now a town of seven thousand people. On its quaint Main Street, businesses tend to be adorned with German names or Germanic spellings like Das Peach Haus, Kaffee Klatsch, Marktplatz, and Sunday Smokehaus, so they fit right in with other businesses around town whose namesakes have monikers like Jaksik and Schwettmann and Dietz. Luckily for us, Frank has been to Germany and understands this language. "That's the Peach House over there," he explains.

We are here vaguely in search of barbecue's German roots and know nothing about barbecue in Fredericksburg specifically. So we are easily swayed by the pretty young woman who works at Schwettmann's Emporium. "She looks German enough," Frank says. She tells us to try a place called Pardi's at Birck's.

Pardi's at Birck's is an old, large, red-barn-like building along Main Street. In a covered area beside it is a row of brick barbecue pits. A regular down-home restaurant, Pardi's at Birck's makes its own doughnuts and has a full menu; barbecue is only a small part. We take a seat in the large dining room. In it there is the clang of flatware and dishes and the sound of familiar conversation that suggests that many of these people eat here every day. We order a barbecued lamb chop and some pork ribs. The meat arrives; it looks great but tastes as if it has been drenched in salt. The lamb chop is not so bad because it is very thick (and a bargain at $3.50), but the ribs are almost inedible.

The scenario is similar at Ken Hall's Texas Barbecue. Hall, a former football standout, also has a covered area next to his restaurant with rows of cinderblock pits. The meat here is both tender and salty in the extreme.

Though no one recommends it, we stop at Burrer's Barbeque, the youngest of the three restaurants. It is a small, clean place on Main Street, an old building nicely redone with hardwood floors, a German flag, ceiling fans, wood paneling, and a metal barbecue pit beside the restaurant. The place used to belong to Brad Burrer's grandfather, who sold beer and soft drinks

Charlie Riddle, Pit Boss SONNY BRYAN'S SMOKEHOUSE **DALLAS, TEXAS**

Bob BOB'S SMOKEHOUSE **SAN ANTONIO, TEXAS**

until 1984. Brad, a fourth-generation Fredericksburgian whose family moved to Austin when he was a young boy, decided he wanted to go into business for himself. After an apprenticeship at an out-of-town barbecue place, he moved home and opened his own restaurant. His pit was custom-built from a length of oilfield pipe.

The menu here is limited to beef brisket and sausage. The brisket is cut into large chunks and served on a bun with onions and pickle and a light tomato barbecue sauce. It's excellent and not too salty. We ask Brad about the connection between Germans and barbecue. His parents have visited Germany, he tells us, and over there they eat a lot of grilled meat. That, he says, is as big a connection as he can draw.

Southside Market, Elgin

Ernest Bracewell has recently had surgery on his knee. His wife beside him, he leans on a cane as he walks across the cement floors of his cavernous restaurant. Through the glass doors at the front, past the tables and chairs, slowly, past the ice cream station in the middle of his restaurant, and behind the two lines of people waiting to order barbecue. We wait for him at a table in the rear dining room.

By the time he arrives we have already eaten and, especially impressed with the brisket and the sausage, we have asked to speak to him without knowing that he was home recuperating and would have to drive here. We wait, retasting the two sauces on the table: the barbecue hot sauce, a thin,

vinegary liquid with pepper and spices congregating along the bottom of the various liquor bottles that contain it, and the thicker, tomato-based sauce, still thinner and less sweet than a Kansas City or a Memphis sauce. It's rather bland, we think, but perhaps it's a major concession for people in this part of the country who don't like sweet, tomatoey sauces.

When he arrives at our table, Mr. Bracewell tells us about how he used to call on Southside Market, selling meat for Armour & Company when it was "closing up and shutting down and doing all that kind of stuff." Rather than wait for the other shoe to drop, he left Armour and in 1968 bought this place. The restaurant was downtown then, and the previous owner was a personal friend of Lyndon Baines Johnson, so the future president was in there all the time. It was an all-Democratic town then, but now you get those "fence jumpers," he jokes, before telling us that he himself votes for the man, not the party.

Having bought Southside Market only twenty-five years ago, Mr. Bracewell is not an expert on its early history; it was established over a century ago, in 1892. But he tells us what he knows.

The meat that was left over, they'd take those excess pieces of meat and grind them up and make sausage. They called it hot sausage and that's really how it got its name. It was hot with pepper too, but it come right off the pit. They get it right off and go out there on their wagons and eat it.

The guy was pretty smart in thinking up the ways to get rid of the excess meat that he had

instead of losing it. He made something people liked and they kept coming after it.

Meat and crackers and soda water is all you would get if you came here years ago. When I first came they didn't even serve brisket. They just served beef steak, pork steak, and sausage. That was about it. We never had beans till a year ago.

I never put that sweet sauce in until back during the 80s when we had the influx of Yankees here. They wanted the sweet sauce, sweet sauce, sweet sauce. The hot sauce was the kind of sauce that they started making here when they started making the sausage. If I eat sausage I still want the hot sauce; I don't want the other.

We use oak wood. Hickory is bitter. There's plenty of hickory around here, but I don't know anybody who uses it. You use mesquite, on this sausage, they'll throw it back in your face. They say it don't taste right; it gives everything a twang.

Sonny Bryan's Smokehouse, Dallas

Charlie Riddle is a small, wiry man, polite and quiet. In this tan-brown building that derives so much of its identity from fading paint and old, creaking grade-school seats, he stands guard over what remains of R.L. "Sonny" Bryan's ways and recipes.

A year or two before he died, Sonny sold the restaurant. The buyers have opened a couple of fancy places under the name they bought, one in a mall, one in the Texas Moline building in a trendy area—that one has business cards on the walls and a long list of imported beers. There are advertisements for the catering service, the new "mini-buns," and ("a great gift idea") Sonny's smoked turkeys.

But the original Sonny Bryan's—"Since 1910"—is famous for being the same as when Sonny passed away, so perhaps out of fear of messing up a good thing, they haven't even spruced the place up. There are tree stumps outside on which people sit, and inside there are small wooden chairs with the desktops attached. And they are exactly as uncomfortable as you would imagine them to be, even though grown men in suits and grown women in pumps sit in them and lean over beers and plates of ribs and onion rings at lunchtime. "It just makes you feel you were at a barbecue place and not a fancy restaurant," Charlie says. "Kind of a novelty, I guess you'd call it."

Charlie came into this twenty-one years ago. Since Sonny's death in 1989, the new owners notwithstanding, he has managed the place and its idiosyncrasies. Every day they cook exactly 800 pounds of brisket and 120 pounds of ribs. They cook the ribs about four hours, the brisket about seven, but it's the weathered two-prong fork, not the clock, that determines when the meat is done. "If it goes in and comes out easy, it's done," he says. "We cook forty-eight briskets a day and I stick forty-eight briskets a day. If it's not cooked, I cook it some more." At closing or once the meat has been sold, whichever comes first, they lock up.

"When I sell out, I close," Charlie says. "It goes back to not being greedy. If you cook 800 pounds and you sell 800 pounds, there's no carryover. That's the way we've always done it. If you change anything about this place, it won't work."

Bob's Smokehouse, San Antonio

Bob Wells at sixty-nine is an oak tree of a man. He has defeated cancer, and though scarred from the battle he remains, at 5'6", 243 pounds, unbowed in posture and spirit. He speaks quietly and confidently in a raspy voice. Without humor. Spooning out words in small servings as if careful not to waste any.

San Antonio barbecue is on its way to becoming a footnote until we find Bob's. The food at most of the places we try tastes obligatory, as if they barbecue there because, as part of Texas, they are supposed to do so. But at Bob's the meat—pork ribs, lamb breast, smoked sausage—is cut-with-a-spoon tender and the rich spices have been gently and thoroughly smoked into the meat. Bob keeps his sauce hot in plastic coffee percolators. It's a subtle, tomato-based sauce, gently flavored with very little pepper. Steam rises from it as they pour it over the meat. And the cobblers, which Bob's wife makes, sometimes apple and sometimes peach, close the meal with sweet finality.

Sitting in his original restaurant (there are three now), Bob tells us about how his parents died when he was young, how he was stationed in the South Pacific during World War II, and how he opened this place because his father had told him, "A job is for a lazy man, not a smart man."

I really didn't have to learn how to barbecue. Barbecue was just like a gift for me. It ain't nothing that I went to school for. Actually I inherited barbecue. My daddy was a barbecue man, the very greatest.

I think we had better barbecue in those days. My daddy could kill and barbecue a whole calf. The legs, the tail, the hocks. I ain't that good. We only barbecue what's designed for barbecue now. Brisket, shoulder clod, and the short ribs. That's all we barbecue in this modern time, but my daddy barbecued the whole thing, and it was all good, good barbecue.

When you barbecue from the ground you ain't got all this chemicals, this steel. Steel is the worst thing to barbecue with. It's no man can barbecue with steel. You got the chemicals in steel and that stuff gets in the barbecue. I got bricks in my pit, and what is bricks made out of? Sand. So you still got some of the same ingredients you got in the ground.

See people got these little barrel pits in they back yard, I like to give them a tip. And the tip is go buy 'em a bag of sand and put it in the bottom of the pit. First, the pit gon' last three times as long, it ain't gon' rust out near as fast. Number two, it keeps some of this chemical out.

I would say that your best barbecue wood would be hickory nut wood with the nuts on it, walnut, pecan. That's what people say is the best barbecue wood. But I say the best barbecue wood is mesquite. Why is that? I know I got the best barbecue in the United States and I use mesquite.

It's not barbecue sauce as far as I'm concerned if it don't match mine. Now if you can find another one that can match mine, then I'll call it a barbecue sauce. There ain't but one sauce made that I would recommend a man to and that's Kraft. Kraft got about as close to a barbecue sauce as I have tasted.

When I started my barbecue sauce I kind of used them for a copycat. But I improved mine at a much

The Hinze Family HINZE'S BAR-B-QUE **WHARTON, TEXAS**

more of a high level than Kraft. That's why I say they the only somebody in the world got something similar to a barbecue sauce.

I named the place Bob's then because I wanted to cut down on my neon letters. You know, money. I wanted to make it short as I could make it. But the onliest name that was ever on that place was some little letters I put on my front door say Bob's Den, so I never had to buy a neon sign.

Hinze's Bar-B-Que, Sealy and Wharton

All this foolishness about counting the damn calendars on the wall of a restaurant, or looking for some beat-up old place to eat because poor folks whose places are beat-up have an unerring sense of culinary aesthetics, is just that—foolishness. Given the increasing costs of land, labor, and capital and the increasing marketing sophistication in the restaurant industry, the days when a person could open up a cookshop on the corner armed with little knowledge beyond the culinary are all but over. Many of the small restaurants that are vestiges of this era survive, not on the strength of their balance sheets, but rather on the sheer grit of the owners.

Which is to say that when we pass Hinze's Bar-B-Que in Sealy as we are driving along Interstate 10, we decide to stop despite the restaurant's large new sign and antiseptic fast-food-chain appearance. Once inside, Frank decides us on staying to eat because they have some meringue pies with the meringue browned and whipped up real high. It's cafeteria style, so I go through the line and order for both of us, making sure to get some of everything: ribs and brisket, beans and coleslaw, bacon-onion potatoes, pecan pie, and also the lemon meringue.

Before I can set the tray on the table Frank yells, "Muh-RANG-gay pie!" and grabs at the lemon meringue as if it is a time bomb that can be defused only by quick ingestion. He begins spooning pie far faster than he can swallow it. The other patrons are eyeing me, concerned that the asylum has let out so deranged a charge with such scant, slack-muscled supervision. Only once he has finished the entire slice of pie does Frank look up from his plate, a bit winded, meringue on his upper lip and cheeks. "Now that was some muh-rang-gay pie!" he says.

But like a good book, a good meal should have several climaxes, as a meal at Hinze's does. Most barbecue restaurants with full menus rely on the meat being so good that diners will overlook the fresh-from-the-freezer desserts and the fresh-from-the-can vegetables. Hinze's is without a doubt the barbecue restaurant with the best array of quality food.

First the bread. It's white bread, made from scratch. Soft, but it has flavor. The beans are pinto beans, well seasoned, made from dried beans, not precooked canned beans, not too heavy on the cumin and other Mexican spices that Texas barbecue places usually exaggerate. Instead of the usual frozen French fries, Hinze's serves onion-bacon potatoes. The coleslaw is made with vinegar rather than the usual mayonnaise. It's lighter this way, a sweet, cool counterpoint to the rest of the meal. The spareribs are well smoked, and the brisket has a nice flavor all the way through, not just on the salty outer edges, with a hint of onion. All in all, it's a wonderful meal.

Once the lunchtime crowd has died down a bit, Walter Carl Hinze, the owner, takes us out back to where the meat is cooked. He shows us how his custom-designed pits have drawers so that, rather than peering over the smoking embers, the chef can pull out a drawer to check the meat. He tells us how he seasons his meat with nothing but salt and black pepper before putting it on the grill to smoke over pecan wood, the brisket for eighteen to twenty hours, the ribs for three or four. Every fifteen minutes or so of that time the meat is mopped with a marinade of vegetable oil, onions, and lemon juice. This keeps it moist and adds flavor.

Walter's is a second-generation barbecue business. He worked for his parents for seventeen years before opening up this place with his wife. The more we ask him about his business and his cooking technique, the more he tells us we need to talk to his parents, specifically his mother. He says she is responsible for many of the concepts and recipes featured on the menu and suggests we visit her at his parents' place in Wharton, about thirty-five miles away.

We meet Mr. and Mrs. Hinze in the kitchen of their restaurant. It's early in the

Edgar Black BLACK'S BARBECUE **LOCKHART, TEXAS**

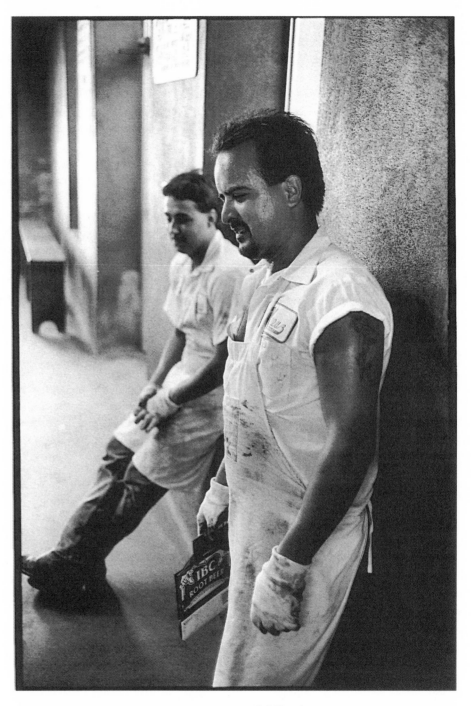

Brief Respite KREUTZ **LOCKHART, TEXAS**

morning, so we begin our conversation amid the steam of beans boiling and the sound of cabbage being made into coleslaw. The family started in the restaurant business with a Dairy Freeze, Mrs. Hinze tells us. She ran it at first while Mr. Hinze was still farming. "The man that had the Dairy Freeze was going to Czechoslovakia. He had kinfolks up there in Europe and they wanted to see him. He thought, well, he was going to sell it to us and we was going to get tired of it and sell it back to him," she tells me.

Mr. Hinze learned the art of barbecue from his father-in-law and his uncle. He practiced it on Sundays. Once he got out of farming he set up a little stand next to the Dairy Freeze. Things did not go well at first. Not too long after deciding to go headlong into the barbecue business, the Hinzes went to see Joe Cotton, whose restaurant in Kingsville is one of the best and best-known in Texas.

"Joe Cotton told us, 'Whatever you do, get out on the highway, on the bypass,'" Mrs. Hinze recalls. "Everybody said, 'Yeah, they're going to rob you,' 'cause we were out there by ourselves."

"Cotton had left from downtown and a bunch of his friends told him he was nuts, but he made a killing," Mr. Hinze says. "He gave us the best advice we ever had."

"The first two or three years I thought I was going to lose everything," she says. "We were opened up about five days a week and we took in about $378 in those five days. We just had this small portable build-ing. It was tough. The bank was calling us two or three times a week."

"We had hell for a while there," he says.

"The reason I started the pies is 'cause we were so slow and I wanted to get people in here," she says. "The first year I started rum poundcake. So then after that I started the pies, and now I wish I wouldn't have started sometimes. The day before Thanksgiving we baked over three hundred pies that one day."

"Right now I'm semi-retired," he says, "but I can't get her to get semi-retired."

"What am I going to do with myself at home?" she asks.

Black's Barbecue, Lockhart

It's the food that makes us want to meet Edgar Black. Not the Jell-O or the boiled eggs or the other items on the cafeteria-style steam table, but the barbecue. Black's own succulent sausages, made in the back of the building, are Frank's favorites in a state where good sausage is common. The ribs are excellent but the pork loin, well seasoned on the outside and thoroughly smoked on the inside, is the highlight of this place.

We return to interview the owner, but it turns out to be a bad day for it. Edgar Black is upset this morning—something about a city council lawsuit and some land he owns. We ask questions about barbecue, and he seasons his answers with reflections on his involvement in this town's civic life, by which he means to say that he has given much to this place and doesn't deserve to be handled so roughly or, he thinks, so illegally.

We begin at the beginning, the founding in 1932 of a butcher shop and grocery that barbecued only what meat was left over. But we quickly arrive at 1949, when Edgar Black made his mark on his father's business, by then a sit-down barbecue restaurant that made its own sausage from scratch. And whether he would be as eager to tell a white writer this I don't know, but what he tells us is that he desegregated the business in July 1949, five years before the Supreme Court decided *Brown v. Board of Education.*

"I saw that it wasn't right," he tells us. "Separate restrooms and all that kind of mess. Completely ridiculous today. Some of the people said, 'Where're the colored gonna sit?' I said, 'They can sit anywhere they want to sit.' They said, 'That's gonna hurt your business,' and I said, 'If it does I don't want those people anyway.'"

Black started a petition in his church pointing out how silly it was for a town this size to build two high schools, one colored, the other white. So they built one school, later integrated the swimming pool, and ultimately desegregated the Little League.

Black's Barbecue bills itself as the state's oldest barbecue restaurant operated by the same family, but it is more famous for the signs that advertise this fact than for the fact itself. Unlike its two competitors in town, Black's is not on the highway and the lion's share of the barbecue business in this town comes off the highway. So Black's has to call attention to itself with huge, obnoxious signs, signs that seem out of character for this reflective, white-haired man. If they are out of character, however, they are no more so than the jackalopes and crocheted shawls and T-shirts and bumper stickers ("There are only two places to eat: Black's Barbecue and home") on the walls.

Black's troubles with the city council seem ironic when you consider the fact that a few years ago he was named Lockhart's Most Worthy Citizen. The irony is not wasted on him. "That's what I told my sons, I'm going to get a big plaque and put it up. 'From Lockhart's Most Worthy, 1988, to Lockhart's Most Wanted, 1993,'" he says.

Kreutz Market, Lockhart
∞

… and here is the great irony. The classic Texas barbecue place doesn't sell brisket or ribs or beans. It doesn't even have sauce.

Classic, then, is origin and architecture, pit and plate. Classic is an honest simplicity, much envied and much copied.

They pronounce Kreutz "krites" or "kroitz," and they call it a market because it was started as such. It still is a market, but now, rather than barbecuing only the meat that doesn't sell, they cut meat specifically for barbecuing. Only now ninety percent of the shop's business is from the barbecue restaurant and only ten percent from the meat market, which also sells groceries. The German immigrant who started this place, Charlie Kreutz, sold it to his sons in 1907, and they sold it to a brother-in-law four years later; then in 1948 the Schmidt family bought it. The Schmidts still own it, the brothers Don and Rick having bought it from their father.

Outside this huge, red-brick building are rows and rows of post oak—a cemetery of firewood, or perhaps a garden, the older wood graying, the new wood reddish brown. As you enter the building, you feel the heat of the fireboxes at either end of an L-shaped pit. You walk past one and stop at the counter to order meat.

Point One. In the classic Texas barbecue places (or in their neoclassic imitators), you order the meat right in front of the pit and you order it by the pound. It is pulled off brick barbecue pits whose doors are made of metal and opened with the assistance of the counterweights attached to them.

Kreutz sells beef shoulder clod, prime rib, pork loin, and hand-tied rings of the eighty-five percent beef, fifteen percent pork sausage which they make here early every morning (twelve thousand rings in an average week) in the refrigerated room on the other side of the long hall from the dining room. They cut the meat on an old butcher block that stands in front of the old brick pits. They wrap the meat crudely in butcher paper and hand it to you with your choice of bread or crackers.

Which brings us to Point Two. In the classic Texas barbecue places they serve the meat on butcher paper. "Texas plates," Frank calls them. As Rick Schmidt explains it, the place started as a butcher shop, and what do they have in a butcher shop? Butcher paper. They also don't serve "Texas toast" or garlic bread. They serve crackers for the old-timers who remember when that's all they served, and bread for everyone else.

The antechamber, where the pits are and where it is always hot despite the great height of the old ceiling, is separated from the dining room, where you order your side dishes, by a pair of glass doors. The dining room is long and also has a high ceiling. There are rows of plain tables and chairs, no forks or spoons, and no barbecue sauce. There are, however, knives chained to the tables to cut the meat, little paper trays full of a mixture of salt and coarse-ground black pepper to be scooped out with fingers and sprinkled on the meat if you want, and hot sauce.

At the counter where the woman cuts cheddar cheese into chunks, you can also order soft drinks, beer, and condiments like onion and avocado and tomato sold by the pound.

Point Three. In the classic Texas barbecue places, they always sell beer and Big Red, a soft drink synonymous with Texas. In Tennessee and the Carolinas and Kentucky, the barbecue places mostly don't sell beer.

On Friday afternoons, in a long, cement-floored hallway between the dining room and the meat market, Rick Schmidt and his friends sit on benches and drink beer and talk and tell jokes. We interrupt him this Friday, and as his friends yell their own answers to my questions in the background, Rick tells me about this place.

He uses the term "evolution" to describe how much of its tradition came about. When the barbecue place started, there was already an established grocery store that sold vegetables and soft drinks. It was just natural that the meat and the side orders would continue to be sold in separate places. People didn't use barbecue sauce then, so here they still don't. A lot of people did buy hot sauce from the grocery store, put it on their barbecue, and leave the half-empty bottle. Other customers assumed these half-empty bottles were provided by management and began to request them. So hot sauce is on the table now.

Years ago people told Rick's father that he needed to remodel the place. It was too old, too run down. They were right about its being old and run down. But the old man waited, changing nothing, just gritted his teeth and waited. As Rick explains it, people started writing about the place and now it's considered "antique."

"If you took this place and drew it up on a piece of paper and described it and took it to a banker and said, 'I'm going to open up a place and this is how I'm going to run it,' he'd laugh at you. But it works here," Rick says. "The hardest thing about running this place is not to change things."

That's Point Four.

Burying the Meat XIT RODEO AND REUNION **DALHART, TEXAS**

XIT: Of Icons and Emblems

Dalhart, west Texas. We are everywhere surrounded by the cowboy, his icons and his emblems. The four-footed, the four-wheeled, the broad-brimmed, the bow-legged, and the slow-cooked, all kicking up that dust which carries with it the scent of animal pens and open spaces. Dust rising and converging along a plain road leading to that infinite, cloudless sky which rests on the farthest visible point.

"Up here it's still open country. It's mostly pasture and farmland," Terri Abbott tells us as we drink cold beer and recover, her from the burying of the meat, us from the long drive. "To dress up is to wear creased jeans and polished boots and your best hat. The farmer and the rancher and the cowboy are still very much mainstream—and when we go to different parts of the state, it's not that way."

To which her sister Robbi adds, "The cowboys around here, to them it's their horse, their pickup, and their woman. They got a cool home and a good wife sitting beside them, meat and potatoes and a cold beer, and they're fine."

"You know the movies about the Old West?" Terri says. "The traditions and the culture are still very much ingrained here."

The traditions of the Old West are certainly still alive in the XIT Rodeo and Reunion. In 1882 the state of Texas had much more land than cash, so it gave three million acres to a Chicago corporation in exchange for the construction of a new state capital. Those acres, known as XIT, made up the world's largest ranch then under fence. It was so large that the cowboys working in the northern part didn't even know the ones working in the southern part, two hundred miles away. The east fence was twenty-seven miles from the west fence. It took six thousand miles of barbed wire to enclose the whole thing.

XIT has long since been sold and parceled off, but the city of Dalhart, near the southern extreme of XIT territory, holds an annual reunion in honor of the old cowboys, only one of whom is still alive. Up in age, he doesn't make it out to Dalhart. But much of the rest of west Texas won't miss the event with its rodeo and dances, free beef stew, watermelon, and barbecue.

I have never been to a rodeo before, and hadn't felt I'd missed much. Rodeo is rural and western—in short, much of what I am not. But here in this grandstand surrounded by these Texas families and the shrill anticipation that the next cowboy might either ride his bull with hobby-horse ease or be thrown off it in the direction of his own death or paralysis, I am attracted to the drama of it. Larry Pennington, the announcer, is so thoroughly professional that he can make a neophyte rodeo watcher feel at ease. He explains without condescension the details of rodeo scoring and cowboy technique. It is as if he begins every sentence with "I know you know this, but the point of this event is …" And it's helpful. I didn't know, for instance, that the point of bull riding is not to stay on the bull as long as possible, but to ride the bucking bull with I-don't-give-a-damn style, making certain to follow the specific conventions but only for long enough for the rider to imply that he could've stayed on the bull a week if he'd had half a mind to.

"Keep your eye there on chute number seven," Pennington's voice and its echo instruct through the loudspeaker. "Cowboy's just about ready. Eight seconds of a hurricane fixing to go down in chute seven. He's taking those final wraps I told you about earlier. Then he'll scoot up on that hand hold, get as close to it as he can, squeeze that fist as tight as he can around that loose bull rope, drop his legs down on the side of the bull, then he's got to squeeze with his legs, keep that free hand swinging in the air, and weather that eight-second storm. Larry Williams is the cowboy. Hightop's the name of the bull."

Pennington repeats many of his lines over and over. But he's cool about it, and you don't get bored. There are only so many ways to describe the limited proceedings here. When the cowboys are ready, they signal that the gate is to be opened so the bronco or bull will exit the pen and begin the competition, and Pennington yells, "He says outside! Let's go with him!" Unfailingly he describes bull riding as "eight seconds of a hurricane." And when the bulls win and the cowboys are cast summarily down to earth, Pennington drawls, "Threw him right back in there. Blew him out quicker'n uh two-cent piece of bubble gum!" But Pennington also tells us that bull riding is consistently voted the most dangerous contact sport in the world by the American Sportswriters Association. So when a bullrider doesn't do well, Pennington is understanding and implores his audience to be likewise. "Your applause is all that cowboy is going to take home this evening. Give him a hand."

Rodeo is not merely a game, Pennington says, but rather the exhibition of those very skills necessary for even the modern cowboy to do his job. Sometimes he just says it plain like that, and other times he adds the larger frame around the picture, saying by way of preparation, "Folks, I want you to sit back and relax and watch one hundred years of American culture rolled into an eight-second ride."

As evening falls and Pennington is packing up his microphones and equipment and the rest of the XIT crowd is preparing for a night of Texas two-stepping, I talk to him in the announcer's booth about cowboy culture. A tall cowboy from (where else?) Dodge City, Kansas, Pennington used to be a rodeo man himself. Calf roping and bull dogging were his specialties. He competed for twenty years before he tore up a knee real bad. Now he stays in it by announcing, which is not bad money, he says, but he also does some auctioneering.

"Where'd rodeo come from?" he begins. "It came from the old days of the cattle drives and things. The way it really got started was the ranch hands from different ranches would meet at a certain location and they would have bucking contests and roping contests, the ranch hands from one ranch pitting their skills against the skills of the ranch hands at another ranch." Even today, he tells me, despite the proliferation of pickup trucks, when you have to medicate the herd or separate some of the animals from the others, you still have to be a good horseman and a good roper. It is part of the job.

The development of rodeo clearly follows the same pattern as the development of all art, a transformation that Albert Murray refers to as "the evolution of aesthetic statement." Art begins, Murray tells us, as the playful re-enactment of an occupation or survival technique. When the re-enactment is supervised by a priesthood, it is religious. When it is supervised by referees, it is known as recreation—the act of re-creating. The very etymology of "recreation" makes clear its relationship to re-enactment.

The art of drama, for example, may begin as a symbolic re-enactment of the hunt, a praise of the hunter's skills and an implicit encouragement for young boys to become great hunters. But as it becomes more stylized, as the community grows more tolerant of dramatic action that strays from the strict confines of re-enactment, you forget that this play used to be about a hunter and his game and see it as a broader story, one much less specific in its references to any particular survival skill.

Of course, as you get further from re-enactment and closer to true art, individual personalities and stylistic nuances become more important than adherence to a tradition or pattern. In rodeo, in bull riding specifically, the game or play no longer has any direct relevance to cowboy life. While it may be necessary to break a wild horse so that it will become rideable, there is no corresponding necessity in the case of bulls.

In no corner of culture is this evolution more obvious than in the realm of food art. Cooking obviously began as a means of providing the sustenance necessary for a community to sustain itself. But as food became more abundant, people began to crave the luxuries of rarer, tastier delicacies, and cooks began to experiment with seasonings and techniques for the enhancement of taste.

Dancers XIT RODEO AND REUNION **DALHART, TEXAS**

One theory of the evolution of barbecue is that it developed on the cattle drives as the technique that chuckwagon cooks used to bring flavor and taste to their crudely prepared meals. These cooks, far away from the stoves and herb gardens that people in towns or settlements had, were forced to develop different culinary techniques.

The connection between barbecue and cowboys has become an *idée fixe*, an accepted notion that is no longer questioned. The most common decor for barbecue restaurants is western. In restaurants all over the country, there are little buckboard wagons printed on napkins, there are tables and benches of rough-hewn wood with brands burned into them. If the employees wear uniforms, they tend to be cowboy uniforms. This is true to a varying extent in most of the major barbecue chains. It is less true in single proprietorships, and less true the farther east you go.

So it is not surprising that at the XIT Rodeo and Reunion the real drawing card is the free barbecue. The reunion bills itself as the world's largest free barbecue. "The other stuff's just to kill time till the barbecue is ready," one of the cooks says.

The technique for barbecuing here is not exactly traditional. It may not even really be barbecue. All year the barbecue committee of the XIT event collects wood, chopping down unwanted trees, and hauling off dead and dying trunks. Whatever kind of wood it is, they'll take it. Elm and cedar, not woods known for imparting a delicate smoke flavor in meat, are what they have the most of here.

A day before our arrival, 1,100 pounds of choice chuck roll was seasoned and wrapped—first in brown paper bags, then in burlap—and then tied with wire. Days before that the bulldozers dug two pits, each seventy-five feet long, four feet wide, and five feet deep. Ten feet of wood was stacked in each of the pits. Last night it was set on fire and allowed to burn down to coals. You can feel the heat of these embers on this barren patch of land near where the rodeo is being held. Contrary to what the Veras say about smoke making its way through the aluminum foil in which they wrap the barbacoa, the barbecue men here claim that the smoke imparts no flavor.

"We don't smoke it," Carl Finch, one of the barbecue hands, tells me. "Elm wood smells like trash if you're smoking. All it's for is the heat. It makes it like an oven underground. We do it this way because we have so many people to feed."

I begin to research this connection between barbecue and the cowboy lifestyle Saturday when, just like everyone else with little to do after Saturday's XIT parade and before that day's rodeo, I go to the Dallam-Hartley Counties Historical Museum. Books I find there—such as *The XIT Ranch of Texas* and *6,000 Miles Under Fence: Life on the XIT Ranch of Texas*—contain occasional references to the food that was eaten back then. Sourdough biscuits and beef were the staples. A calf was killed every other day. Meals might also include some combination of potatoes, eggs, butter, syrup, coffee, canned vegetables, pie, and dried fruit. Almost nothing is said about barbecue.

Later, I call B. Byron Price, executive director of the Cowboy Hall of Fame and Western Heritage Center in Oklahoma City, for some guidance on this point. He is compiling a book of chuckwagon recipes and histories. He has found little mention of barbecue in the sources that he has scoured; the absence is easily explained, he says.

"Barbecue, because of the time involved, would not have lent itself very well to an activity like trail driving, where you moved every day and sometimes twice a day. That wouldn't give you an opportunity to sufficiently prepare the meat to effect what I think we traditionally associate with barbecue. The same would be true of roundups. I haven't seen a single mention of a barbecue sauce, much less any recipe of any kind. Barbecuing became obviously more prevalent later on, I'd say from about the last quarter of the nineteenth century to World War II.

"Where I have found the use of the term was in those instances where there was time available, for example cooking at headquarters or when a wagon stayed in a headquarters for a length of time. Most of the time I found it in the context of ribs, as opposed to beef on a spit or whatever."

Although prime beef may be in part raised by cowboys, it is not raised for cowboys. Cowboys, like diamond miners and oil refinery workers, aren't generally paid with a percentage of their product. So barbecue may have been associated with the

XIT Rodeo Queen XIT RODEO AND REUNION **DALHART, TEXAS**

West while not necessarily having been associated with cowboys per se. But that still leaves open the question of why the image of the cowboy and barbecue have become inextricably linked.

"I think part of it comes from the centennial of 1936, when Texas was kind of introduced to the world and the Texas image got a shot nationwide," Price says. "It had been sort of a regional phenomenon before then—the big hat, the big brag, all the cowboy stuff."

Many of the oldest Texas barbecue restaurants were already open by 1936—Southside Market, Black's, Kreutz. But at that point they were selling mostly sausage. Their menus looked very different from what we now think of as a menu in a barbecue restaurant. Price's theory, which is plausible, suggests that the story of cow-boys and barbecue has been composed in the modern era to fit our vision of an idealized past. Or, perhaps more to the point, cultural history has been rewritten so as to make it more readily marketable.

☜☞

Back at the barbecue pit, a noose sways gently from the teeth of the bulldozer. Predictable jokes are being mouthed, stuff about how good it was to know Loyd Johnson and how it would be a shame if something was wrong with the barbecue and they had to hang him. For his part Loyd is quiet, laughing at the jokes, but uncomfortably, I think. He seems damn near sure they probably wouldn't hang him, even if the barbecue wasn't quite right. But he also seems anxious to taste it and let them taste it, so all this speculating can be put to rest.

With great ceremony Loyd takes the first roast out of the pit, cuts open its wrapping, and drops a long, stringy piece of hot, dripping meat down his throat. He smiles and everyone applauds. The whole barbecue crew digs in then, opening up a couple of the steaming roasts and tasting the meat. Loyd's smile was justified. The meat is beautifully seasoned, plenty of salt and pepper and garlic powder. All that seasoning plus the fat and juices from the meat have been sealed within the paper bags, so it's very juicy.

All this time the noose, itself an icon dusty with disuse, sways gently in the wind.

Mrs. Softa OTTO'S BARBECUE **HOUSTON, TEXAS**

Sexual Implications

Bright Lights on a Small Stage

Primarily outdoor cooking is man's work and man-sized menus and portions should be the rule.
James Beard, *Cook It Outdoors*

Once when I was real young and Mom was in the hospital, Dad fixed eggs and rice for my sister and me. I remember that time as the first time I ate that combination, and sometimes now I'll warm some rice in a buttered skillet and scramble some eggs to go along with it, plus maybe some crisp bacon. A lot of people don't think they would like eggs and rice, so mostly I make it when there's no one else there. And always when I eat it I think of Mom being in the hospital and Dad fixing it for Migel and me.

Then there was when we bought the yellow barbecue pit from Sears. My father would stand in front of it tending ribs and hot sausage and pork chops and chicken. I was the one who mixed the vinegar and water and punched the holes in the top of the jar used to put the fire out.

Who else was there? The faces are a blur now. Some of the people I associate with these family times became friends later and couldn't have been there then. But in each memory there are the men drinking beer and hard liquor and standing around the pit and carrying on a running commentary about the cooking. I know there were women there and I can always see my mother's face in these memories, but somehow the other women, even the ones I know were there, are a bit faceless. I can see and hear all the lawyers who worked with my father in 1971 on the trial of the Black Panthers. Specifically, I see Ernest Jones, who I realized even then embodied an effortless cool that epitomized what a boy with any ambition at all should aspire to. But what of Edith, his wife?

In the kitchen my mother was baking beans and making potato salad and corn on the cob and garlic bread. I remember her putting slices of bacon and cheddar cheese on top of the beans and telling me (though perhaps this was later) that you shouldn't put celery in potato salad because it holds water and makes your salad soggy. There were no crowds in the kitchen commenting; it was just the two of us, as my sister has always viewed cooking as the province of other people.

Bob Richardson, my cousin, does the family barbecues now. He has an unerring sense of the dramatic, and his charms are both natural and well honed. He's a bachelor now, and is known for showing up at Christmas and Thanksgiving dinners with empty Tupperware in hand. His freezer is filled with plastic containers of Christmas gumbo and Aunt Doris' red beans, each neatly dated. Despite this inclination to be cooked for, he can cook and is especially proud of his barbecued shrimp (a misnamed New Orleans delicacy) and his barbecued ribs. But he makes clear that his cooking is an event. This will not be just the ordinary, garden-variety smothered chicken with rice and gravy and potato salad and sweet potatoes and green peas and stuffed mirlitons that our grandmother used to make to go in front of the thin chocolate chip cookies with the pecans in them. Rather, his presence in front of the fire is an occasion.

Even Reginald Williams—whose mother, Mama Ella, could stew a chicken so good it'd make you want to slap your own mama—did and still does the family barbecue. And I still remember that Fourth of July when he barbecued over by Mrs. Smith's house and made me know anew that it was possible to get great barbecue in my home town.

It's amazing when you think about it. It is possible for a man to cook one half of one meal two or three times a year and be splashed with compliments and attention. Maybe it's like praising children for accomplishing something that would be no accomplishment at all for an adult. But when you have an ear tuned for the reception of flattery, it's hard to hear even the most obvious strains of condescension.

It would seem odd at first glance that men cook so little at home. Men have always been professional chefs, so it is not the act of cooking itself that is unmasculine. But cooking one's daily bread (as opposed to cooking to earn one's daily bread) is a different situation. Take Nathaniel Burton, the co-author of the greatest of New Orleans cookbooks, *Creole Feast*. He never cooked at home; his wife did the cooking there, and he ate whatever she prepared. Similarly, I imagine that when the great fashion designers need buttons mended on their suits, they don't do the work themselves. The difference lies not so much in the distinction between professional and amateur as it does in the difference between public and private, onstage and backstage.

So if a man is going to cook at home, there must be an occasion, something almost ceremonial. The folklorist Thomas A. Adler titled his article on men cooking "Making Pancakes on Sunday: The Male Cook in Family Tradition." Other days are cereal-and-milk days, breakfast being merely a stop en route to school or work. But on Sunday, once you plant your feet under the table for breakfast, you are where you're going.

Men also like to have signature dishes. Unburdened with the responsibility of preparing something appetizing on the other six days of the week, they take one dish and invest it with such excitement and anticipation that they are never asked to vary the menu. After a week of cornflakes, pancakes work well. Better still are banana pancakes or buckwheat pancakes, delicacies with extra adjectives in front of their names.

Of course any *real man* has a toolshed filled with specialized implements for accomplishing repairs and other tasks that only a real man can accomplish. It is the same in the kitchen. Adler cites the example of a man who bought a small flourmill to grind the wheat for his whole-grain pancakes. This was necessary, he claimed, because the vitamin E in wheat is lost almost immediately after grinding. Adler suggests that the "ritual" had more to do with the ceremony of weekly grindings than with vitamin potency. A less ambitious patriarch might settle for an expensive skillet, a cheaper imitation of which could not possibly conduct heat to wheaten batter or beaten eggs in the appropriate way.

All this is true in barbecue, only the themes sound there with greater resonance. First of all, barbecue requires the taming of fire, and it was the act of taming fire that first lighted man's path out of the cold drafts and raw-meat dinners of cave life. Any prehistorian worth his testosterone can tell you with certainty that it was a man, not a woman, who first bent fire to human will. Women are perfectly capable of cooking in controlled environments, of starting fires with pilot lights and adjusting the heat with knobs, the logic goes, but from the beginning of human time, men have lighted fires from sparks and beaten small flames into blazes. It is this image of themselves that men cling to.

In more recent times men have preserved these skills as boy scouts and campers. What are these activities but the voluntary exposure of oneself to primitive conditions so as to prove to the world and oneself that if it were necessary (and God spare us if ever again it is!) we could survive under these conditions? Not all men are campers, of course. Even those who are have not always done well at it, and even those who used to be good at it may have lost the touch. But the man sweating in front of his grill, protected from the savage flames only by a few dozen pounds of steel and the bucket of water next to him, sends a message to himself if to no one else that, though a mild-mannered tax accountant by weekday, he is as fit as any outdoorsman by weekend.

Claude Lévi-Strauss, the French anthropologist, draws a major distinction between roasting and boiling. He posits that roasting predated boiling, as roasting required fewer tools and thus less sophistication: "Roasted food, being directly exposed to fire is in a relationship of *non-mediatized conjunction*, whereas boiled food is the product of a two fold process of mediation: it is immersed in water and both food and water are contained within a receptacle." In Lévi-Strauss's equation, roasting is akin to nature and boiling is akin to culture. The chef and author Alain Senderens writes that "woman = culture; man = nature" —from which it can be concluded that man = barbecue.

The tools of barbecuing, like the saws and hammers of a man's workshop, are a specialized lot. The forks and spatulas are large, man-sized implements. There's the charcoal starter to woo the flame and the hose to subjugate it. And of course the pit.

Much like a man's enthusiasm for finally buying the expensive riding mower or jigsaw that he needs, there is an enthusiasm for buying the proper (read expensive) barbecue pit. The pit by its very size, weight, and expense must communicate that this is a man's tool. A pit like this is obviously not to be brought out on just any occasion. Rather, it is reserved for the Fourth of July or Cinco de Mayo or Juneteenth or some other day that has already been made large by history. The event itself then provides the introductory fanfare for the entrance of the cook.

At a barbecue, as large numbers of friends and relatives arrive, the back yard is transformed from private into public space; it becomes a stage. No matter what time the guests are told to arrive, there will certainly be meat still cooking on the grill and everyone will at least walk over once or twice to check it. The man barbecuing will be either very tense and neurotic to reinforce the message that this is a difficult, manly job requiring undivided attention, or relaxed and cool so as to make clear that the fire is so subjugated that it poses no threat to the women and children present.

The final opportunity that barbecuing gives a man to prove he's a man is in the creation of his sauce. Not all barbecue sauces are hot, of course, but hot barbecue sauces are deemed appropriate opportunities for a man to demonstrate how much pepper he is man enough to ingest. In this regard barbecue sauce is much like chili, another *man's* dish. By creating a sauce so hot that the women and wimps are unable to eat it, the *real men* reassert their membership in the all-male club.

Jim "Arkansas Trav'ler" Quessenberry, a world-champion pit man, sums up the overall connection between men and barbecue this way: "It's the caveman in us. I think that's why you see more and more men barbecuing. It's a macho thing. Playing with the fire and being outdoors, bragging about how good you cook, it's got all the macho rush to it without any of the violence. Also women don't really pursue it very thoroughly. That's one territory they don't try to invade. They kind of leave it to us."

In the Province of Men

Women barbecue cookers are not rare, but neither are they common. At the root of Lem's Barbecue in Chicago are the recipes of Mrs. Lemons, from whom her sons learned their trade before moving up north. Half of PDT Barbecue, one of the most successful teams on the Kansas City Barbecue Society competition circuit, is Donna McClure, who shares equally in competition duties with her husband, Ted. And from my own childhood I remember Mattie Bivens Dennis, who always did the barbecuing while her husband poured the drinks and told the jokes until the meat was ready. But in an age when women drive schoolbuses and run major corporations, it seems odd that they aren't better represented in barbecue.

To an extent, women *don't* barbecue because men *do* barbecue. All the factors that conspire to make barbecuing masculine also contribute to its image as not feminine. In her article "The Joys of Cooking: Sex Stereotyping Among the Pots and Pans," Johanna Ezell notes that traditional cookbooks deserve much of the blame for society's image of what is and is not appropriate for a woman to do. "American cookbooks have traditionally been written by women and for women," Ezell writes. "It is one sphere of print communication which has been dominated by women. Because of this, we can assume a cultural continuity in cookbooks—threads of thought and areas of concern are passed through succeeding generations of authors and readers—the readers often becoming the next generation of authors."

Ezell cites the example of a 1938 book, *The Working Girl Must Eat*, which advised the working "girl" to "learn how to cook a steak properly and as he likes it ... the girl who can broil a steak well, make good coffee and light fluffy biscuits, will be forgiven many sins and omissions." Ezell quotes also from Catharine Beecher's 1869 book, *The American Woman's Home*, which offers an explanation of the husband's duties: "To the man is appointed the out-door labor—to till the earth, dig the mines...transverse the ocean...conduct civil, municipal, and state affairs, and all heavy work, which most of the day excludes him from the comforts of home."

"The tradition of stereotyping is still carried on actively in many of the less important books published," Ezell writes. "For instance, it appears that a man can appropriately cook barbeque, or any form of game. He can do any kind of camp cooking. He can have specialties of cooking meat, or fish (particularly if he caught the fish himself); he can have a specialty of making salad. He can bake bread, particularly if it is sourdough. He can mix drinks."

A final factor in the disinclination of women to barbecue is no doubt the belief that they have enough work to do already. According to the Barbecue Industry Association, men are more likely to do the actual barbecuing, but women are more apt to decide when the event will take place and what will be barbecued. Add to that the responsibility of shopping, making the side dishes, and cleaning up, and many women are no doubt relieved that they are not called upon to do anything else.

These factors notwithstanding, we encountered several women who barbecue and/or run barbecue businesses.

Mrs. Lula Hughes SOUL SISTER **WHARTON, TEXAS**

Otto's Barbecue, Houston, Texas

Mrs. Softa wears nice dresses and jewelry and doesn't look like she works here. She looks like she's going to tea. Or perhaps she does look like she works here, not because it's a barbecue place, but because, as the photos on the walls tell you, this is President Bush's favorite barbecue place.

Lighted cigarette ever present, Mrs. Softa is friendly and direct and speaks through the clouds of smoke she blows.

Otto was her father-in-law. Otto was from Shiner, Texas, an old Czech town, and he made hamburgers from the meat he sold in his grocery. Later the barbecue came. Now the two businesses can't fit in the same building, so they are in buildings next to each other. The barbecue is real good, but the hamburgers, for which they still grind the meat themselves, are great.

Mr. Softa inherited the business when his father died, but his wife tells us he doesn't really want to be in it. He started doing this when he was ten. He remembers how even on cold days whenever a customer ordered a beer he had to stick his hands in the tub of ice to retrieve it. Even now sometimes when it starts to get cold, he complains about his fingers.

He doesn't want to be in it. She doesn't want to be anywhere else.

She's worked here ever since the kids—seven of them, the youngest now twenty-six—were grown. She doesn't cook the barbecue; she just manages the place.

It was her idea to let the guy use the Otto's name and Otto's barbecue for a new hamburger and barbecue place he's opening. She pushed her husband into it. The guy expects to do $20,000 a week during lunch at this new place, but everybody thinks that's a little high. Mrs. Softa predicts that if he does do that kind of volume, then Mr. Softa will remember how the whole thing was his idea.

Soul Sister, Wharton, Texas: Wherein Miss Lula Hughes Meets the Two Nice Gentlemen

Because Hinze's was so good, we were curious and optimistic about barbecue on the other side of the tracks in the Texas town of Wharton. We found this place, a skinny little building next to the old Daton Grocery Company, but only by asking everyone we saw for directions and then being further encouraged by the man who responded to Frank's question "Is it good?" by saying, "Shit yeah! It's the best."

Once inside, sitting in the booth below a tapestry in which cowboy dogs are playing poker, we order some brisket and ribs. Soul Sister, in her large brown pants and red sneakers, returns from the back with our order. As we eat our food, we watch her as she eats some brisket herself and also watches soap operas on television. We eat enough to learn what we think and decide that the ribs are good, though not the brisket so much—this to ourselves—and then to her, "We're doing a book on barbecue, can we talk to you for a minute?"

"Yeah," she says, looking up from her plate, "but I don't have no money. I'm going to the hospital, to the doctor, to a specialist." Which leaves me wondering whether I asked her the same question I had asked the other hundred people I had interviewed. I try again, this time making certain to invest my tone with all the polite humility that you learn when your grandmother is from Maringouin, Louisiana, knowing that if you know anything you must be sure to tip your hat twice to the white folks in these towns just in case, but remembering now also that black folks can be standoffish and even mean if you don't approach them just so.

"I'm too busy," she says above the sound of the television, though there is no one even passing along this street now, much less passing through this restaurant. I say whatever I say and she responds, "I have to go to the bathroom. I don't have time for all of this. You should have told me what you wanted before you ordered your food." And I try once more, telling her that we can come back later, perhaps in an hour. "An hour, two hours, three hours, I'll be here till seven o'clock," she says, but it sounds as if she means she'd rather that we not come back.

It's drizzling outside; the clouds promise a downpour. Frank would like to take her up on her offer. But it has become a game now; the obstinacy in her has bred persistence in me and I want to go back if only to see what she'll think of next.

When it's an hour later and we have driven on what seems like every road of this town, we return and she tells us that she's been sick since June the seventh (bad disk) and if she don't do good by the twenty-sixth they say they gon' send for her. Plus she had a massive heart attack two and a half years ago. I don't want them to have to send for her in the middle of the interview, so I relent and offer to forget the whole thing, but she reminds us that we're here now, so we might as well go through with it.

She got into this, she says, because years ago people would smell the barbecue around her house and they would hang out in the back yard playing dominoes and cards and carrying on. "I told my husband, 'Just as soon go into business if they gon' gang up behind my house like that.' So I started out from there."

She shows us the old pit in the back, which was already here when she moved into the place and on which she can cook up to twenty-one briskets, but in which she burns only oak, no charcoal. As she talks, Frank snaps pictures; she seems to appreciate the attention. He comments on all the photos of blues musicians on the walls, then asks about the family photos. She tells us about her husband, now deceased, and her brother, Jim Kearney, who used to play football with the Kansas City Chiefs, and her son, who is fifty-one. And she tells us that she named the place Soul Sister because back in the 70s if the men didn't know your name they would just say, "Hey, soul sister," and she decided to let those words live in this place.

By now we have learned what we have come to learn, and besides, the sun is coming out; we are anxious to get back on the highway before the sun changes its mind. Aided by Frank, who has been inclined toward the exit since the moment he gained entry, I begin reciting closing lines. But she feels like talking now, so we tarry another moment. Then Frank, feet pointed firmly exitward, begins muttering things like "This sho' has been" and "In the future we hope to recall" and other such Memphis-style verbal acrobatics that when translated mean simply that the sooner we get out of here the sooner we can look back on our time together, and the sooner we can look back on it the more inclined we will be to look back on it with favor.

We inch out as slowly as is appropriate, trying not to dash doorward while she is in midsentence, but nonetheless what she finally says, she says to our backs. "Yaw'll nice gentlemen," she calls. "I enjoyed yaw'll."

And then finally, perhaps to herself, "Nice gentlemen."

New Zion Missionary Baptist Church, Huntsville, Texas

The church needed painting. Bro Ward was a painter and he came out one Friday with Sis Ward, he to paint, she to cook his dinner.

He remembers the scent going out across the road and the people coming over and buying his dinner before he got any. She remembers that he didn't get angry that time, but the next time, when they came to finish, she was certain to put him some on the side while he painted. She sold the rest of the barbecue she had made. That was a dozen years ago.

The church was a small building, she recalls. Most of the people were old and weren't able to support the church. So the Wards started this barbecuing to raise money. Many of the members are still old, but they have a new building now. We sat in it one Sunday while a guest preacher preached on the subject "You can get what you want, and lose what you got."

The church is new, and the building next to it, where the people from the highway and from the town crowd in to eat sliced beef and ribs, is also new-looking on the inside. On the outside, where the pits are, everything is black with soot. The pits are old. A fan sits by the firebox of one pit to blow the smoke across the meat. Smoke is everywhere.

Sis Ward doesn't do the barbecuing anymore. Hasn't for years. Men do it now. "Write this down," the tall man in front of the pit says. "Out all us doin' the barbecue, ain' nar' a one of us got no good back."

Matchstick clamped in the corner of her mouth, Sis Ward oversees three other women in the kitchen. Pots of beef boiling before they go out on the grill. Pots of potatoes boiling for salad. Napkins being folded; sliced white bread being tucked into plastic baggies. She constantly checks the various stations, seeing that everything is in place.

"I tell you one thing," Sis Ward says. "You gon' have a hard time keeping up with me cause I'm gon' be moving." Which seems hard to believe because at 11:45 no one is here. I have time to look at all the newspaper articles and the *Texas Highways* magazine article that has made this place nationally known. I'm reading an article, standing near the door, at 11:50 when the first customers come in.

At 11:55 there's a line.

Amazing Grace, Kansas City, Kansas, and Kansas City, Missouri

The Grand Emporium is a long, narrow, old building. Dark, nearly windowless, and thoroughly marinated in years of spilled beer. By day, at least this day, it's empty except for a few men nursing beers at the bar.

But by night it's a blues club. The walls are papered with posters announcing bygone engagements of Eddy Clearwater, Jimmy Valentine and the Heart Murmurs, and a couple of hundred other acts. Behind the bar is a smaller, less formal poster that announces "Grace Herself Makes All Our Food Items."

Grace Harris' reputation is based largely on the fact that one of her sauces has won a "Best in the U.S.A." at the American Royal Barbecue Sauce Competition. She has her own after-hours joint across the river in Kansas City, Kansas, H-M Old Southern Style. But she also cooks barbecue and other items for the Grand Emporium.

I started cooking at age ten. My grandmother always cooked for a living and she'd put me up on a flour can and I'd be tall enough to cook.

I spent most of my life in Kansas City. My father was from Mississippi; my mother was from Louisiana. So I had all kinds of cooking around me. My mama's people were Creole and my daddy's people were Indian and Caucasian. We came here in the 50s. I have always had a goal from my childhood up, I wanted to go into business for myself.

I started working for Mr. [Otis P.] Boyd, I think it was like 1961. I didn't do no food for Mr. Boyd, I worked as a waitress. My main thing was seeing how I could work with people. I learned the business from Mr. Boyd and I bought a brand-new car in one year's time. At that time, out of all the barbecue that was around here, I thought his was the best. I was there just a couple of weeks ago; I had the lamb breast.

The next place that had real good barbecue was Hezekiah. Hezekiah was the only person in the city with barbecued pigs' feet and snoots. We would go to the Rosedale on Friday and Hezekiah on Saturday. We used to call Rosedale the greasy bag cause they were wrapping their barbecue in newspaper then. When we went to Rosedale we had ribs. When we went to Hezekiah we had pig feet and pig snoots.

I was the very first person in the city that started coming up with different kinds of barbecue sauce. I've got thirty different ones and all of mines are different. I don't serve them. I have an international sauce. What I mean is, the only places you would make that kind of sauce would be places like Liberia. I have a Jamaican barbecue sauce. It is called jerk barbecue sauce. And I have a wine barbecue sauce. I have all different types of flavors of

sauce, some of them I don't want to list. I got a lot of them in the closet—recipes that I got wrote.

Then after I got into business myself I was the very first person in the city that came up with that beef sausage. Everybody else followed. Everybody was doing pork but nobody was doing beef. Then I decided to come up with a chicken sausage. I did it a couple of times, but not enough for someone to catch on. And then I came out with a combo. I made it one time in a festival and it went over real good. I named it a combo cause it was a combo of different stuff and it was a hit. I only did it that one time 'cause I knew someone would be trying to copy it.

And I was the very first person came up with a rub. And when I came up with my barbecue rub everyone else came up with one. But I never have put my real rub in a contest, but everybody thinks I have.

After everybody jumped on the rub, I came up with another thing, which is called a dip. It's completely different. You prepare your meat, then you dip it.

The point is, it's just like if you were a fighter and somebody said, "Oh well, they're gonna bring out so-and-so today to try you." Every time somebody think they coming towards me, I move. I do fifty-six different coleslaws.

I wasn't treated very good being a woman, you know. Just a couple of years ago a buddy of mine and I entered a contest and we got there and the guys were all happy to see him, but they told him, "You know, you could have left Amazing Grace at home." When they said that it made me feel kind of cold inside, but I never showed it. To me it's a challenge because of me being a lady. I have to earn my respect; that's what keeps me going. Most of the barbecue people are mens.

Amazing Grace Harris THE GRAND EMPORIUM **KANSAS CITY, MISSOURI**

One of the real reasons that I was really so determined to make this work was like when I started my business one time I was setting up around City Hall and I had a booth set up and this guy walked up to me and he called off all the other barbecue places that were there and he said, "I don't know what you doing here when all these other places are here." And I looked at him and I told him, "Honey, it's enough for us all." And I smiled at him and so around about four o'clock he came back he said, "I see you going home." But I never told him I had sold everything I had. By four that evening I didn't have anything left and the rest of the barbecue places were still there.

I had a dream I wanted my own car, my own house, my own business, and I wanted to go to Washington, D.C., to the White House. I went to Jimmy Carter's inaugural ball and I stayed there five days. All of the things that I wanted to do, I kind of done most of them. I just have one more goal now, and I'm hoping the good Lord will bless me with enough money that I can put all thirty of my sauces nationwide, all over the world. I don't want them to be limited to the United States; I want them to go all over the world.

Still Life with Grill MOE'S BAR B Q **EAST ST. LOUIS, ILLINOIS**

CHAPTER
FIVE

Chicago/East St. Louis
Midwestward Migration

Prominent among the technological advancements that gave rise to barbecue in the Midwest was the mechanical cotton picker.

From the days of Reconstruction until the middle of the twentieth century, the dream of many African-Americans in the South was to move up North and put as much distance as possible between themselves and the unreconstructed lash of postbellum bondage. Initially this talk of Negroes moving up and emancipating themselves didn't go over real well with the white people. But no matter how little you paid them or how much you threatened them, the Negroes remained inexplicably determined to leave home.

Refined in the 20s and 30s, by the late 1940s mechanical cotton pickers were having a major impact on the economy of the South. According to the figures of Howell Hopson, a Mississippi planter, picking a bale of cotton by machine cost him $5.26. Having the Negroes pick it by hand cost him $39.41. Each machine could pick as much cotton as fifty people. The Negro's stock was soon trading at an all-time low. Faced with the prospect of a sudden surplus of Negroes, Southern whites were less inclined to impede their flow northward. There were other factors influencing the northward migration of black Americans, of course, and the cumulative effect of these forces was quickly felt. "In 1940, 77 per cent of black Americans still lived in the South—49 per cent in the rural South," Nicholas Lemann wrote in his book *The Promised Land*. "Between 1910 and 1970, six and a half million black Americans moved from the South to the North; five million of them moved after 1940, during the time of the mechanization of cotton farming. In 1970, when the migration ended, black America was only half Southern, and less than a quarter rural; 'urban' had become a euphemism for 'black.'"

Many of the older barbecue restaurants in this region, like Arthur Bryant's in Kansas City or Lem's in Chicago, were started by black migrants from this era. And just as "urban" came to all but mean "black," eating barbecue came to all but mean going to the black side of town. Barbecue has spread itself out geographically, but in places like East St. Louis and the Southside of Chicago, the culture of barbecue remains especially rich and predominantly black.

A Crisp Extravagance: East St. Louis

Snoot sandwich.

The words married in my ear like reluctant lovers at the end of a shotgun barrel. Whatever a snoot was—and I didn't know then—it had the sound of something that should be thrusting itself between the bars of a cage rather than between slices of bread.

Joe Davis first told me about them. Joe Davis, Philadelphia disc jockey and youngest son of Miles Dewey Davis, Sr., patriarch of a family renowned for music making, pedigree pig raising, and—as I was to learn—snoot consumption.

I encountered those two words again, years later, in the *Wall Street Journal* in an article on the economy of St. Louis. There they were, in the first paragraph, being barbecued at a Jefferson Avenue church fundraiser, serving both as food and as symbol of economic decline.

In Chicago, still later, I ask Uncle Vince about snoots. For forty-six years he has been married to the former Dottie Davis, the sister of Joe and Miles the younger. Uncle Vince grew up on the west St. Louis side of the river and knows about snoots, but cannot cook them. With a sip from his Mason jar–shaped mug of iced beer, he tells us about the one time he tried to make snoots as a surprise for his trumpet-playing brother-in-law. Short on luggage space, he went to the trouble of putting them in his golf bag so they could make it onto the plane. All to no avail. "Motherfucker, why you fuck up my snoots?" Miles said, or words to that effect.

So while he is barbecuing a rack of ribs on the patio, which he does expertly, he enlists the assistance of Boonie, an East St. Louis transplant who has been his neighbor now for several decades. Boonie is a slight man, less than five and a half feet tall from the top of his baseball cap to the hem of his light blue pants.

"You talking about the hog' face," he says, tracing the outline of his own face to indicate clearly that the snoot is composed mostly of the cheeks. "The first thing with snoots is you got to cut 'em on the inside or they'll curl up on you. You have to cut 'em."

"Score 'em," Frank says.

"Yeah," Boonie says. "Put 'em on the grill fat side down. And you don't put nothing on it. Not even salt and pepper—hey, it's gon' have its flavor.

"With snoots it's a constant thing of turning 'em. Turning 'em over, turning 'em over, turning 'em over," Boonie says, moving his hands like a three-card monte player on a New York sidewalk. "You don't want to burn it, tha's the reason you keep turning it. It takes about two and a half hours, but you can tell when they getting together. When you crack it," he says, his right hand tapping an imaginary snoot with an imaginary knife handle, "it just crumbles."

∞

What we know of East St. Louis before arriving here is mostly bad. The three words of its name are the shorthand that people in the Midwest use when they are trying to capture the mood of American decline without boring you with the details. They say simply, "You know, like East St. Louis." In the Northeast words like Newark and the South Bronx are used with similar efficiency.

And, avoiding the details, I can tell you that the feeling of East St. Louis is the feeling of decay. Without knowing whether its golden age was genuine or not, I can tell you that empty spaces stand out in almost every block, like so many missing teeth in an ill-kept mouth. And there are the boarded-up store-fronts and the broken windows that increase exponentially when people move away. Some of these people, it seems, left long ago.

There are many barbecue places, but if the number of restaurants is any indication, chop suey is the staple here. There is probably not a ten-block stretch in East St. Louis that does not contain a chop suey restaurant, or the boarded-up remnants of one. Not even the fast-food chains have managed that kind of penetration.

What we know about snoots when we arrive is mostly what Boonie has told us. We stop at the first barbecue place we see, but it's closed. We stop at the hatmaker's shop next door, hoping someone there can give us a lead on where to get good snoots. Though it's well after the posted hour for opening, the door is locked. Minutes later, as we are getting back into the car, a woman emerges cautiously, asking if she can help us. We ask her what she thinks of the barbecue place next door. "Everybody has their good days and bad days," she says, leaving it to us to figure out which days predominate at her neighbor's restaurant. She does have a favorite snoot place, she tells us—Mary's. There, she says us, they have really good snoots.

Mary's is open, but not for the sale of snoots. There are a number of products on display behind the plexiglass that encloses Mary's counter—candies, potato chips, and one package each of various pain relievers, lotions, and feminine hygiene products. We could buy a fish sandwich, some fried chicken wings, or any of the sundries on display, but the snoots, a woman yells through the plexiglass, won't be ready until about noon.

We are trying to get an early start in our search, but we discover that the barbecue places here don't open early. So we stop in a barbershop, one that has caught our attention because it too is next to a closed barbecue place. While Frank is in the chair, he maneuvers the conversation around to the subject of snoots, asking whether the place next door has decent snoots. We are told that it doesn't. The middle-aged man who has more or less been leading the conversation does know where the best snoots in East St. Louis are, though. Moe's, he tells us. "It's right there behind the VFW hall. If Moe is doing the cooking, that's your best snoots. And tell him Bobby Jones sent you."

Behind the VFW hall is right. Driving through the VFW parking lot, we see a genuine, unmistakable rib shack, one of those buildings which, like diners, are a fading light in the American cultural cosmos. There is a hand-scribbled sign leaning against the wall. It says, as best I can make out, "MOC Bar B Q," but with its dripping paint and the letters running into one another, it really can't be read. To its right is the screen door through which you enter the small white building that houses Moe's. The building is perhaps twenty feet long, divided by the counter where customers order. Its pale green walls with their dusting of soot are lit, though dimly so, by three bare light bulbs hanging from the ceiling. In the left corner in front of the counter is a pile of oddly shaped blocks of wood, each roughly six inches by six inches, but none exactly the same shape or dimension as any other. On the wall, handwritten, is Moe's menu:

MENU

SNOOT	$2.75
SNOOT CHIPS	2.75
RIB TIPS	3.00

RIB SANDWICHES

SMALL END	$4.00
MIDDLE CUT	3.75
LARGE END	3.50
WHOLE RIB	11.00
HALF RIB	5.50
PORK SANDWICH	2.75
BEEF	2.75
COMBO (rib tip and snoot chips)	4.00

The young woman behind the counter tells us that Moe has gone out. But despite the fact that Bobby Jones specifically said that this place has the best snoots "if Moe is doing the cooking," we order a snoot sandwich.

She first puts a slice of bread on top of a piece of tin foil. Then with a pair of ice tongs she removes a brown piece of meat from the grill and places it on the bread. Then she dips several tablespoons of barbecue sauce onto the snoot, puts another slice of bread on top, wraps it up in tin foil, wraps that up in newspaper, puts it in a bag, and presents it to us. In the car, under a shade tree, we unwrap and eat.

The snoot announces itself on the tongue with a crisp extravagance of grease. It's not nearly as light as the conventional pork rinds that you can buy off the potato chip rack. They are more like cracklins with their combination of crisply fried fat on one side and the hard, crunchy skin on the other. It's the skin that gives you the most trouble. It seems that no matter what angle you take the snoot from, it's hard to bite into. Though it does have a soft underbelly, the snoot is well protected by an armor-like shell.

We refuse to give up. This is the local delicacy, so there must be some way to eat it. Finally Frank adapts a trick he learned from his daughters' rottweiler, Sheba. He maneuvers the snoot around to his hind teeth, where he can get a better grip. He closes his eyes and bites with renewed vigor but marginal success. "This is damn near uneatable," he says in frustration. With three quarters of the sandwich left, we give up.

We try two or three other barbecue places, most of them recommended, none of them outstanding. Our enthusiasm wanes. (We try Mary's again. "He just put 'em on," the woman says. "They should be ready about two o'clock, but call first to be sure.") To make matters worse, finding true barbecued snoots is an increasingly difficult proposition, even here. More and more barbecue places are turning to the deep fryer to cook their snoots. The snoots are boiled first, the excess fat scraped off, and the remains deep-fried. Since frying guarantees a crisp snoot, and since a splash of barbecue sauce masks any taste differential, the snoot chef, no matter how accomplished, is finding himself increasingly replaced by the fry man.

"I can't believe that what we are getting is real snoot sandwiches," Frank says, incredulous. "People can't be clamoring for this shit." But they are. "I try not to eat a lot of 'em," the waitress at a coffee shop tells us. "Why not?" I ask, assuming that she can explain the snoot phenomenon to us from an impartial distance. "If I start," she says, "I just can't stop." We get an almost identical reply from a barmaid. "I love 'em too much," she confesses.

There is another pattern we notice. Everyone has a favorite snoot place, and as far as they are concerned, it is the only place in the city with good snoots. All other places are unsanitary or their food is inedible. In all restaurant categories people develop emotional attachments to their favorite places, attachments that often defy reason. But this loyalty has a more personal, almost vindictive edge when it comes to snoots. The waitress at the coffee shop swears by the snoots at a place called Bud's. She doesn't seem to know or care that they are deep-fried. "I don't eat no more snoots from there," the barmaid says of another place. "I know somebody almost broke they dentures on a snoot from over there." Her suggestion is that we try Bolden's.

At Bolden's you order through a little hole in the plexiglass and they slip your food to you via a drawer. Human contact is kept to a minimum. Bolden's sandwich is a slight improvement over the other ones we've had. The main thing that separates one snoot from another is the ratio of the hard crunchy parts to the soft crispy parts. If you can get enough crispy parts, then the crunchy parts are a nice change of pace. But if you find yourself biting around the whole snoot without getting a tooth in edgewise, it destroys the whole experience.

Having tasted what strikes us as the closest thing to a good snoot, we try to talk to Mr. Bolden. "First of all, I don't have the time," he says gruffly. "Second, I don't want to be bothered."

(Back at Mary's circa two p.m., we ring the bell on the outside of the plexiglass to order a snoot. Through a small speaker a bodiless voice says that the snoots aren't ready. "They should be ready about six—but call first." "They must be cooking elephant snoots over there," Frank comments. "They real hard to cook.")

The main reason for returning to Moe's is to take a picture of it. The building has a face and feeling that Frank likes. Moe is there when we return. He is a shy, older man with worn shoes and work clothes. He's very kind, but there's a problem, he tells us. He doesn't own the building. The VFW owns it. "I can't do nothing without they tell me I can do it," he says. "If you want to take any kind of pictures you have to talk to them."

The VFW hall is a lounge, for the most part, where veterans and their friends can drink and socialize and on special occasions have barbecues and memorials. There have been a couple of lively debates

Taming the Flame MOE'S BAR B Q **EAST ST. LOUIS, ILLINOIS**

at the hall in recent years, someone tells us—the usual exchanges of views, but punctuated with exchanges of blood and bullets. So beyond the doorway to the club there is a metal detector like the ones at the airport. I empty the change from my pocket and go through, but my tape recorder sets the detector off. As I begin to take it out of my pocket, one of the men sitting at the table inside says, "Come on in. You don't have no pistol, do you?"

The hall is a long building with a bar extending nearly half its length. The room is darkened by red shades over the fluorescent lights; trails of smoke circle above dozens of lit cigarettes. They sell liquor either by the drink or by the set-up (a half pint of liquor, a bowl of ice, a glass or two, and a chaser). The codes of dress and conduct are communicated to the newcomer by a series of hand-lettered signs posted on the walls. NO SHORT SHORTS. NO ATHLETIC SHIRTS OR SHORTS. NO HALTER BLOUSES. MUST WEAR SHOES. MUST BE CLEAN. NO WEAPONS ALLOWED, VIOLATORS WILL BE PROSECUTED. NO SNEAKERS. There are nearly half a dozen NO PROFANITY signs spread around the club. East St. Louis veterans are apparently very offended by foul language. No one questions my jogging suit and sneakers.

The commander of VFW Post 3408 is Ronald C. Rattler. Sitting at one of the tables near the bar, he approves the picture-taking idea with little hassle. Frank and the commander walk across the parking lot to let Moe know and to make an appointment with him for us to come back early the next morning.

Back inside the hall, Commander Rattler points to a man at the bar whom he introduces as the world's greatest snoot cooker, his friend Paul. Over a half pint of Seagram's extra-dry gin and some grapefruit juice, he is talking with a friend, Billy Riley. (Both are wearing sneakers.) They turn around in their barstools and, speaking loudly over the Will Downing version of "I Tried," we discuss the history and preparation of snoots.

Like Chicago, he tells us, East St. Louis used to have a lot of packing houses. The most desirable portions of the hog were packaged to sell. The black folks managed to end up with the less desirable portions, chief among them the snoot.

"At one time the packing houses used to give 'em away," Paul says, "and the blacks learned how to cook 'em different."

"Most black people come from the South anyway," Billy says. "We used to eat chicken feet, the backs, the necks. All that shit. You could buy ten backs for about a dollar."

In preparing snoots, Paul tells us, the first thing you do with the snoot is trim the excess fat from it. Next, he says, there is a big white vein that runs through the snoot called the leader vein. That must be cut out. Also, sometimes the butcher will leave part of the snout (rhymes with "out") on the snoot (rhymes with "suit"), and that must be cut off. Then you score the fat side of the snoot to keep it from curling up.

"A lot of people deep-fry them, a lot of people boil them and then put them on the grill, but I prefer the old-fashioned way," he says. "Neighborhood I live in, I'm the only one don't have a gas grill. I don't fuck with no goddamn gas grill. It's all a matter of taste and whether you want to do it right.

"Depending on how much lean and how much fat is on the snoot, it takes approximately two to two and a half hours to cook them. I usually start mine with the meat side down and I use charcoal most of the time. I try not to turn my snoots more than two or three times while it's cooking. By the fourth turn, it's done. It's crispy. Like a pork rind."

"Yeah, but it taste better than a mu'-fucking pork rind," Billy says. "Not to change the subject, but you guys eat tripe? We eat all kinds of shit down here. As long as you cook it right you acquire a taste for it. I eat snoots 'bout once every two or three weeks or so. I couldn't eat them every day. Now, chicken you could eat every day."

"Around here, we eat everything on the hog but the oink," Paul says.

"We eat pig ear sandwiches," Billy says. "I put some of that hot sauce and mustard and onion on there. It's just like eating a bologna sandwich to me. And I tell you something else," he adds. "With all the people that have moved to Chicago from here, if you opened up a snoot place in Chicago you could make a lot of money. A lot of money."

"That gentleman right there taught me one thing about snoots," Paul says, pointing to a man seated at a nearby table. "If you want to keep your snoots fresh, no oven, no foil, just put 'em in a brown paper bag."

"Why you do that?" Frank asks. "Keep 'em crisp?"

"Yeah."

"What does the bag do?" Frank asks, perplexed.

"You have to ask the bag that."

East Meets West

Leaving the VFW, driving west toward the river and St. Louis, you pass the brightest and most shining objects in East St. Louis, the advertisements for the floating gambling hall, the *Casino Queen*. A Cap'n Crunch–looking cartoon figure with a white face (one of the few here), white mustache, and blue navy suit points you in the direction of the boat. Other than the bridge over the Mississippi River, the casino is just about all that connects East St. Louis and the city with the almost identical name across the water. It is a long-distance call between East St. Louis and west St. Louis.

The two cities are as different as rich and poor. In St. Louis there is the huge silver arch; there are skyscrapers and fancy hotels, a Federal Reserve Bank, and several colleges and universities. But in East St. Louis we couldn't even find a post card with that name on it. There is probably not a building taller than a few stories there. At one elementary school, the playground is the vacant lot between the school and the railroad tracks. And although parts of St. Louis are as impoverished and underdeveloped as East St. Louis, what stands out on the Illinois side of the river is that other than the vacant lots, the run-down build-ings, and the diminishing number of occupied houses and businesses that are open for business, there is almost nothing.

East St. Louis wasn't always like this, though. "East St. Louis used to be the fastest li'l town on the map," Boonie told us.

Except for a funeral a few years ago, Joe Davis has hardly returned since he left for college. "It just doesn't turn me on now," he says. "It wasn't like that when we were growing up. I wouldn't trade that experience for anything. There're a lot of good memories there, but it's very painful to see the city that way."

We are staying with Frank's cousin Adrienne and her husband, Hasmukh, over in St. Louis. Their home is a peaceful departure from the norms of either St. Louis. Hasmukh is from India, and both he and Adrienne are followers of the Gurumayi, an Indian guru. The air at Adrienne and Hasmukh's is perfumed by burning incense, and there are candles burning on altars here. The rows of shoes at the door indicate to you that in this house it is customary to remove your shoes. And there are pictures of Gurumayi and Baba Muktananda and blue-skinned Indian gods like Shiva and Lord Krishna and Brahma, and also a pink-skinned Jesus.

Neither the pig's ears nor his snoot are talked about here except in connection with our work. This is a vegetarian household. Hasmukh's cousin Pratima, who is living with them, has prepared rice, curry, an eggplant dish, paratha, and fresh fruit. Frank and I indulge in what has become rare for us in the last six months, the consumption of vegetables.

Morning at Moe's

When we arrive at Moe's it is nine o'clock Saturday morning, and several of the odd-shaped blocks of wood are already blazing in Moe's pit. More odd-shaped blocks of wood are being unloaded from an old pick-up truck with patched sides. The pit, consisting of a brick frame and a grill, is built into the far wall of the place. The red bricks are now covered with soot. There is no cover.

While the fire is roaring, Moe cleans his grill, first sweeping it off twice with a broom and then mopping it down once. As the fire burns off the detergent he uses, he rinses two slabs of ribs in the sink to the right of the grill. That done, he places the ribs on the grill, bone side down. No seasoning.

Yesterday Moe cooked a batch of snoots about half done, leaving much of the grease in them. He takes them out of the refrigerator and places them one by one on the grill. The fire crackles as the grease drips down.

Moe, whose given name is George Sheared, is from Helena, Arkansas. He came here as a teenager, following a friend, and ended up working at the packing house. Retired now, seventy-five years old, he says that he learned this trade not in Arkansas but in East St. Louis. "I knowed what a snout on a hog was," he says, "but I didn't know what a barbecue snoot was. Hadn't heard of it till I came here." I notice that he's cooking a lot of snoots and very

Dancing THE V.F.W. CLUB **EAST ST. LOUIS, ILLINOIS**

few ribs. "The snoots draws 'em," he says. "That's what draws 'em."

Adjoining the barbecue place is a screened-in patio with some worn-out picnic tables and chairs as well as a few file cabinets. It looks as if this building is, or will be, a seating area for Moe's if the veterans' organization ever completes the promised renovations. Overhead, stuck among the rafters, are several dozen white crosses. I can't figure out their purpose. Moe, searching for their exact function himself, answers cryptically but also poetically. "That's when, Memorial Day, people that passed. See the names on them? They spread that all up front—the veterans that died."

As he turns the ribs, he explains to us his unusual method of cooking them. They are on the side of the open pit, away from the direct flames, and they are unseasoned. "The way I do, when the rib get half done, then I make a bas'ing sauce. I draws my grease out first, before I put any seasoning on it. Otherwise the seasoning just ends up in the pit. In my bas'in' sauce I use onion, a li'l mustard, and some ancest," he says, picking up a bottle of Accent flavor enhancer to show us.

By this time the snoots have stopped sizzling so much, indicating that most of the grease is out of them. One by one, Moe removes them from the grill and puts them in a white enamel pan. He takes one, and then, much as the woman did yesterday, he puts it on a piece of bread, puts some sauce on it, and wraps it in aluminum foil and newspaper. He presents this package to us and we thank him.

I don't know if this snoot is just better than all the rest or if we are developing a taste for snoots, but we eat it and even enjoy it. Between the two of us we still can't finish a whole sandwich. But the several bites that we do eat taste good.

"You know," Frank begins, "if we opened up a snoot place in Chicago—"

And that's where I cut him off.

It's always bad business for an amateur to enter the prognostication business, yet I'll hazard a prediction. Even while eating the best snoot of my life, and even though snoots can maintain their crispness over great distances with the help of a brown paper bag, I'm willing to predict that the snoot sandwich will forever remain a local delicacy, known mostly to East St. Louis natives and people writing books about barbecue.

James P. Lemons LEM'S BAR-B-Q **CHICAGO, ILLINOIS**

Wait Till We Get to Chicago!

Frank beams when he says these words as if they were a magic lamp which, if whispered over, would disgorge great things in a puff of colorful smoke. "Wait till we get to Chicago!" is the solution to every problem on the road, from bad barbecue and cheap hotels to long drives and fruitless interviews.

Chicago is Frank's other home town. It's more memory than place. It's Catholic schoolgirls and letter jackets. It's working at McDonald's in the days when French fries were fresh-cut and your friends could pay a dollar for a few burgers and get four quarters change. It's the warm shiver of Chicago winters recalled while driving through Texas in summer.

Frank was a star athlete then. He played at De La Salle in the Catholic leagues. Each time we pass a high school he makes a point of telling me how well or badly they fared in football games and track meets thirty years ago. It is in this incremental way that I learn what I take to be the central lesson: there are a lot of Catholic schools in Chicago.

This city is home to many of the great heroes in Frank's own barbecue cosmology. There is Uncle Vince, who barbecues *every* weekend; Caesar Collins, the man who originated the famed "Mumbo" sauce; Lem, as in Lem's, Frank's mythic standard for great barbecue sauce; and Lem's brother, who, at least in Frank's memory, has a smoke-darkened ridge above his forehead, the result of peering over his barbecue pit for so many years. As with Hawkins in Memphis, there is a slight familial connection between Frank and Lem's. Frank has a niece who used to work there.

On the way to Chicago, Frank tells me the story of the first time he ever had barbecue. It was in Memphis and he was six years old. He and his friend Julius Robinson were playing in an alley. Julius' father was barbecuing and Julius snuck Frank a small taste of the meat. Beg as he might, Frank couldn't get another morsel. Thus began this obsession. Five years later Frank had moved to the Southside of Chicago, his craving for barbecue intact, but in Chicago he found that the culture and ritual of barbecue was a very different thing.

Memphis barbecue places open a little before lunch and close a little after dinner, and in that way barbecue maintains an air of respectability. People have business lunches in Memphis barbecue restaurants. But on the Southside the barbecue joints don't open until about two in the afternoon, and they don't close until almost midnight on the early nights—which is to say they open and close when the night people wake and retire. On weekends, the places close three or four hours later, about the same time the after-hours joints are closing. It is possible to enjoy barbecue in Chicago in the afternoon or early evening, but barbecue here belongs to what the writer Albert Murray in *Stomping the Blues* calls the Saturday Night Function, that "ritual of purification and affirmation," which, not unlike the Sunday Morning Service, helps people prepare for the stark realities of the come Monday workaday world. After all, Murray reminds us, "not all ceremonial occasions are solemn."

Lest we forget, as Murray points out in *The Omni-Americans*, to be American is to be mulatto, and by inference and extension, to be part Mandinka and part Yoruba as well as part Irish and French (not to mention part Sioux and Apache). For many of our west African ancestors, of course, singing and dancing were unashamedly part of their rituals, even the specifically religious ones.

So if there can also be ceremony on these late Saturday nights, ceremony echoing Africa at least to the extent that it is not formal in any European sense, can barbecue not be said to be the secular communion of these devotions? The devotees are here each and every Saturday the Lord sends, and for that matter they stay until the small hours of Sunday morning. Theirs is a fellowship of dancing and drinking, and these people, only some of whom will make their way into church after daybreak, end their ritual with the consumption of the sacrament that will help them get ready for work.

Which means that for Frank barbecue has never been just food. It's all tied up with the things that made you want to hurry up and be older and then grown. It's going to the prom and getting your first car and all those other landmarks on the road to becoming an adult. Much of what a young man on the Southside looked forward to in those days was taking his best girl to some blue-light party in a no-air-condition basement and steaming the paint off the walls with the sweaty to-and-fro of adolescent passion while Smokey Robinson and the Miracles sang "You Really Got a Hold on Me" or the Diablos sang "The Wind." But after that, before the kiss goodnight, there was the piling into the car of whoever had been able to borrow one, and the driving to the barbecue joint.

"We used to go there at like three in the morning," he tells me, "but we couldn't afford no barbecue. We'd just get some hot links. Or if you were splurging, you would save your money and buy a dinner and you and your girl would split it. Then you had to ride down the street throwing bones out the window. That was eating barbecue on the Southside."

And even now, this many years later, doesn't Chicago still mean looking up ol' Beau, Frank's main man from high school, and checking out some of the nightspots and heading over to Lem's to get some of those good ribs? The ones that don't get right till late at night?

Chicago Style

When we arrive in Chicago this particular afternoon, Edwin "Beau" Phillips is not home yet. Frank remembers the Rib Joint, a barbecue place near Beau's house where we can begin our research until our host arrives. We pull into the parking lot and I see Chicago barbecue architecture for the first time. Barbecue places here are small and don't have seats. They remind me of those old Dairy Queens, where the only space for customers was a small area in front of the counter that could quickly become crowded in the summer when ice cream sales were most brisk. Rib joints here also feature a wall of plexiglass, like those in New York cabs, designed to minimize human contact and the risk of robbery.

And the menu on the Southside of Chicago is different. Often there are no soft drinks for sale at the counter. Rather, outside the plexiglass, in the area where patrons order, there is a machine that sells them. There are no beans, no slaw, no barbecue sandwiches. Only ribs, hot links, bread, French fries, and fried chicken wings. The ribs are served on a bed of French fries, set afloat in sauce and covered with a few slices of white bread. There are four different cuts of ribs—the small end, which is the most expensive, the center cut and the large end, which are slightly cheaper, and the rib tips, which are the tougher top portion of the spareribs. Meat isn't sold by the pound here, only by the slab or the order. The small end is usually a little more tender than the rest of the slab, so even when we are not in Chicago Frank always asks for them.

Once our order arrives, I ask Frank where we are going to eat it. He looks at me strangely and says, "In our office." As we walk into the parking lot, most of the cars are driving away, large bags of barbecue peering over the windshield from the passenger seats. But there are several patrons—radio on, bones flying out the window—conducting businesses similar to our own. Frank opens up the bag and places it on the armrest that separates the driver's seat from the passenger seat. Taking out the first rib, he looks over at me and explains, "This is eating at your desk."

The flavor of the ribs at the Rib Joint is the flavor of the best backyard barbecue. The meat is tender but firm; it doesn't approach the falling-off-the-bone standard. The sauce is sweet and tomato-based and not very thick. There is also a distinctive flavor that is hinted at in the sauce, a dash of cloves perhaps, or maybe allspice. It is so faint that it doesn't come out in every bite. Just as you are concentrating so hard on trying to identify it, it disappears, only to resurface just as you've given up ever naming it.

After polishing the last bone, Frank grips it between his thumb and forefinger and shakes it at me. "This," he says with that same air of superiority that Brer Rabbit expressed upon his escape to the briar patch, "is barbecue."

The Artful Beau

Before driving off we get an order of short ends to present to Beau. He and Frank go back to high school football days when, after being sidelined by an injury, Beau was the team trainer. That's still his role really, commenting from the sidelines, offering encouragement or ridicule depending on his mood or his perception of what you need at the time. We'll be out in the middle of nowhere at one of those KIDS STAY FREE motels on the highway and the phone will ring. On the other end will be a fanatic demanding to be included in the book. "Lotus? Lotus Elie? This Bobbicue Bobby! You writing a book on bobbicue? How the hell you gon' write a book on bobbicue without talking to me? Shit! My sauce so good they serve it over caviar at the Palmer House Hotel." Or perhaps it will be Abdul, the imam of barbecue, offering me a recipe for whiting rib tips. "They small, but they good!" Just as I begin readying the pen the caller turns out to be Beau.

Since his mother's death Beau has been living alone in the house he grew up in. He knows the quality of the hotels we've been staying in and so you can tell he's happy to be able to offer us our own rooms in this Chicago rowhouse, even if the mattresses are lying sheetless and flush on the unswept floor. Of course the whole time he's showing us the place he's making up some house rules and explaining them, reminding us that this ain't one of those rooms-by-the-hour hotels that he claims we are used to staying in. "… And there's soap in the bathroom," he says. "Don't be afraid to use it."

Beau's is a bachelor rowhouse. Even though the dining room table could accommodate eight people, it is covered with so much debris that he has to move the magazines and television guides and bills and important papers to the other side of the table in order to make enough room for a rib plate. Beau swears that he rarely eats barbecue except when Frank is in town, but the attraction between him and the ribs is instant and genuine. A crowbar couldn't have come between them. Between bites of ribs and sips of beer, he and Frank go through the roll, asking about high school friends and sweethearts.

I quietly go to bed.

Moo & Oink

This is the weekend before Labor Day, a holiday created in tribute to the American worker. Since the whole point of our research is to examine the connections between barbecue and American culture, I begin calling labor unions. After all, Labor Day is a big barbecue holiday, and to me it seems logical that a union would have a big barbecue for its members. I know that many of the jobs have moved down South, where barbecue is generally more plentiful and unions are generally less so. But I have taken courses in the history of the labor movement, and, its recent demise notwithstanding, I have been led to believe that the unions remain strong enough to at least purchase the requisite meat and charcoal for a small barbecue.

I call union after union—nationals, locals, federations—but ours is a different country now. The image I had of worker solidarity being forged both on assembly lines and in front of Labor Day barbecue grills is false. Judging by the reactions of union officials, you'd think I was asking if they were sponsoring a right-to-work rally.

Vince Wilburn is not kin to Frank by blood, but like all the young people in this Southside neighborhood, Frank grew up calling him Uncle Vince. And Uncle Vince possesses such an instant and unassuming warmth that you don't feel uncomfortable calling him Uncle Vince even at the end of a first meeting.

Uncle Vince is famous for his backyard barbecuing. But he's been invited to someone else's backyard for Labor Day. When we tell him about our search for a union barbecue, he pans that idea. Rather than looking for union activity, he suggests

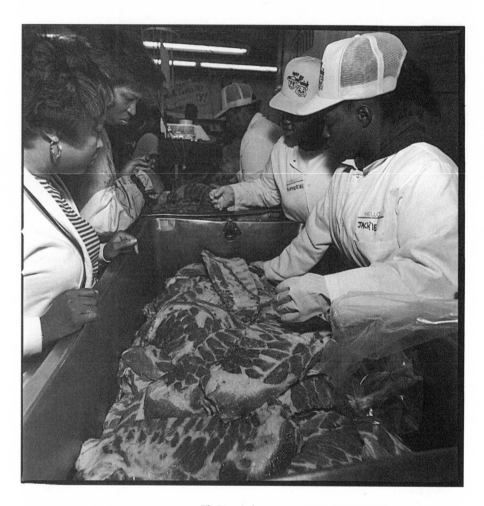

The Raw Side MOO & OINK **CHICAGO, ILLINOIS**

we go to barbecue preparation central. "You need to go to Moo & Oink," he says. "You just need to see it. That place is jam-packed with people buying ribs and hot links for Labor Day."

To really appreciate the phenomenon of Moo & Oink, it would help to know about Elijah Muhammad, the Georgia native who founded the Nation of Islam and ultimately headquartered his movement for the betterment of "the so-called Negro" in Chicago. Islam, of course, is hell on swine eaters, and the Nation of Islam is especially so. But the influence of the Nation of Islam extends far beyond Muslims. Among those who find Islam a bit too strict for their personal taste (and Mr. Muhammad's version especially so), there are African-Americans who are sympathetic to the "do for self" rhetoric and the dietary dictates of the religion. There is something palpable about dietary cleansing, real or imagined. Under the strictest of such regimens you can get the feeling of moving closer to God on a thrice-daily basis. But renouncing the culture that nourished you is difficult. (I know the difficulty well. I myself once renounced meat for several years, but only under the blinding influence of a vegetarian seductress.) So you get a lot of black folks who are trying to do right, whatever that is, but who find themselves of two minds on the subject of pig meat—people like my friend Gaytra, who once told me that she did not eat pork ... except for bacon and ham.

So the corner of Stoney Island Avenue and 71st Street is a crossroads in a sense other than the obvious one, for it is at this address that one finds a Muslim complex featuring Mosque Maryam, Muhammad University of Islam, and the National Center of Minister Louis Farrakhan all staring across the street at Moo & Oink, a meat market that, judging from the crowd here on this Saturday morning, could be hosting a convention of swine eaters. It is on a corner like this one that I imagine Gaytra would become especially perplexed. On the right Brother Minister's striking edifice calls out with forceful, final-call rhythm, "My beautiful African sister, you can't get to paradise with pork grease on your lips!" and on the left you have the silent mooing and oinking, the first steps toward the gentle sizzle and beckoning aroma of frying bacon.

The parking lot of Moo & Oink is filled. You have to look for someone backing out in order to find a space. People are streaming into the store. "What they giving away in there?" Frank asks one woman. But, steady walking, she doesn't hear him.

"Moo, Oink and much MUCH MORE!" says one of the many signs painted on the side of the building. "Whatever the menu don't pass up our quality and savings," says another.

Moo & Oink is like one of those big discount stores that keep the merchandise on the floor rather than in the back to give the impression that their prices must be good since they haven't wasted any money on prettying the place up. We step inside but don't get much further. The line reaches almost to the entrance. "Step down, fresh ribs!" a voice yells from the other side, over the piped-in sound of B.B. King singing "Never Make a Move Too Soon." Stepping around, we see that if you are not buying ribs, you can walk right into the store. For those people who are buying ribs, there are several vats of them, fresh and frozen, babyback and spare, and three scales on which to weigh them. There are more than a dozen clerks working the vats. Clad in white butcher jackets and Moo & Oink baseball caps, they thrust latex-gloved hands into the vats and resurface with slabs of ribs.

Moo & Oink is primarily a meat market. You can buy a wide variety of meats here, from frozen frogs' legs ($6.99 a pound) and Danish pork ribs ($14.90 for a ten-pound case) to Indiana Pork Ribs ($38.70 for a thirty-pound case), fresh pork spareribs ($1.69 a pound) to lamb breasts ($.59 a pound). But the market also sells a large array of regular grocery items like cornflakes and paper towels.

The store, which has two locations, is owned by the Levy and Lezack families, who are cousins. It seems as if the only white faces in the store are those of family members. Barry Levy, who runs this store, enlists the aid of Herbert Lee to give us a tour of the operations.

As we walk from the rib vats to the frozen meat section to the freezer, Herbert tells us about coming to Chicago from Liberty, Mississippi, in "nineteen and sixty-eight. I started on what you call the raw side of it, in the slaughterhouse," he tells us. He's been working at Moo & Oink since 1977, so he knows which ribs are which.

"Spareribs comes from the side of the animal—where bacon comes from," he says. "The tip is on top; if you take the tip off the sparerib, you have the St. Louis cut. Back ribs are what you get if you take the meat off of pork chops. Baby spareribs are the spareribs off a smaller pig."

Everyone in Chicago seems to have his or her own special barbecue sauce for sale, and Moo & Oink stocks all of them. Customers can get the national brands anywhere, Barry tells us; these local offerings are a point of distinction. There is the famous Mumbo Sauce at $7.99 for a gallon. Charlie Robinson's award-winning Barbecue Sauce and Curt's Boss Sauce at $9.29 a gallon. And Moo & Oink's own High Five Sauce, which at $6.49 is the store's biggest seller.

Lem's

The Southern community Nicholas Lemann uses to illustrate his points about the great black migration north is Clarksdale, Mississippi, which was fine for his purposes. But perhaps more central to the history of Chicago barbecue is Indianola, a community sixty miles down the road from Clarksdale. It was Indianola that produced Caesar Collins and the three Lemons brothers of Lem's Barbecue fame.

When we arrive at Lem's it is still early. Chicken wings are frying and sausage and ribs are being barbecued in preparation for the afternoon and evening crowds. It's a small place with the barbecue pit on the right wall, a deep fryer along the back wall.

Opposite the deep fryer is the counter and the wall of plexiglass through which orders are taken and filled. Two or three employees move constantly between the storeroom in the back and the kitchen area, carrying boxes of ribs and hot links, putting raw chicken wings into the fryer.

We stand in the middle of this traffic as James P. Lemons tells us about how he got to be in the barbecue business. A short, reddish brown man, Lem is the second of the three Lemons brothers. He moved from Mississippi to Chicago in 1942, when he was eighteen years old. When asked why he left home, he answers with weighty simplicity in that sandpapery, back-of-the-throat voice of his, "Years ago, you know how it was."

He worked as a dishwasher and then as a cook, he tells us, but he and his brothers wanted to go into business for themselves. Armed with their mother's recipe, they chose the barbecue business. In 1952 they opened the first Lem's. One of his brothers has since died and the other has retired from the business, leaving only James and his employees to work the nineteen-hour days and nights that he says the business requires.

When Lem first arrived in Chicago, there were not nearly as many barbecue places as there are now. It seems that as more and more Tennesseans and Mississippians moved up from down South, they opened more and more barbecue places. In 1951 Leo Davis, who owned a sheet metal business, designed the metal-

bottomed pits with the plexiglass hoods that have come to be synonymous with Chicago barbecue. Before that invention, brick pits were used.

The Chicago barbecue menu, Lem tells us, evolved out of expediency. "Years ago, you'd go out to the Swift Company and they'd have the chitterlings out in a barrel and you'd take as many as you wanted," he says. "They used to throw away the rib tips, back in the 50s. We were the first barbecue house to sell them. We would charge 49 cents for rib tips, 69 cents for short ends, and 99 cents for a slab." Now rib tips are a staple. Barbecue places in Chicago used to sell coleslaw, Lem tells us. But as the price of the ingredients as well as the cost of the little paper containers to pack them in went up, the rib joints started serving fries and bread as their only side dishes.

Lem cooks his ribs about thirty-five to forty-five minutes, depending on how hot his combination of hickory, oak, and charcoal is burning. Slow cooking, he tells us, doesn't improve their flavor. In an average weekend he sells six to eight hundred pounds of ribs. This weekend he expects to sell nearly twice that much.

Much of the tradition and the design of Chicago barbecue joints is a direct result of concern about crime, Lem tells us. Most places stopped sit-down service back in the 1960s even though crime wasn't the problem then that it is now. "Seemingly customers just enjoyed it better when they had to get in the car and eat it," he says. But these days the real advantage to the take-away barbecue joints is that if you keep people moving, and you limit the space in which they move, you are less likely to have what Lem calls "an incident." Ditto for the plastic glass that separates the patrons from the employees. "It takes away from your relations with your customers," Lem says, "but it's like an insurance policy. If you want to stay alive you put it up. Crime ain't that bad around here, but you can't take that chance."

Lem's ribs aren't ready by the time we finish talking to him, and Frank is hungry. Of course if you're writing a book on barbecue you're never supposed to get tired of eating it, especially if you're in Chicago or any other city that's famous for it. You're supposed to ignore that feeling of lethargy and irregularity that can come from a strict meat-and-bread diet. Since ketchup was declared a vegetable by a dearly demented former president, you are to assume that the barbecue sauce you've been eating is sufficient to add balance to your diet. But every now and again you can admit to having a craving for something else.

So now Frank insists that we check out a Southside soul-food restaurant. The one he chooses is a long, old-fashioned place with a counter on the right side, a few booths on the left, and the kitchen in the back. Apparently it's run by West Indians. There's curry and oxtails and rice and peas on the menu as well as a perfectly good selection of down-home soul food. Which is why it's a mystery what possesses Frank to order the gumbo. When it arrives there are carrots in the bowl.

I say nothing until he finishes. Then I reach across the table and remove the polished bone of a chicken wing. Gripping it between my thumb and index finger, I shake it at him to emphasize the gravity of the lesson. "Son," I say with the same air of superiority that Brer Rabbit expressed once he was safely out of the wilderness and back home in New Orleans, "this ain't gumbo."

Southside Saturday Night

Frank has told me how much fun it is to hang out in Chicago on a Saturday night. The amount of fun he recalls having is directly proportional to the amount of liquor he drinks during the telling of the tale. "You better take a nap," he warns me. "Here in Chicago we hang out a little later than you're used to."

I believe him and get excited. I nap first, then pretty myself up a bit. We've been on the road for three weeks straight now, so my hair is lurching skyward and my clothes have creases in all the wrong places.

It's about eleven p.m. when we leave the house, me driving and Beau in the front seat next to me, indicating with his beer bottle which way I should turn. Even if I'm in the dark, Beau knows exactly where we are going and how we are to get there, so he dispenses directions sparingly as if there were a shortage. What he concentrates on are his meditations on matters moral and religious. He speaks with a slow cool, like that gangster in all the Mafia movies who explains what will happen if you don't pay

the boss his money. He lifts his beer bottle infrequently as he talks, using it only to point directions or highlight the most important points. Since he works at the Safer Foundation, a not-for-profit organization designed to serve ex-offenders, Beau spends a lot of time explaining life.

"I try to tell 'em, 'Man, if yaw'll wouldn't commit crimes, a whole lot of people would be out of work,'" he says. "All those judges and clerks and lawyers you see in the courtroom, they'd be out of a job. See, these brothers have power and they don't even know it. If brothers stopped committing crimes this whole thing would just shut down. But you can't tell 'em nothing."

How can you react to such perplexing insight?

Frank, sitting in the back of the car, already two beers closer to nirvana than he was an hour ago, nods with exaggerated enthusiasm. "Yeah!"

Beau isn't all the way clear on what it is we want. Our first stop on this Southside Saturday Night is a nightclub in downtown or somewhere, far from the heart of the Southside in both distance and decor. Ever artful, Beau whispers something to the man at the door and then gestures toward Frank and me. We try to look natural in the way that suspects in a police lineup do. Whatever he says works, and the three of us walk in, our money intact. This place is one of those clubs that someone has spent a lot of money decorating and where the waitresses are all real pretty but they've heard all your best lines several times already that very night, so you are left only with the intangible pleasure of being alive in an era when it is stylish for pretty waitresses to wear miniskirts as they strut purposefully to the seductive accompaniment of pop love songs.

Once it is abundantly clear that we will learn nothing about Southside nightlife here, Beau promises to take us back across town to the Other Place, a nightclub that he says is what we are looking for. There is another soliloquy in the car, this time Beau telling us about how women in nightclubs are always trying to get you to buy them a drink and how he would rather watch television at home than indulge in the impoverishing pleasure of watching a woman's bar tab and his monetary assets move rapidly in opposite directions. "Woman got to be crazy!" he says, and I know that if he still had a beer bottle this statement would have been seconded by it. As it stands we are left only with Frank, two beers plus two cognacs minus one trip to the men's room closer to nirvana, saying "Yeah!" from the back seat.

The Other Place is on 75th Street. It's on a strip of clubs and barbecue joints so there are fine cars cruising up and down, their drivers moving slowly enough to check out and be checked out. Even from the outside you can tell the club is full because there are no parking spaces on the street.

Beau knows everyone on the Southside, it seems. We walk into a conversation on the corner between some acquaintances of his. After a minute Beau tells them what we are doing in Chicago. Pointing to Lem's lighted sign two blocks away, one of the men tells us that that's the best place in town. "They say Lem sold his soul for the secret to that sauce," one of them says. This remark sends Frank into an orgy of gesticulation. Gripping an imaginary pen in his right hand he scribbles invisible words feverishly on his left palm to let me know that I should write this down. Finally someone has said out loud what he always suspected to be the true genesis of Lem's barbecue sauce.

At the door of the Other Place, Beau goes to work again, whispering something to the money collectors, gesturing toward Frank and me. This time he is only thirty-three percent effective; he gets in free but we have to pay.

Rather than move forward, time in the Other Place has elected to spread itself out. Around the walls there are autographed publicity shots from the 1950s, one of Dizzy Gillespie, one of Freddy Cole, one of Redd Foxx looking strangely out of the corner of his eye at a transvestite performer. But there is also one of the young trumpet master Wynton Marsalis. The disc jockey's play list, though mostly current pop hits, also includes Ray Charles's old hit, "Night Time Is the Right Time." And there are people here representing each of the generations touched by these songs and these stars.

The dance floor is tiny and thus always crowded. Between the tables, which are crammed together, and the spectators eyeing the dancers, there's little space to maneuver. The ceiling fans notwithstanding, the room is a perfect promoter of sweat and thirst. All of which means that each of the four bars in this not very large room does good trade. There are television monitors all over, so even from the back we are able to keep up with the dancers' progress.

Before long Beau introduces me to Maceo, the owner of the Other Place. A tall man, he's wearing a black suit, an open-collar shirt, a white Panama hat, and a flat gold chain. Speaking loudly over the sound of the music, Beau tells him that we are here in search of something related to barbecue. This as his introduction, Maceo begins to give me his version of the history of barbecue.

"Barbecue originated in the Chicago stockyards," he says. "Whitey would throw the ribs away and the blacks would go and get them out the garbage can. Chitterlings too. Barbecue didn't originate in no storefront. It originated in the alley, in a schoolbus. Collins was the first to put it in a storefront. When whitey found out that blacks were doing that at the stockyard, they started selling them. Just like Southern fried chicken, see, blacks started that too. Places like Ella's and Charlie's. That's when Kentucky Fried Chicken came in to kill all that."

I ask him about the Southside and how or whether it has changed over the years. In response I get an extended, unexpected history lesson. "It changed with urban renewal, which was really *nigger removal*," he says, spitting the words out as if they were a bad taste.

The whole time we speak Maceo is looking out over his club, monitoring the monitors and generally making sure. He does this mostly because it's his job to know what's happening, but also, I think, because looking at these people and this place is in some way a reminder of what is and what could have been. Though his words are packed with emotion, he has none for Beau and me. While others dance and talk and laugh, he's smileless, listening to the cash register and looking out for potential trouble.

"They didn't want to see the major cities in America go like Gary, Indiana, went—all black," he continues. "So what did they do? About 1947, 1948, they downgraded the educational system in the black community, paid the street gangs to terrorize the people, they funded the Blackstone Rangers, they let the drugs get in here."

"It's a devious plot, ain't it?" Beau says.

"It's a national conspiracy," Maceo says coldly. Again as if the words tasted bad. "Until they stop this, America will never be the same."

"The same as what?" I ask, but he doesn't hear.

Just then a man stumbles up and takes Frank loudly into his confidence. In a drunken whisper he says, "I made a mistake and walked into the ladies' bathroom."

"Tonight?" Frank asks.

"Every night," he says, giggling.

⬯

We decide to leave the club a little before closing—it's three-thirty in the morning—so that we can hit a couple of rib joints before

it gets too late. Of course each of us remembers seeing the NO PARKING, VIOLATORS WILL BE TOWED AT OWNER'S EXPENSE sign in the parking lot of the Kentucky Fried Chicken stand. Of course none of us remembers being the one who said it was irrelevant in the wee hours of morning. So none of us takes responsibility for the fact that the Living Legend has been towed.

Knowing that funds are low, Beau offers to get us a free ride to his house, where we can pick up his car and drive to the place to which ours has been towed. He flags down a police car and begins talking to one of the officers, gesturing again to us as if we were orphaned puppies looking for a good home. Whatever Beau says falls on sympathetic ears. He beckons to us to come on as he works out the final details. The cop on the passenger side says to Beau, "You're a retired policeman, tell me what I'm going to tell headquarters."

This surprises me a bit, though it shouldn't, knowing Beau. It is true that Beau served for years on the Chicago police force and served, it can be said without exaggeration, with distinction. But the definition of the word "retired" would have to be stretched a long distance to apply it to the conditions surrounding Beau's departure from uniform. Suffice it to say that he left the force under sudden and unforeseen circumstances without so much as a word of thanks from his superior officers.

"Tell 'em you're assisting a citizen in distress," Beau tells the officer.

"Yeah, a citizen in distress," the officer says.

"Yeah," Beau says, "from out of town."

"Yeah," the officer says, "an out-of-town citizen in distress."

"Yeah," Beau says, reassuring him. "Out-of-town citizens in distress."

The three of us jam into the back seat of the squad car. Once it starts moving, the officer on the passenger side says, "If you're a retired policeman then you know my father."

"That's your father?" Beau says, upon hearing the name. "I used to see him at the dog shows."

"That was his hobby," the officer says.

As the conversation progresses it becomes clear that this man's father had been an officer for many years but somehow had lost a degree of respect from younger policemen. The younger man was clearly hurt by this downgrading of his father's reputation. Beau assures him that the younger officers just didn't understand.

"Your old man was all right," Beau tells him, pausing as if picturing the scene. "Yeah, I used to see him at the dog shows."

As we get out of the car, we thank the officers for the favor, and they say it was no problem. The younger officer seems on the verge of thanking us. The ride has done him good.

⬯

Beau's Volvo, though silver like the Living Legend, farts blue smoke when asked to go more than thirty miles per hour. As tow yards are invariably plum out the country and nelly out the world, we hear much

The Electric Slide LABOR DAY, 1993 **CHICAGO, ILLINOIS**

farting and see much smoke and get slightly lost. Ever since we realized that the car had been towed, our Saturday night in Chicago has felt like a complete loss. In what I choose to accept as an admission that he was the one who told us it was okay to park at the Kentucky Fried Chicken lot, Beau assures us that somehow he can revive the evening.

"I might have to take you to a place where you have to knock a certain way," he promises. "Knock knock knock. And when they answer, you whisper through the little hole, 'Yeah, small ends.' " It's a beautiful promise made perhaps more so by the fact that as we are retrieving the car the sun is crawling skyward and by that time even the after-hours places are certain to be closed.

Southside Sunday Morning

We spend Sunday morning, Frank, the Legend, and me, in Hyde Park and then in other parts of the city.

First, breakfast of coffee and juice and layered pastries. We're on a clean, sunlit street now, in a delicate gourmet shop. The customers are paired and conversing, some of them. Others are walled off by newspapers as in a complex of modular office cubicles. May I help you?—the women at the counter smiling as each customer walks up. These are white faces mostly, of which we've seen few in the part of Chicago we've been in.

We move on to some bookstores and to other little shops that suggest themselves as we walk or drive past them—the sunlight warm, but the breeze crisp and cooling.

Then just driving around this Chicago because this one is new to me. It's rowhouses still, but the walls are of a less dull color. Rowhouses still, but seeming not crammed together like poor relatives, just close in the sense of some old city in Italy or France. Driving now past the mansion where Elijah Muhammad lived before moving west to preserve his health.

And I ask Frank if we are still on the Southside. He says yes, but we're in Hyde Park, which is different.

In the park along the lake, behind the Museum of Science and Technology, the men of Phi Beta Sigma and the women of Zeta Phi Beta are reuniting at a barbecue. There are blue and white balloons and tissue streamers, blue and white T-shirts and shorts. They're older now; they have brought games along for their children to play. They barbecue chicken wings and rib tips in an inexpert, backyard way. Some of them haven't seen one another in twenty years. It's the reunion, not the food, that matters.

We return now to the regular Southside, and it's like a curtain dropping. It's not so much dirty as dull. Sunlight is somehow filtered differently here, as if through gauze or mesh. We drive down Drexel Avenue where John H. Johnson, the publisher of *Ebony* magazine used, to live. But we also drive down State Street in front of the Robert Taylor Homes, block after block of identical bricks and mortar. "This is the largest public housing complex in the country," Frank says, "thirty stories by damn near thirty blocks." He says this

and then trails off, first boasting of the distinction and then growing aware of its tragic implications.

Later, after many blocks of silence, he says only, "Life is desperate up here."

We spend the early evening driving up and down 75th Street in search of Caesar Collins. Frank thinks looking in the phone book and getting exact addresses is for sissies. So we drive up and down the street around where he thinks he remembers Caesar Collins' barbecue place being twenty years ago. I know only that I'm looking for a sign with Caesar's name on it, so I try to read every sign we pass. I can see then why Frank believes he can find a place he knew that many years ago. Much of the Southside looks as if it hasn't changed since then. The signs here are all large, neon, 50s-era signs that light up the night and blur into one another as you see the procession of them down the street. You still see these signs on old movie theaters in a lot of cities, but seeing so many of them on this street makes plain how little this area has changed. It is understandable that these older businesses would not have altered their signs; doing so would have been tantamount to altering their identity. But the fact that this street is a sea of old neon suggests that younger, newer businesses have not come in.

And Frank breaks through the sounds of blowing horns and booming car stereos, speaking more to himself than to me, as he says again, "Life is desperate up here."

Meanwhile, we check out Kenny's for Ribs, which also specializes in pizza. You

Steppin' Corleone and Li'l Pumpkin THE STEPPER'S CONVENTION CHICAGO, ILLINOIS

have to bite these ribs; they aren't especially tender. But they're good, backyard-style ribs with a nice amount of salt and pepper and smoke. Eating Kenny's ribs in our office, I begin to realize that there is a similarity to all the Southside ribs we've had. Most of them are cooked on the exact same type of pit, and they are cooked relatively fast. And the sauces, though each is unique, all taste as if they have a common ancestor.

When we finally find a barbecue place on a corner near where Caesar Collins' place used to be, we ask the woman behind the counter if he is still around. He's alive, she tells us, but he's no longer in the rib business. Someone else tells us that he's selling pesticides now.

Soft-Shoe Without the Tap

We decide to give Saturday night another try, this time on Sunday. There are posters all around advertising a "Steppers' Convention" at the East of the Ryan Motel on 79th Street. Stepping, Frank tells me, is a special dance native to Chicago and preserved there by old-timers and their young converts. It's the dance that he used to do coming up, he says.

The East of the Ryan ballroom is a large, plain room with a bar in the back, several rows of tables and chairs in the middle, and a dance floor up front. Beyond the dance floor is the disc jockey and his crates of albums and compact discs. The steppers are dancing in pairs—hand-dancing, we used to call it. They dance toward each other, embrace and perform an embellishment, a circle or twist, then separate, connected only by their hands, touching always.

From the stage, the disc jockey talks between and during songs, like the deejays used to do on the old AM radio stations, only he conducts the proceedings with taste and subtlety. "That was Harold Melvin and the Blue Notes with Sharon Page," he says. "Some people spend their whole life searching, but remember, love is just a step away"—and the volume goes back up on the music— "here at the Steppers' Convention."

We make our way to the stage and I introduce myself to deejay Sam Chatman. He's cool. A fortyish man working the mixing board, wearing his black silk shirt with the white figures on it. He's glad to talk about stepping, but he has to be excused every now and then to find a record or to acknowledge someone in the crowd. "Lisa in the house"—music fades up, then immediately back down—"out there looking like new money."

"Ninety percent these people here started with me when they were fifteen years old," he tells me. "I was the first person to do high school stepping parties. Stepping is just a whole different thing. The appearance, the dress. It's relaxed. When you go to a disco party you lose your curls; you sweat. These people come looking good and they leave looking good. And there's a stepping party in Chicago every night. If you a stepper you know where they are.

"Stepping music is whatever the beat is. It can be jazz; it can be country and west-ern. We don't classify R&B or jazz or pop. It's either stepping music or it's not."

Much of the music he plays is 70s-era rhythm and blues, but there seems to be no common denominator. The saccharine strings of disco music might follow the wordless pop of so-called jazz fusion, and might itself be followed by a carefully selected song from the current top ten. "I give them a conversation when it's a new record I'm playing," he says. "I might say something like 'This is for all of the real motherfucking steppers in the house.'"

One of the favorite tunes is Toni Braxton's "Another Sad Love Song." It is played three or four times during the night, and the floor fills up each time. It's a perfect steppers' vehicle. Its rhythm is subtle, sock cymbal largely, so there is the sound of gliding across the floor contained in the music itself. Braxton's voice is smoky and held in check by a tortured restraint. She manages a masterful mix of groans and exclamations, sounds that recall both tearful catharsis and an understated accompaniment to carnal ecstasy. The song is about the compounded sadness of hearing songs of lost love on the radio while lamenting one's own lost love. It's a song about songs like the song itself, and somehow the graceful movements of the steppers take on their own sympathetic sadness in deference to it. Each partner is already a partner, but each dances as if the face and body across from the dancer's own is a mere prop, a catalyst in cahoots with Braxton, conspiring to exhume the corpse of an old love affair so that the singer will not be left to lament alone.

The whole time Sam and I are talking, Frank is standing on the side of the stage, dancing with himself, reminiscing in tempo about the days when, or so he tells me, he stepped. The deejay eyes him and makes an impromptu introduction from the stage. "Two brothers up here writing about barbecue…"—music fades up and down—"They trying to step on the side…"—fade up and down—"looking like Pee Wee Herman and his cousin…"—fade up and down—"Any ladies who want to teach them to step, *please* come up."

Frank is the one stepping. I'm doing my job, minding my business, checking out the scene with the cool dispassion of a professional observer. Then suddenly I am pulled to the front and center of the dance floor. Frank and his partner have their lesson to the side of the stage, away from the critical eye of the professionals. My instructor, a woman of thirty-some years in black leggings and heels, drags me where the scarcity of my talent can be witnessed by all.

We face each other and hold hands. She teaches classes in stepping and so grips my palms with the gentle confidence of a professional. "Kick left, kick right, cross left over right, cross right over left," she tells me. But this is a recipe for how to step in the same way that "First you split an atom" is a recipe for the manufacture of an atomic bomb: the information is useful but by no means exhaustive.

Truth be told, dancing has never been my strong suit; I used to try to talk my way through the fast songs and then ask a girl for a dance on the slow records, thinking that in the close darkness of those ballads my meager talents wouldn't be so easily detected. And now my inadequacy eventually prompts my instructor to abandon the traditional instructions and enter the realm of metaphor. "Move like you're having sex," she says.

The deejay, no doubt because of his years of experience, is able to mathematically pinpoint the source of my problem. "This motherfucker got three left feet," he says into the microphone loudly, just in case the amplification is not enough to carry his voice into the crowd. "He dance like his feet hurt."

Mercifully, the song ends. My partner, visibly disappointed in her own performance as instructor, politely excuses herself. I make my way over to the corner, where Frank is doubled over with laughter. "He dance like his feet hurt," he says, chuckling, with his characteristic sensitivity. During the entirety of my labored performance, Frank was ensconced in a dark corner of the stage where I couldn't see him. "Shee-it," he assures me, "I was stepping my ass off!"

Owing to our sudden celebrity, a fifty-ish man in a black hat and a black-and-white-checked sport coat comes up to us and announces himself. "I'm Steppin' Corleone," he tells us. "Corleone has been my name ever since I started doing fashion shows. I was Sir Corleone then. This was long before *The Godfather* and all that shit was out."

I had noticed Steppin' Corleone on the dance floor, and he had acquitted himself well. In this young crowd, he is clearly an old master and proud of it. "What the young people are doing, they lindy hopping, they free styling," he says. "These guys are from the 80s and the 90s; I'm from the 60s and the 70s. I look at my stuff as soft-shoe without the tap."

While we are waiting in line to try some of the barbecued rib tips they are selling, we are told by our deejay that tonight is Li'l Pumpkin's birthday. He invites her to the front of the stage and asks that everyone clear the floor.

Li'l Pumpkin is a tall, thin woman enclosed tightly by black spandex and adorned with earrings from the lobes to the tips of her ears. When she makes it to the front, the deejay introduces her. She is not the only Pumpkin present tonight. "That's Li'l Pumpkin, yaw'll," the deejay says. "You know Big Pumpkin got a big booty. Li'l Pumpkin got a li'l booty." Everyone who wants to dance a birthday dance with Li'l Pumpkin is told to line up on the dance floor. A couple of dozen people, men and women, line up. As the music plays, Li'l Pumpkin dances with each of them for several measures and then moves on.

"Pumpkin, you know what somebody told me?" the deejay comments from the stage. "They told me it's hard waking up by yourself on Monday. Sometimes it's hard," he says, "and sometimes it's soft."

Much of what is remarkable to me about stepping is that it seems to be unaf-

Dancers EAST OF THE RYAN MOTEL **CHICAGO, ILLINOIS**

fected by recent dance fads. Neither the Soul Train dances of the 70s nor the Black Entertainment Television rap video movements of the 90s have had an impact on what is happening here. The steppers range in age from their early twenties to their late forties. Seldom do you find so diverse an age group able to enjoy the same music, let alone dance together to it. In that regard, this "convention" is an enclave and its participants singular devotees blessed with a rare skill, the ability to block out certain external influences and concentrate on their own program.

But the whole Southside seems to be that way, a self-contained, self-containing land and people and culture. In the last thirty years desegregation changed other black neighborhoods. As black people began to patronize white establishments, businesses in black communities declined and closed, opening the way either for urban blight or for new businesses to move in. But Chicago remains one of the most segregated cities in the nation. Even without knowing the results of the academic studies that have shown this, you can see it along the streets on the Southside. There are almost no white people walking around here who look as if they live in the area. In most cities, chain businesses like convenience stores and fast-food operations have tended to supplant older, mom-and-pop businesses, but here on Chicago's South Side, black businesses—among them many barbecue joints—have survived.

Not only has barbecue survived here, it has evolved to a certain similarity that is also remarkable. Granted, the Southside is only one part of Chicago, but it's a large section of a large town, and there are people here who hail from many different parts of the United States. Barbecue in a place like Kansas City has a long tradition, one that is primarily black in its origins. But Kansas City also has newer restaurants, some black and some white, that look different and serve different foods and have expanded the range of flavors available. Chicago, at least its sprawling Southside, seems unmoved by new technology in barbecue cookers or nontraditional barbecue meats or anything else that is going on outside its borders. The ribs at every restaurant we have visited are cooked to roughly the same degree of tenderness, the side dishes are identical, and the sauces, though distinct, are also very similar to each other when compared with the great range of sauces in other locations. It's not unlike eating benichen, the national dish of Gambia. In that tiny west African nation, from one side to the other the taste of that dish varies only slightly.

"This is a culture that feeds on itself," Frank repeats often. Time has not stood still here, but neither has it marched forward. Rather, it has done a dance, stepping now forward then back, leaving much as it was. It is difficult to imagine Corky's or Luther's or Tony Roma's opening a place here, much less opening a successful one. For the foreseeable future, this is apt to be a haven for small, local restaurants.

And that approaches an explanation of what Frank means by "Life is desperate up here," that mantra he has chanted more times than I've bothered to note. Driving along 75th Street, searching for Caesar Collins, he stared through the windshield and said these words as if they were related to Chicago, but it becomes clear that the words have more to do with Frank himself. Here now, not on a casual visit, but on a mission to rediscover those old places and feelings. Here now not just to pause briefly over beers and greetings both polite and hollow, but here to be asked and to ask himself in a conscious and sustained way what it was like and what, if anything, those days and places and people might have meant. Here now, looking through these moving windshield wipers at a Southside Sunday evening and seeing this conjoining of past and present, Frank recalled the coldness of the Chicago wind, how over in the Lake Meadows complex the high-rise apartment buildings were so far apart that the wind had plenty of space to sharpen its icy blade before slicing through every layer of your clothing.

And Chicago winters could be cold for many reasons.

These memories escape sporadically and in monologue, not as concise narrative but as individual episodes in a catharsis. The coldness of relatives, the kindness of strangers, that absence that comes when you've spent your last money and there's so much else to buy. These things go hand in hand with those memories of that young Stewart boy, himself hand in hand with young love or perhaps hand in glove on the baseball diamond. For every one of these football teams whose home schools we pass, there is some building where Frank lived after his father kicked him out. "You ever live in the YMCA?" he asks. "I did. The room was so small you could open the door, shut the window, and take a shower all at the same time."

And then before I can ask a question or make a comment, he is silent.

⌒

Having missed out on the rib tips being sold here, we leave East of the Ryan hoping to catch some of our fellow steppers on a barbecue binge. The deejay has told us that he has cured himself of the late-night barbecue habit. "The barbecue joints are the only thing open, but the worst fucking thing in the world you can do is eat barbecue that late at night. I don't do it no more. It'll have me tossing and turning all night." He recommends Leon's, but only the one "in the 'hood. The Leon's taste different uptown. We put sauce on our fries and all that shit. They don't go for that."

Despite his advice we go first to Lem's and arrive just in time to hear the counter man tell a customer, "That's it. We just sold the last one."

"Man, I came all the way from the northside to get some Lem's," the customer says. The counter man digs up some odds and ends of ribs. Showing his find to the customer he says, "I'll sell you all this for nine dollars. I got some fries but they not hot."

Sold.

I walk up and the counter man asks another employee if he wants to sell his ribs. "No," the man says, and continues his sweeping.

So we do end up at Leon's and we take home a slab of small ends. The aroma wakes both Beau and his appetite. He comes to the dining room in his underwear. Frank takes one bite for the sake of research and then goes off to bed. I eat a couple of ribs, but fatigue ultimately gets the best of me as well.

⌒

We leave early the next morning, before Beau is up. So my last vision of him is the one I caught glancing over my shoulder as I went upstairs to bed. "These ribs kinda dry," he had said as he ate the first of the ribs we brought him from Leon's. "I guess that's why they gave you so much sauce." Having finished the ribs and the fries, Beau was tearing the bread into thirds and dipping the strips into the little plastic barbecue sauce containers. Having finished the bread that came with the rib plate, Beau went to the kitchen and returned with a loaf of his own bread. Tearing those slices in thirds, he dipped them into the remaining sauce and repeated to himself and to me, though I was by that time most of the way up the stairs, "Yeah, that's probably why they gave you so much sauce."

Quess with Slab JIM QUESSENBERRY **BIRDEYE, ARKANSAS**

CHAPTER

SIX

Arkansas Travels

Our first experience with Arkansas barbecue was on a drive from St. Louis to New Orleans. Frank and I argued about whether to take the long way and stop at as many of the places along the highways in Arkansas as possible. Unfortunately, I won. We stopped at nearly a dozen of these places, each worse than the one before.

We returned to Little Rock right after the Fourth of July, when most barbecue places were closed—or, to judge from our experience, most of the good ones were closed. Our first lucky break was finding the Great Southern Sauce Company, a gourmet shop and mail-order operation specializing in salsas, pasta sauces, hot sauces, and barbecue sauces. Randy Ensminger, the store's owner, put us in touch with Bill Walker, a veteran of the barbecue competition circuit. He and his wife opened Walker's Bar-B-Que Company in Little Rock a few months before we arrived there. The food is excellent—sweet, succulent loin ribs that made us wish we had discovered the place sooner.

We found one other outstanding place in Arkansas. As a result of our stay there, I have one piece of unfinished Arkansas business:

Dear President Clinton,

Chuck Primus, a fellow native of Hope, Arkansas, now owns a barbecue restaurant. (Frank says, "You should remember him. Yaw'll used to go to separate schools together.") The food there is very good. Primus has asked us to let you know that when next you are in Hope, you are welcome to come by and get some free barbecue.

It's an offer well worth accepting, Mr. President. Especially if you also get some of the homemade lemonade.

Take care,
Lolis Eric Elie

The Arkansas Trav'ler

∽

By the time we meet Quess he has already sold the family farm over in Birdeye, Arkansas. He has already geared up, slowly and deliberately, farm sale proceeds in hand, for another run at the barbecue sauce business.

We meet him first at his colorful booth in the row of colorful booths along that dusty road at the Memphis in May barbecue competition. THE ARKANSAS TRAV'LERS, the sign says, the team having taken its name from the old state song. Also on the sign is a caricature of a huge, red-haired, red-bearded man, a Gaelic goliath with tiny little legs, grasping a trophy won in a barbecue competition. Except for the lower extremities, that's him. Generous in proportion and nature, he directs us to the cooler for beer and to the pit to have a taste of his whole-hog entry.

The hog is sitting up on its stomach, plenty of meat left, but many of the bones are showing from where it has already been tested and tasted. The meat along the loin is whiter and drier, like pork chops, and the meat along the hams and shoulders is darker and juicier. Quess's hog, without sauce, has a sweet flavor. It is too tender to slice, so I pull a few patches with a fork from this section and that, then eat them with my hands. The white meat, pink from the smoke, gently falls apart in my mouth. I pick up a long, juicy strand of dark meat and dip it into some Sauce Beautiful, Quess's product. It's a Memphis-style sauce, sweet, not real thick, with plenty of vinegar and black pepper.

As we eat, he tells us how these competitions started off as a hobby sixteen years ago and then got serious. He was at the first Memphis in May competition and has been at every one since. He's won various smaller competitions and placed in several categories at Memphis in May over the years. But his reputation is based primarily on one grand feat accomplished twice. In 1985 his team won the Irish Cup International Barbecue Contest at Galway Bay, Ireland. They couldn't make it in 1986, but the following year people were clamoring for the Arkansas Trav'lers to go back across the water and bring the cup home for the red, white, and blue. And the team did just that.

He goes to other competitions, but the expense and the trouble of packing everything up and putting it on the road have forced him to cut way back. That weekend in Memphis—food and hotel rooms, entry fees, the hog, team T-shirts, gasoline, and the rest—cost him about $7,000. They didn't even place this year, but still Quess has a sentimental attachment to Memphis in May.

He tells us about growing up in Birdeye, Arkansas, and how for the Fourth of July all the men would stay up all night and barbecue goats—everybody drinking and having a good time together, the black men mostly doing the cooking, the white men having bought the liquor. And Quess would whine and moan because he was too young and they made him go to bed long before all the stories had been told and the goats pulled off the fire. He stayed up until after Dave Block, an ancient man, had collected all the glands and entrails that went into his "sillulin," but long before it had finished cooking and way long before anybody would work up the courage to actually taste this strange-smelling stew—which, as far as anyone knew, originated and died with Mr. Block—he went to sleep.

That story decides it for us; we accept Quess's invitation to come to Wynne, Arkansas, a town neighboring Birdeye. Wynne is now home to the production facilities and international headquarters of Sauce Beautiful.

Wayne is a small town, and the liquor store there looks like a living room. There's a counter in the front, but to pick out your brand you have to go behind it and pass in front of the sofa and the television. The whole time Charlya is being real friendly, finding out who you are and what your business is there and why she hasn't seen you before.

"Quess?" she says. "You here to see ol' Quess? I should've known when you bought Johnny Walker Red." It is clear that everyone knows everyone here and that Quess is a celebrity. There are no commercial barbecue places around here she'd recommend. When people want barbecue they either do it themselves or pay Quess to do it.

We get to the house, a small, ranch-style house on the corner. There's not much room in the kitchen, so the Trav'ler is sitting on the living room couch, "doctoring" on some ribs and a brisket that are almost done, slathering Sauce Beautiful on them and sprinkling Spice Beautiful, his barbecue rub, with abandon. Before he wraps them in foil and places them back on the grill in preparation for their grand entrance at table, he takes a liberal taste.

"Mmm, mmm," he says, licking his fingers. "If I had a twin I'd marry him!"

Between sending the boys on errands to check this or get that (Lee, age twelve, and Michael, age ten) and teasing Michael about Natalie, the cute little girl who has been hanging around in a manner that might suggest budding romance, Quess tells us the tale of the birth of Sauce Beautiful.

"I was working on some barbecued brisket—which is an all-night chore, not unlike whole hogs—and I'd go out there and work awhile, get my fire stoked up, go back in and go to sleep four or five hours, go back out and check on it again. During one of these little sleep spells I dreamed I made this sauce, I dreamed the formula. It was just vivid in my mind when I woke up. I really kind of found it to be funny, but in my own thoughts I said, 'If I don't get up and go in the kitchen and throw this together, it won't be there tomorrow.' Basically the sauce I put together that night is the recipe that I do now, with a few little modifications here and there."

They started marketing the sauce in late 1989, but the company that was manufacturing it for them was itself in financial trouble. The harder Quess and his wife, Donna, worked to get new customers, the further behind the factory fell. So they shut down completely, taking two years to regroup. They bought this place in part because the building next door came with it and in that building they have the vats and blenders and other equipment they need to mix their sauce and put it in the eighteen-ounce bottles with the Arkansas Trav'ler caricature and the cute blue-green tartan labels on them. The business is fledgling, but the sauce is catching on again within a hundred-mile radius of Birdeye. A company in the Northeast seems serious about importing a few hundred cases a month, and there's also the possibility of resurrecting the interest that the Kroger chain had expressed before Quess, fearful of taking on yet more business than his finances could handle, backed out.

Dinner this day is a brisket Quess has barbecued and a pork shoulder and a few slabs of ribs, to which Donna has added some wonderful potato salad and trimmings. Quess always puts some sauce on the meat before returning it to the grill for its finish. So the meat is sauced and spiced beautifully. Arthur Lee McDaniel, Quess's partner since short-pants days, has joined us as we wash down slice after slice of rich meat with bottle after bottle of cold beer. Frank looks up briefly from his plate to ask Quess what makes him think barbecue is on the upswing—in other words, what makes him think there is a demand for yet another barbecue sauce.

"You want to know my theory on why barbecue is taking off?" Quess responds. "Several reasons. One, the European market has fallen in love with it. I tell you why. The Europeans, they got to watching *Dallas* and stuff like that on TV, and it was sort of like the old cowboy shows. It was something interesting to them, going outside and having an outdoor sport that didn't take any exertion. Anytime Europeans fall in love with something, you have that backlash over here. Also, times are tough. What can we do to entertain ourselves? There're only two things we can do. We can sit on our buns at home or we go out in the backyard. So what are the two things that are really taking off? Furniture sales and barbecue."

This theme of hard times would play well in many parts of the country—inner cities, former military installations—but here in farm country it plays especially well. After dinner we drive around this cluster of towns, revisiting the birthplace of sillulin and the Quessenberry homestead. We pass the land that Quess grew up farming and returned to farm after spending a few years away in Memphis. It has already been made clear to us that Quess barbecues because he loves to cook (and to eat), and that Donna, who is a schoolteacher, enjoys it but is also attracted to the family business aspect of it—she and Jim and the boys all work together mixing and bottling the sauce. They've bet the farm on this thing, and that decision was no doubt born in part of the courage I hear in her voice when she talks about it.

But what becomes clear on this drive is that, barbecue business or no, it's unlikely Quess would still be farming. There may be nostalgia in his voice as he talks about those old days, but no regret.

"Take wheat," he begins. "When I came back here in '75, which was eighteen years ago, wheat would be selling for $3.50, $4.00 a bushel. Now it'll bring $2.80 or $3.20 a bushel. In 1974 soybeans got up to about $8.00. In 1979, before President Carter boycotted the Olympics and embargoed the grain and every-thing, soybeans got as high as $12.00 a bushel. Soybeans are now about $5.50 to $6.50. Rice back in the 70s was bringing $5.00, $6.00 a bushel. Now it's bringing about $2.50 a bushel.

"The real pity of that is the fact that everything else, the inputs and all, have gone

Chuck Primus CHUCK'S SMOKE HOUSE BBQ **HOPE, ARKANSAS**

up. Hell, labor in the late 60s and early 70s was $1.00, $1.50 an hour, labor now is $4.50, $5.00 minimum wage. Fuel back then, tractor fuel, cost 18 to 25 cents a gallon. Now it's about $1.00, $1.25. Equipment. A good hundred-horsepower tractor back then would cost you $8,000. A hundred-horsepower tractor now would cost you $40,000. A good top-of-the-line combine back then would cost you $10,000; now it would cost you $85,000 to $100,000. You can see there's no way. Course there's this supplementing and stuff the government does and all that crap, but that's just pitching money down a hole."

But for barbecue, Quess tells us, the outlook is good. Things were looking good before they were set back, and this time he's going into it even more fully committed. A little luck and Sauce Beautiful and Spice Beautiful will be national. Arthur Lee can quit the long hours and back-breaking work he does as a full-time cowboy and come aboard with ol' Quess.

So much might happen, but there's one thing that won't: there won't be any turning back.

Hope:
Chuck's Smoke House BBQ

By now the interview is over and we have already told him that the ribs were very good and also the brisket and that the fresh lemonade (with free refills) has brought the original down-home definition back to a phrase which has degenerated to mean only that the water has been added to the powdered chemicals on the premises rather than at some distant drink-mix refinery. By now we have discovered that along Highway 67 East in this small Arkansas town best known for pachyderm-sized watermelons and a presidential favorite son, it is possible to have good barbecue and to have it, at least for the moment, free of the noise of other patrons. Free of the music of ringing cash registers. We have told him, Chuck Primus, this other Man from Hope, that we are writing a book about barbecue, that we are traveling around the country visiting scores of restaurants trying to get some sense of this food and this life and this country. He's interested in that.

And by now he has told us about this town and his story in it. The crude melodrama of working at the bakery where so many other people work and where so many of the workers are black but none of the people working in the air-conditioned rooms are. About quitting his job at that same factory because his hope has been to own his own barbecue place—a family business where the wife and kids would chip in when things got busy. And how, as if to dream this dream was to dare disturb the very universe, his wife told him, en route to her exit, that a black man couldn't hope for a successful business here, especially one on the highway rather than in "the quarters" (his words), that area where the Negroes have lived and worked and barbecued since the not-so-distant days when the lash flew freely.

He has told us this pit used to belong to the Reverend Hale, a minister who taught him to barbecue and whose widow sold the pit to Chuck. We also know by this point that the best weekend for barbecue sales in Hope, Arkansas, is in August when the annual Watermelon Festival takes place, an event at which crowds will be lined up literally down the block. He has already begun to cook for it. But even that will mean no financial reprieve because the church will get the profit from that day, in accordance with the tradition started by the Reverend Hale. Which is only right.

Only his mother chips in now, he tells us, making the sweet potato pies and lending moral support.

And then this question.

"Let me ask you," he says above the sound of the cartoons his counter man (nothing else to do) is watching. "You've been to barbecue places all over, right? It always takes a time to get on your feet, right? To start making money?"

What to say?

We have seen many new and struggling places. But what I am thinking about is how we spent last evening in a restaurant like this one, less than a year old, where the problem since day one has been what to say to the customers when the ribs are sold out. A place that, or so the owners told us, has been profitable since the first day of business. This notwithstanding, I am preparing to say with conviction, as if it were as true as stone, that barbecue places as a rule start slowly and build themselves up. There will be time, I am preparing to say, there will be time. My mouth is open as a party of five elderly people walks in. One man, leading his fellows decisively to the counter, places his order.

And in that gesture hope is vindicated.

Dawn Patrol GRAIN VALLEY BARBECUE COMPETITION **GRAIN VALLEY, MISSOURI**

The Competition Circuit

In the real world, most people don't know a brisket from a butt and feel not the least bit impoverished by their ignorance. But like Trekkies or bungee jumpers or Civil War re-enactors, competitive barbecuers spend weekends in their own orbit. They worship their own gods, they speak their own language, and they think the ability to distinguish a brisket from a butt is no less basic to a civilized existence than are lounge chairs and chilled beer.

The barbecue season runs from spring to fall, corresponding roughly to the baseball season. On any weekend during the season there are apt to be half a dozen to a couple of dozen competitions taking place across the country. What most surprised us was that there are tens of thousands, if not hundreds of thousands, of people avidly involved in a hobby that we had not heard of before.

Barbecue cookers would ask us what competitions we had been to. Whenever we mentioned Grain Valley they would look at us quizzically. Grain Valley is a small place and hosts an even smaller cookoff, and neither the place nor the cookoff is much heard of outside Missouri. But it fit into our schedule and so we went. It was a good place to begin, small and quaint.

Grain Valley

The winners and losers, indistinguishable now, have drawn their cookers, campers, coolers, and station wagons into a circle as if preparing more for external attack than for internal competition. Nineteen 10-by-20-foot campsites shoulder to shoulder on the Grain Valley High School lawn, accompanied by nearly as many kinds of barbecue rigs. Interstate 70 roars in the background a few hundred feet away, but it feels more distant than that. This circle is its own city, complete with life's necessities—food, drink, music, and portable toilets.

It is early yet—Friday evening. Judging won't be until tomorrow at noon. There is time in the morning or later tonight to barbecue ribs and chicken and other quick-cooking items, so most people aren't preparing their

Competitor MEMPHIS IN MAY **MEMPHIS, TENNESSEE**

Tracy Hawkins and Her Turkey Flambé GRAIN VALLEY BARBECUE COMPETITION **GRAIN VALLEY, MISSOURI**

competition entries yet. The smell in the air is from hot dogs and hamburgers.

Before we begin acclimating ourselves, Frank makes a suggestion. "Look, neither one of us knows whether any of these people can cook," he begins, "so why don't we make a little bet, just enough to make it interesting?"

"How much would make it interesting?"

"I could be interested for a hundred dollars," he says.

Frank's interest in betting has a lot more to do with the state of his financial affairs than it does with any concern about the outcome of this event. When he's not being a book author, he's a freelance photographer. Freelance photography, I have learned from Frank, is not the most lucrative profession.

∞

The northwest quadrant of the circle belongs almost entirely to the Tuttle family and its three generations of barbecue cookers. Ed "Grandpa" Tuttle, who goes by the name Ol' Smokey in competition, used to captain a team consisting of his wife, his three sons, his daughters-in-law, and his young grandchildren. Chips off Ol' Smokey, they called themselves. But the sons and their wives and kids have since formed separate, smaller teams. When Rich and his wife, Bunny, began marketing KCass barbecue sauce ("We put a little kick into every bite"), they were put in the professional category and had to start competing in that division.

The KCass team is conducting an experiment. Though they've been at this for eight years and own a barbecue rig as large and impressive as most of the ones out here, they're cooking on two small smokers. "We went back to basics," says Bunny. "That's how we started and that's how we won. And we did it to prove a point. People can come out here on a smoker like this and beat people on a smoker like that"— and she points to an especially large rig.

That rig belongs to Roger's Barbecue, the Sugar Creek, Missouri, team whose candy-apple-red smoker is shaped like a U-Haul trailer with a chimney. Roger Evans, a sixtyish man with gray hair and a gray beard, has more than $20,000 invested in his pit and the pickup that pulls it. The five couples who make up Roger's Barbecue are a favorite to win. They won the Grand Champion Kansas City Barbecue in 1991.

If the size of the campsite and the complexity of the rig are any indicators at all, Jason Levine and his KC Barbecue Factory team also stand a good chance. While most teams have an open-sided tent, a few lawn chairs, and a table or two, the Barbecue Factory has a fence surrounding its site, which gives it a backyard feel. Jason, a lineman with Missouri Public Service, paid $10,000 for the huge smoker onto which the kitchen is attached.

Most contestants expect to get only two or three hours of sleep tonight. Some of them sleep cramped in chairs and covered with blankets, others are a bit more comfortable in campers or vans, but all sleep uneasily, prepared at any hour to get up

and check a gauge or baste a brisket. Even if there is more than one team member to monitor the meat, the air of excitement here is enough to make sound sleep difficult.

By midnight things are quieting down. Many of the hangers-on have gone home. The place to be is at the Hawk's Bluff site. With an average age of thirty, they're the youngest team here. Cindy Hawkins, the team leader, is removing her smoked wild turkey from one of five small bullet smokers they have lined up. The turkey was shot by Cindy's husband of eleven years, Tracy. "My little Pilgrim," she says, looking at him with adoring sarcasm.

Cindy, wearing a white chef's hat with a light attached to it, is clearly in charge, often yelling instructions. She has a reclining chair set up near her smokers so that her sleep won't interrupt her cooking. Though there are about half a dozen team members who help out, she limits their assistance. "They call me Jemima," she says. "I just don't trust nobody cooking my stuff."

After nearly six hours of walking around and talking to contestants, we have met fewer than half of the people who are competing out here. No one has offered us any barbecue yet, and without tasting I have no idea who has a chance of winning. As we drive back to our hotel, Frank is wearing a Cheshire cat grin. I ask him if he knows which team he's putting his money on.

"No," he says, "but I'm not worried. I have me a system."

At five a.m. a small stream of smoke is rising above each campsite. A few teams stir, but mostly it's the designated cookers, alone with forks and tongs, who are awake and watching the pits. "This is about my favorite time in these contests," says Greg Hartnett. "Sun's just coming up and everything is calm."

The Great American BBQ & Spice Company, while now primarily the name of a barbecue team, is also the name of Hartnett's fledgling mail-order business. A Chicago native, he says he discovered real barbecue not in the Windy City but in Louisburg, Kansas, where he moved several years ago. "When I first came down from Chicago I figured, 'These Kansas City hicks, they don't know what they're doing.' I thought I was going to show them," Greg says. "I didn't win anything." Eventually he learned, and four months ago he bought an Oklahoma Joe smoker, the $2,000 model with the firebox on the right end, the cooking chamber in the middle, and a vertical element that looks like a hot water heater on the other end.

Beneath the Confederate flag and the huge Pabst Blue Ribbon can that sports his name, Bob "Buck" Snodgrass is cooking on the latest in his series of homemade cookers. He calls this one a Cajun cooker. It consists of three and a half inches of fiberglass insulation enclosed in particle board. "The theory behind this kind of cooker is that the moisture will penetrate into the meat and keep it from drying out," he says.

As we begin to talk about Kansas City barbecue, I mention the few places I've been so far. Mrs. Snodgrass stops me when I say Arthur Bryant's. "If you knew what was in Bryant's sauce you wouldn't eat there," she tells me. Otis P. Boyd has already explained to me that the secret ingredient in Bryant's sauce is tomato juice that has been allowed to sour in the front window. The fact that the juice is allowed to go sour is what, according to Boyd, made the health department bar Bryant from marketing his sauce commercially. But according to the Snodgrasses, Boyd is wrong.

"I knew Arthur Bryant personally," Buck tells me. "He was a super-nice colored guy. His original sauce was made out of pig's blood. He would set it in the front window and let it ferment." Though Buck loves the barbecue at Bryant's, he says, he orders it without the sauce.

While I'm working, Frank is carousing with the Wood Brothers, drinking as much of their Wild Turkey as can fit in a cup. They are a four-man team, but only two members are here today. Sporting the generous proportions of a nightclub bouncer, Jim Nesselrode (Drift Wood) is a professional chef who studied, among other places, in Switzerland. Jim Closson (Burl Wood) is an engineer for California-based Electro Test, Inc. "In the miscellaneous category, we're entering venison we caught ourselves," he tells me. "It's what you would call a slow-footed Missouri deer."

The quietest campsite is that of R&R Barbecue. Almost every other place you go has a number of people cooking and talking, but here there are only two, Jack Williams and his fifteen-year-old son, Matt. Jack, a fortyish man, is clearly thrilled to be here. I ask him about his cooking techniques and he responds with evangelical fervor. As we talk, Matt looks on, but there is an unmistakable lack of enthusiasm on his part. His parents are divorced and his other two siblings are elsewhere today. I get the impression that this is the day set aside to be with his father, even though perhaps he would prefer to be elsewhere.

Owing to a shortage of judges, Frank and I are appointed to the judiciary. We dutifully report to the cafeteria, having no idea what a barbecue competition judge is supposed to do. They seat six of us at each table, and no sooner are we settled than the discussion of next weekend's competition begins.

Gary Wells, the president of the Kansas City Barbecue Society, stands at the front of the room and attempts to set the proper mood. "People out here have been cooking all night, so we ask you to take this seriously," he says. "When the entries come to your table, you need to assume that everything has a nine [the highest score], and go down from there. The first category is ribs. Everybody loves ribs, but be careful. You're going to eat a lot of meat today. Pace yourself."

The contestants have been provided with white styrofoam containers to put their entries in. Every half hour or so they must turn in an entry for a different category. According to KCBS rules, the

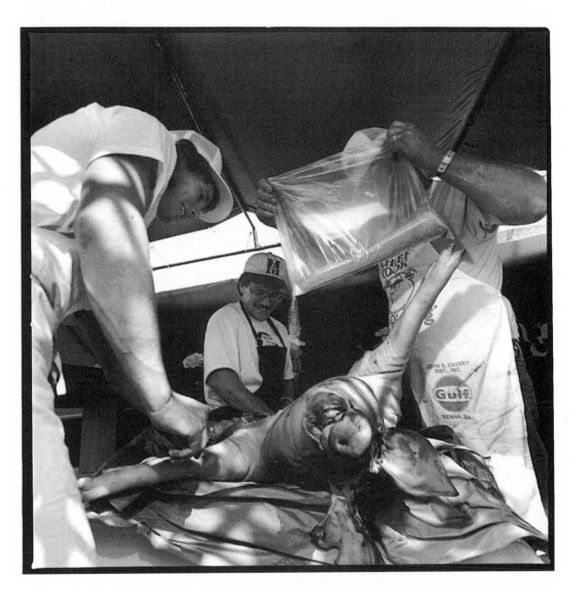

Preparations MEMPHIS IN MAY **MEMPHIS, TENNESSEE**

Shoveling Coals by Night BIG PIG JIG **VIENNA, GEORGIA**

Cajuns in Competition MEMPHIS IN MAY **MEMPHIS, TENNESSEE**

only garnish allowed in the box is lettuce and parsley. As we are hearing the last of the instructions and taking the judges' oath, the containers of ribs begin arriving. Each team's container comes to the judging area with a number assigned to it. There another number is assigned to it, so that only the computer knows which entry came from which contestant.

The entries are to be judged on taste, appearance, and texture/tenderness with the taste score being doubled once the scores are tabulated. The judges at my table are evenly divided between men and women. We are instructed not to speak while judging so as not to influence one another's opinions. Each container has six to eight ribs in it. We look at the ribs first. Even in that initial stage there is some indication of which ones have a shot at winning. The best-looking ribs could be advertisements for a nice restaurant: they are neatly cut and laid out on the parsley and lettuce with artistry.

After about ten or fifteen minutes all six of us have finished marking our scorecards and we begin comparing notes. It becomes immediately clear then how subjective the decision is. Everyone else at the table had a clear winner among the ribs, an entry I didn't really like. One of the ribs had a lot of black pepper on it, which I liked. No one else did. One entry came with a sauce that looked like black tar. I liked it and so did another judge. We were alone. It is also clear that, regardless of how much time and energy these people are spending on their cooking, most of the entries are not very good. There is, however, a broad range of ways in which the entries are not good: ten-der with no flavor, tough with no flavor, tough with flavor, and so on.

By the end of the ribs category, convinced of how wrong the other judges are, I feel more confident. In the remaining categories—chicken, pork (not ribs), beef brisket, miscellaneous—the subjectivity of the process continues to make itself obvious. After the poultry scorecards have been turned in, I retaste one chicken entry that most of the table has been recommending; it strikes me as flavorless. Beef briskets have two distinct textures to them. One side is very lean and looks much like any other roast. The other side is richly marbled, lined with the fat that makes it tender and juicy. I am certain that everyone agrees that the fat side is better. How could they not? They don't.

In the end, once the scorecards have all been turned in and we have tasted some of the best entries from other tables, we begin to talk about barbecue in general. It is then that I get a third guess as to the recipe for Arthur Bryant's sauce. "I think it tastes like Comet and ketchup mixed together," offers a fellow judge.

Before the judging is over, Frank is asking me which team I'm placing my money on. He refuses to say a word about his system until I pick my horse. I decide to go with KCass. They seemed like nice folks and it'd be nice to see them win it all on their backyard equipment.

Frank laughs. "The Wood Brothers are going to take it," he says, and then he reveals the secrets of his system.

The quality of a team's barbecue varies, Frank says, in direct proportion to the quantity of alcohol the team members imbibe. There's no way to know how much someone has been drinking, but in Frank's system you don't need to. He bets on whichever team is the most generous with the alcohol in its possession. Though Jason Levine poured his beer freely at the KC Barbecue Factory, he lost: in the event of a tie, whiskey beats out beer.

By the time the contest organizers come out to announce the results, people have already begun to pack up. Everyone gathers in a large circle within the larger circle of campsites. Gary Wells announces the winners category by category. The teams I had expected to win haven't done well at all. As it is announced that KC Barbecue Factory has placed third overall, Frank kicks himself. The Great American BBQ & Spice Company places ninth. Buck Snodgrass is tenth, the Wood Brothers eleventh, Boastin' and Roastin' twelfth, KCass thirteenth, Chips off Ol' Smokey fifteenth, and Hawk's Bluff eighteenth.

The name called most often is R&R Barbecue, the father-and-reluctant-son team. Because their site seemed small and lonely compared with the others, I'd counted them out of the running. Each time they win a ribbon Jack runs up. He's real excited, and he has a sort of egotistical run/strut, the physical manifestation of the bragging rights he has earned here. All the people from the other teams cheer, and you can see how good it feels to him. He grabs his son each time to come up with him and to accept the award with the requisite braggadocio. At first Matt clearly doesn't feel it. Then, as the prizes begin mounting—"First in brisket, R&R Barbecue!" "Second in poultry R&R Barbecue!"—Matt begins to get excited. When the grand prizes are announced, R&R Barbecue has won first place overall. Jack poses with the trophy as if he's just single-handedly won the World Series. And Matt suddenly looks as if the two of them are on the same team.

Given the fact that both of our teams finished so far out of the running, I am certain Frank will forget about the bet. There's clearly no honor to be had in the winning of it. Judging from the look on his face as I suggest this, you'd swear he owed me money. Without a word, he simply holds out his hand for payment.

Big Pig Jigs

I

Stan Gambrell is the city administrator here in Vienna, and he came with his cousin Johnny Cothran up from Milledgeville, Georgia. We were playing cards one day and I said, "We've been barbecuing all our lives and I'm the best barbecuer in the state of Georgia." He said, "Naw, man; you not. John T., down in Vienna, he's the best barbecuer in the state of Georgia." So one thing led to another, one beer led to another, and we bet fifty dollars on who could cook the best pig. That's really how it got started.

Charles "Charlie Mac" McCullar
Milledgeville Misfits
at the Big Pig Jig

I am told that the Jaycees of Covington, Tennessee, originated organized barbecue competitions twenty-two years ago, ten years before the birth of the Big Pig Jig. I have no grounds on which to dispute that history; I just prefer Charlie Mac's story.

Imagine.

Stan Gambrell has been introduced to you on this Big Pig Jig afternoon. You are poised to be the scribe of his story. Gambrell is more than willing to tell it, but as he is in his official capacity, he is very much in the Big Pig Jig spirit, which is to say, though he may only have been drinking socially, he seems to have been doing it in the society of a hell of a lot of people. His is a willing spirit but, flesh being what it is (and spirits being how they are), he prefers to let Charlie Mac tell the story. He whisks you through the smoke of a dozen barbecue pits. As he passes his minister, he carefully drops his drink below eye level and tips the brim of an unworn hat. Then he introduces you to Charlie Mac.

The story Charlie Mac tells involves an afternoon of golf leading to dinner and then to a card game. And it involves the Slosheye Pig Trail, an earlier place and event onto which the Big Pig Jig has been grafted. Truth being what it is—vast and yet surprisingly deceptive—what you will retain will be the tale's edited version, its essence. And as you choose to remember them, both tale and teller, Charlie Mac will become more than the historian of a small village in Georgia. He will become the griot of this whole thing—its Homer, if you will.

These days barbecue competitions are a big deal. They attract moneyed tourists and put places on maps where you didn't know there were places. And they draw competitors from as many different places as there are attitudes toward the spirit of competition. So our mythological origin of barbecue competitions is clearly not large enough to account for, say, the origin of Memphis in May or the Kansas City Barbecue Society. It can't tell us where they get the thousands of dollars in cash and prizes awarded at the largest events. Yet it tells us what we like to think happened. It tells us that beer and friendship and good-natured bragging have more to do with these events than do money and corporate marketing and chamber of commerce promotions and win-at-any-cost tactics. The very innocence of our little tale provides for us the spiritual plot of exactly what did and still does happen—at least in part—at these events.

II

Watch your alcohol consumption. I wouldn't say it if it wasn't an issue all the time … It's devastating to us if you go to the wrong booth.

Mike Cannon instructing judges
at the Big Pig Jig

I'd rather see these guys out here drinking beer than all these potheads running around town. It's a whole different class of people.

Buck Snodgrass
at Grain Valley

Memphis in May **MEMPHIS, TENNESSEE**

The Agony of Defeat MEMPHIS IN MAY **MEMPHIS, TENNESSEE**

Mrs. Fischer is right, of course. These events resemble nothing so much as the pig roasts that the fraternity boys used to have along Locust Walk at Penn or along Rugby Road at the University of Virginia or along whichever street at whichever college you might care to place in the blank. There are differences. For one thing, there are women in this fraternity. Some are cheerleaders and friends and hangers-on, but many teams are also run by or in partnership with women. All the same, the men predominate.

There is an ugly side to these gatherings of mostly men. Consider those things that so define the lives of boys and touch more lightly on the lives of girls: competitive sports, bragging, fighting, tossing back a few with the boys. The years put an ever-larger distance between a man and these things. At a certain point in a man's life the playing of competitive sports begins to be accompanied by the unnerving creak of aging bones. Fights, once as quickly forgotten as begun, become potentially fatal. Competitive barbecue is definitively male, yet it's a noncontact sport, which means that in competitive barbecuing there is the rush of testosterone without the accompanying injuries.

At their best, fraternities are families that we adopt because bloodlines have sometimes grouped us with people that we'd otherwise have little to do with. At each fraternity event you get the warm greetings of fraternal brothers and sisters who may not have seen you since this time last year and who, but for these events, might never see you at all. Like all families, the barbecue family can be distant and extended and not always in the best of touch. Still, when Obie Obermark and Pat Caudle decided to get married, they decided to exchange their vows at the Meat in the Middle competition, which was itself a merger—it was the first event cosponsored by the Kansas City Barbecue Society and the International Barbecue Cookers Association. Obie and Pat's courtship had taken place in part at barbecue competitions, and the people at the competition were in a sense family members they wanted at their wedding.

III

Each time we meet Mason Steinberg he tells us about the barbecue society they started in Omaha, Nebraska. It had twelve members a year ago and their competition offered just $1,000 in prize money. Now they have ten times as many entries and the prize money has increased proportionately.

That's the story of barbecue societies and competitions in a nutshell. It's not so surprising that Southern places like Rocky Mount, North Carolina, and Wichita Falls, Texas, have barbecue competitions. What does surprise is the fact that interest in barbecue is sufficiently broad to support competitions in places far from the center of barbecue country, places like Tacoma, Washington, and Coeur d'Alene, Idaho, and Carlisle, Massachusetts, and San Jose, California.

Organizations like the Kansas City Barbecue Society and the Texas-based International Barbecue Cookers Association feature so-called blind judging; the judges don't know whose entries they are tasting until the winners are announced. These are cookers' organizations, created by and for the people who are actually competing.

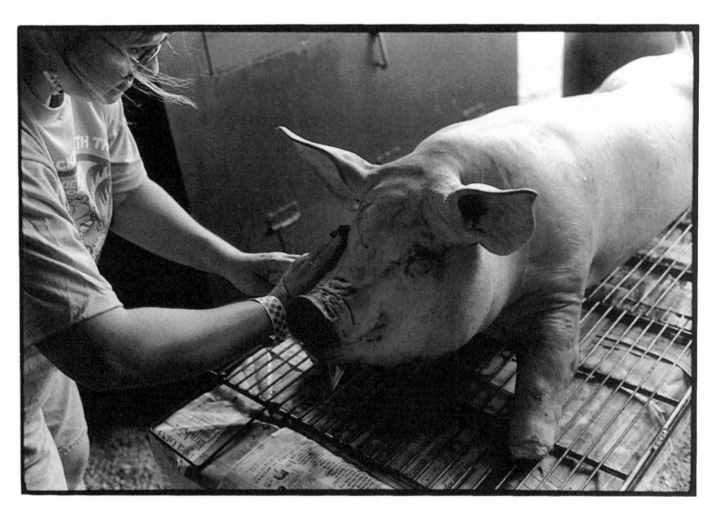

Greasing the Pig BIG PIG JIG VIENNA, GEORGIA

Memphis in May and the contests it sanctions, such as the Big Pig Jig, serve a function not unlike that of a county fair. Large corporations like Federal Express and Hampton Inns sponsor teams at the competitions for much the same reason that they sponsor competitors in sporting events: it makes good marketing sense. Scattered among the large, fancy edifices that these companies erect are the smaller, plainer sites of family teams.

IV

I'd just about give my left nut to win this thing. I don't need it like I used to.
Bill Eason
Little Red Pig Cooking Team
at the Big Pig Jig

This is my hobby number one. People say, "You must be crazy spending all that money on barbecue contests." And I say, "What do you do for a hobby?" and they say, "I play golf every weekend." "Well, how much money does a set of golf clubs cost?" "Anywhere from $180 to $600." That's what I've got invested in the equipment that I use to barbecue. "What's it cost for a green fee?" "Thirty bucks." It'll cost me thirty dollars to come to a barbecue contest and I can bring my wife, my four kids, and we can spend thirty hours together. I say, "Can you take four kids out on a golf course while you're playing?" Ain't no way!
Rich Tuttle, *KCass*
at Grain Valley

One time this guy's fire had gone out; his cooker was cold at three a.m. We woke him up and he ended up winning the whole competition.
Greg Hartnett
Great American BBQ & Spice Co.
at Grain Valley

We like to cook and we're real competitive. There's no other way to show how good you are but to beat everybody out here. We even do contests that pay no money.
Jim Howell, *Slaughterhouse Five*
at American Royal

Let's put it this way: it's a passion.
Marty Edwards, *Swine Flew*
at Grain Valley

We had met Fred Barnett early at Memphis in May. Had watched them—a team called Outdoor Cookery, from Orlando, Florida— season their six hogs inside and out. Had seen them stoke up the "World's Largest Cooker" (weighs eight tons, is twelve feet high and forty-eight feet long, and cooks as many as a thousand whole chickens, five hundred slabs of ribs, or sixty whole hogs) and slice fresh onion onto its firebox just to give their site an added aroma of good cooking. The meat wasn't done yet, but we tasted their lemon-vinegar marinade and the basting sauce flavored with oranges. Both were of championship caliber. Their set-up was large and elaborate, the men dressed in black aprons, white shirts, and gold bowties, the women in black culottes, leopard vests, and white boots. The six pigs they had cooked were dressed up in sunglasses and various adornments. Each had an orange in its mouth, the team being

from Florida. A crowd gathered behind the roped-off area as the on-site judges were wined and dined.

They were confident then. Perhaps cocky.

There are hundreds of contestants at Memphis in May. We walked around the grounds talking to people and taking their pictures, biding time until the results would be in. Then we made a beeline back to Outdoor Cookery's site to see how the team had done. Fred was now out of his dress shirt, wearing a plain white T-shirt. He hadn't made the finals. His head was in his palms.

"This is the worst I've ever done," he said. "I had awful good hogs. Used the same sauce, the same marinade. I just didn't get the right judge. What it amounts to is I spent a thousand dollars for nothing."

On that same day Jim Quessenberry found out he had finished eighteenth out of the forty-eight teams that had competed in the whole-hog division. If he had made the finals, he would have had to gear up to feed and charm another set of judges, but he didn't. He was disappointed but not distraught.

"A lot of times I have to settle these old boys down," he said. "If they say we didn't make the cut a lot of the old boys want to start yelling and throwing stuff. I say, 'So we didn't make the finals. That means we can start drinking!'"

V

Hell, like I say, you don't know the power of barbecue. Hell, you could go into Haiti. I could go in, smoke them some good barbecue, have them people

Oklahoma Joe MEAT IN THE MIDDLE **PERRY, OKLAHOMA**

throwing down their weapons and wanting to celebrate.

Silky Sullivan

international barbecue contest promoter

I'll drive up to some cookoffs and some people get upset—"Damn it, he's here; I don't have a chance"— which is ridiculous. Everybody has the same chance as I have. Others look at it as "We have to be on our toes now; Paul's here."

Last week I did the class down here, I said, "Okay, guys, you can't use the Oklahoma or Texas crutch— that's foil. They wrap everything in foil and that just basically steams everything and you lose a lot of flavor and marking. Just cook it slow; I cook my brisket sixteen to nineteen hours. You get it just as tender and have a better-tasting product by not wrapping. And they say, "It'll get black," and I say, "Hey, black is beautiful."

Paul Kirk, *the Baron of Barbecue*

In competition the outfit Harley Goerlitz wears makes him look like a caricature of himself. From the front it appears that this Giddings, Texas, native is wearing only cowboy boots, a cowboy hat, and an apron. He looks like the Texas hick who makes only a minimal concession to citified standards of appropriate dress. It's his gimmick. He's won a bunch of trophies and ribbons and has developed his own line of barbecue rubs and seasonings.

Organized barbecue is like that; it has its list of characters and celebrities, people whose exploits and victories you can follow in the newsletters and by word of mouth.

Paul Kirk, for example. He's been variously called the Paul Prudhomme of Barbecue and the Baron of Barbecue, the latter being the name he uses in competition. His waistline is large, though not nearly so large as that of the Cajun chef, and while his influence may be similarly narrow by comparison, the Baron has exerted considerable influence in his chosen sphere. By day he's the head chef at Trinity Lutheran Hospital in Kansas City. At night and on weekends he's competing ("We do at least fifteen competitions a year") or teaching barbecue classes ("Everything I do is on timing"). He and his pit man, Steve Holbrook, have won most of the major competitions at least once. And while the two of them make a good team, it is the third team member who seems to be the good-luck charm. The Baroness, as Frank and I nickname her, is Paul's teenage daughter. She does little in the way of cooking, but she is as much a fixture at competitions as the Baron is, proudly bounding up to accept the prizes whenever they win.

Oklahoma Joe is another barbecue figure of renown. Outside the KCBS sphere of influence, people use all kinds of barbecue cookers, Pitts and Spitts out of Texas, JR's out of Arkansas. But wherever KCBS competitions are held, nearly half of all the cookers are Oklahoma Joe's. It helps that the company gives away a lot of them as prizes at the competitions. It also helps that cooking on their hardware Oklahoma Joe and his Hogamaniacs win more than their share of prizes and produce rack after rack of what may very well have been the best ribs we ate in an entire summer of tasting barbecue.

Silky Sullivan is perhaps the most interesting character in barbecue, since he's not really in barbecue in any way you can put your finger on. I talked to him and even saw him in action both at Memphis in May and at his Beale Street bar. But he doesn't compete. He doesn't own a barbecue restaurant. The recipe he contributed to the cookbook *Barbecue Greats Memphis Style* called for a pig and a lot of whiskey. The pig was to be discarded while the whiskey was to be drunk. Yet the internationalization of competitive barbecue has resulted largely from his efforts. He has started barbecue competitions in Ireland and Russia and other far-flung places around the globe.

I asked him how he managed to put these competitions together. His answer, while not evasive, was ample justification for his nickname. "I know how to make the political connections, you know," he said. "I just know how to get in with the people who have the money. If you gentlemen ever want to do one of these competitions, I'd be happy to help you put it together. It'd be easy to do."

VI

Partly the contest is a social-class thing. You have to have money to invest to get into one of these contests, so automatically it's the middle and upper middle class who are willing to do this as a hobby. In terms of it mostly being a white-dominated contest circuit, I think it's a reflection that we're still a segregated society. I can imagine somebody who's not white, not middle or upper class saying, "It looks like a white man's pissing contest to me." And when you look at the judges—are the contests making a conscious effort to reflect cultural diversity among the judges? For the most part you see white, middle-class judges.

My sense is that once people get involved there's this camaraderie that develops, regardless of who you are. It becomes a little barbecue community. But I'm an idealist, so I may be projecting what I want to happen. I think when people are enjoying food together that common denominator can do a lot of bonding that can't happen in any other way. That's just one reason I love barbecue.

> Ardie Davis
> at American Royal

Most of the places are black-owned. All of the famous barbecue restaurants in Kansas City are black-owned. But events like this are predominantly white. Why do you think that is?

> A judge at Grain Valley

How can you compete with a bank or a car dealer and you working at the mill making seven dollars an hour? This is a rich man's game, like automobile racing. We come four hundred miles. Look at us. We rinky-dink.

> Ed Phillips, *the Intimidators*
> at Meat in the Middle

We appreciate our sponsor, Pitts Gin Co.

We thank our supporters, Mixon Chev-Olds, Nature-Glo Hickory Charcoal, M&T Meats, The Steak House, Planters Bank.

> Sign at the Big Pig Jig

It costs $2,000 to $2,500 to be here. Sponsors pay about $1,000. Without sponsors this team wouldn't be here today.

> Gary Cross
> *Sporty Porkers World Class Cooking Team*
> at the Big Pig Jig

I am an on-site judge at the Big Pig Jig. At the first site I am sent to, the man, sixtyish and balding, speaks with a graveness of tone that permeates the whole campsite. He introduces me to his wife and daughter; after the introductions, they say nearly nothing. Among the larger sites, those with the loud music and the matching costumes, that feeling of swagger, this place is lonely and hollow.

The man walks me over to the pit, and though I am there to judge the whole-hog category, he doesn't barbecue whole hogs. He explains that with whole hogs the meat dries out or doesn't taste right or does something it isn't supposed to do, so he has the pig cut in half along its spine.

The meat is good and the old man is okay and I give them all nines and tens, but even as I do it, I know it won't be enough.

Another team at the Big Pig Jig consists of three men, Jim Weiss, Ed Phillips, and Charlie Magness, who make the drive every year from Shelby, North Carolina. The Intimidators, they call themselves, though everyone including them can see that their team and that name work about as well as a hog in house slippers. They don't get here days early to entertain their corporate sponsors as they haven't any. They don't enter many categories because they don't have that kind of money. But they have a good time and are as generous with their food and beer as anyone else out here. We know we're not going to win, they tell me, we just come to have a good time.

☞

You don't have to have a lot of money to win a barbecue competition, but it helps. First of all, the more you compete, the more you learn about the little tricks that go along with winning. Teams like the Vienna Volunteer Fire Department present their entries with a polished perfection that is seldom achieved by the casual competitors. You might be able to spend as little as a hundred dollars to compete in one small competition, but that amount climbs quickly when it is multiplied by the eight or ten events that a serious competitor enters each summer. And no matter how much the officials caution against it, judges can't help but be moved a little by the fancy scenery or winning ways of the better teams.

VII

Before we went to Memphis we never had cooked anywhere but here in south Georgia. In south Georgia everything is vinegar and pepper, no brown sugar. We cooked next to a Memphis team up there in Memphis, and when I saw their ribs and how they had done put that brown sugar and honey on them and glazed them over I said, "Lord, we done come to the wrong damn place now!"

What that told me was the next year when we were in Memphis I had my brown sugar and honey, see. We go to South Carolina cooking—we were South Carolina state champions for two years—we take mustard with us and mix that in. They eat mustard sauce over there. In Tennessee and North Carolina, especially the further up in North Carolina you go, the more ketchup-based it is. In this part of Georgia a hundred miles east of here,

Obie Giving Instructions MEAT IN THE MIDDLE **PERRY, OKLAHOMA**

Skies over Vienna BIG PIG JIG **VIENNA, GEORGIA**

they do it different. We have Brunswick stew here. Over there in Savannah and that area, they don't have Brunswick stew, they have what they call hash and they put it on rice. Here you put rice and barbecue together and folks think you crazy as hell.

That's another thing you have to know. When you have judges in a contest this size where the judges come from everywhere, you have to have a sweet sauce and a vinegar sauce. Regardless of what a person does, when he sauces down some meat he's gonna judge that meat about ninety percent on what that sauce is like. You just can't help it. If you ain't careful you'll get into a sauce-judging contest instead of a meat-judging contest.

That's another thing. Up there in Tennessee, Arkansas, and Missouri, they like stuff smoked. Heavy on the smoke. That brisket up there they cook? They try to see if they can get a smoke ring on it, a little pink ring that smoked meat gets below the surface. Down here, everybody don't like a smoke taste. When we barbecue stuff, a lot of it's over an oak pit and we don't want it to have a smoky flavor. What it does is the juice from the hog drips right down on them coals and you getting smoke back. It's not the thick, heavy smoke you get with hickory. That coincides with this vinegar-flavored sauce I'm telling you about. To us, this barbecue has got a flavor coming from where that juice drips on the coals and goes back up. You don't need a sauce.

J.C. Causey
Vienna Volunteer Fire Department
at the Big Pig Jig

Barbecue contests have taken the focus off of the real old-timers that do it the old-fashioned way. It's

the old chili cookoff syndrome, I call it. If you go to a chili contest, I don't care where you go, the winner is going to taste the same. They always do. The people who do down-home barbecue aren't interested in competing against these people who have corporate sponsors.

Jim Quessenberry
the Arkansas Trav'ler
at Memphis in May

I have to be perfectly honest, they're getting homogenized. There used to be a time when they said the Carolinas was vinegar-based sauce and all that, but they seem to generally be coming toward Kansas City and Memphis. In other words, you wouldn't see a bright yellow mustard-based sauce at a competition in Kansas City. Even though you try to leave an open mind when you're judging, those sauces just tend not to win. The contestants are also very aware that they can't win with those sauces in Memphis and they couldn't win with them at the American Royal.

Jim "Trim" Tabb
veteran barbecue judge

It was once truer—if not ever absolutely true—that west meant beef barbecue and east meant pork. But with people moving from region to region and with restaurateurs opening businesses based not so much on what is regionally authentic as on what has proven to sell well in other places, it's easy to find pork barbecue in Texas and not impossible to find beef in Tennessee, Georgia, and South Carolina.

Competitions exacerbate the trend toward homogenization. If you compete in

a small event with local judges, you can reasonably hope to win by preparing barbecue the way your father or grandfather did. But if you hope to make the big time, Memphis in May or the American Royal, you can expect to find judges and teams from all over the country. Your best chance at winning is to cook in a style as similar to that of proven winners as possible. This movement toward uniformity accounts at least in part for the popularity of basting with apple juice and cooking indirectly and barbecuing poultry with fruit woods rather than the oak or hickory that is used for pork and beef. Because so many veterans of competitive barbecue go on to open restaurants, the influence of competitions makes its way into the mainstream by that route.

Much like certain varieties of fruits and vegetables that didn't travel well or didn't have a sufficient shelf life, certain barbecue techniques are dying. It's easy to blame the competitions, but the truth is that the effect of competitions has been overwhelmingly positive. These events set standards for good barbecue. They have developed a large cadre of cookers who take pride in their art and who are unmoved by promises of cooking something more quickly or more easily. So while gas and electric cookers make headway at a disappointing rate, we can take heart in the fact that the palates of an increasing number of people are being developed to the point where they reject short cuts and help stem the tide in that direction.

Boss Bewley A.N. BEWLEY FABRICATORS **DALLAS, TEXAS**

More American Than Apple Pie: The Poetics of Barbecue

Do I contradict myself?
Very well I contradict myself,
(I am large, I contain multitudes.)
Walt Whitman, *Song of Myself*

There are those, wise men among them, who firmly believe that, saints and devils aside (and who can claim to have seen many of either kind lately?) the true, unfeigned character of every man and woman is formed, therefore to be found, in the tugging and wrestling of contrarieties. The opposites he or she embraces.
George Garrett, *Entered from the Sun*

We meet Bob Brasch and Tetsuaki Sugawara at the XIT Rodeo and Reunion. Bob is an American specializing in trans-Pacific trade. Tetsuaki is a Japanese manager. They have traveled together from California, and this is what Bob wants Tetsuaki to see: a barren patch of land out of which men and women have dug a long trench and back into which they have put burning coals and roughly a thousand pounds of raw beef—this plus the beer and watermelon and country music that go with it. Bob wants Tetsuaki to see a barbecue.

Perhaps Bob has already taken Tetsuaki to see Wall Street and the Chicago Board of Trade or the Waldorf-Astoria, places that might be expected to impress a visiting businessman, but I doubt it. I think Bob, who has been coming to XIT for a dozen years, likes to show his visiting associates the side of American culture that shines at a barbecue.

Barbecue is the quintessential American food, perhaps the only one large enough to reconcile the lies and myths out of which the fabric of our national truth has been woven. Barbecue, then, serves as a metaphor for American culture, bridging and embracing this nation's various facets. For if any sense is to be made of the character of this nation, it must be done on the terms that George Garrett has set before us. Its contradictions must not be seen as opposites but rather be seen on a larger, grander scale.

The arrival of Bob and Tetsuaki parallels what happens at barbecue restaurants around the country. The standard answer given in books and articles about where to find good barbecue is that you should look for places with both Porsches and pickups in the parking lot. If the people who can afford to go elsewhere eat there, and if they do so next to the people whose cheaper vehicles suggest they know good barbecue, it must be the right place. And if you count the number of white faces in a black-owned business like Cozy Corner in Memphis or the number of black faces in a white-owned place like Rosedale's in Kansas City, it's clear that it's not only economic desegregation that takes place where good barbecue is served. In

135

an obvious sense, barbecue brings people together.

The references to barbecues in the letters and diaries of Thomas Jefferson and George Washington make clear that this food and the occasions it accompanied were never just for the common people. But even if barbecue was not associated exclusively with poor folks in that period, it certainly came to be connected more with them than with the rich. First of all, it is a Southern delicacy. Northeasterners, who have appointed themselves the arbiters of taste and refinement in this country, have always looked down on things Southern. Even in the South, barbecue was long, hard, dirty cooking. The white people who could afford it often hired black people to barbecue for them. Poor white people had to cook for themselves.

But as the South has changed, so has its relationship to barbecue. The sons and daughters of many poor whites have moved on to middle-class status. Barbecue for them is a link to their roots. They study barbecue and hone their skills in a very conscious attempt to remain connected to the culture they grew up in.

There is no better example of this than Ardie Davis, the Oklahoma native who now dons apron and bowler to become Remus Powers, Ph.B. (Philosopher of Barbecue). Ardie grew up in an environment that was both parochial and racist, he says. His father was an automobile mechanic with a limited education. Ardie left home to go to school and was irrevocably changed. "After you've been to college it's like being in two cultures," he says. "You go home and they wonder why you've gone on to graduate school and got another degree." Ardie, who is a fixture at barbecue contests around the nation, finds in barbecue a way to remain attached to his rural, working-class roots.

Barbecue competitions, the larger ones especially, are not designed merely to determine the best barbecue cook. Events like Memphis in May and the Big Pig Jig in Vienna, Georgia, are corporate showcases where companies can entertain their clients or employees. In that sense these events, like backyard barbecues with similar guest lists, are a way of demonstrating that the host is a "regular guy." Though he may be the president of the bank, he doesn't drink fine champagne and eat caviar—at least not all the time. He can drink cheap beer and eat barbecued ribs like anyone else.

Barbecue also feeds our national distrust of intellectuals and ideas or techniques that are arrived at via excessive thought and erudition. Perhaps Thomas Jefferson, one of his century's greatest political theorists, first gave voice to this contradiction, no doubt arrived at in a room without mirrors. "State a moral case to a ploughman and a professor," he wrote. "The former will decide it as well, and often better than the latter, because he has not been led astray by artificial rules." As Jefferson's own career demonstrates, it is not intelligence that is distrusted, it is intelligence that presents itself as such.

Barbecue is the reflection of a similar sensibility in the culinary arena. The food begins with *l'objet trouvé*, those meats that the butcher used to give away or sold cheaply because they were undesirable. Then, over some crude stove—chicken wire stretched across an old washtub, the springs of an old bed covering a hole in the ground—the meat is cooked. The primitiveness of the implements employed is plain for anyone to see, but what often escapes note is the complexity and delicacy of the technique itself. In barbecuing at its highest levels, *l'objet trouvé* is wrought into *l'objet d'art*. There is nothing lucky or primitive or crude about the proceedings; there is only the quality that results from the work of a master of the craft.

Although the classically trained chef must learn a far greater range of recipes and techniques than an expert barbecuer, it is doubtful that any single dish from the classical repertoire is more challenging to prepare than serious barbecue. Perhaps the most difficult technique for the barbecue cook to master is the cooking of whole hogs. The task requires putting enough fire under the meat so that the thick hams and shoulders are cooked all the way through and the thinner portions of the animal are not dried out or burned. Whole-hog barbecue is an all-day or all-night affair demanding discipline and concentration. Similarly challenging is the preparation of beef brisket, the barbecue meat of choice in Texas. Besides its notorious toughness, there is the problem of its two textures—one side of it richly marbled, the other side lean. Cooking brisket long enough to tenderize it while not drying it out is difficult work that can again be an all-day affair. The techniques involved in these preparations are no less rigorous for their informality.

But not only does barbecue embody the combination of folk roots and high-culture intellectual engagement, it also has the flexibility to go as upscale as the culinary imagination can take it. Although there can be differences between "barbecued" and "smoked," a word common on fancy restaurant menus, there are also similarities. Smoking—as of salmon, for instance—is generally a slower process and takes place at lower temperatures than barbecuing. But the two words are often used synonymously. The delicately spiced "smoked" meats at our finest restaurants are often just upscale cousins to down-home barbecue. And although barbecue sauce can be a mundane ketchupy condiment, it can also be as exotic and personalized as the chef's imagination can make it. Smoked pork loin, when accompanied by a sauce infused with exotic flavors, is no longer mere barbecue; it is a triumph of the culinary artist. The fact that weekend barbecuers can, with little practice or talent, prepare an edible slab of ribs or a credible variation on a bottled barbecue sauce should not be seen as evidence that the barbecuer's art is easily mastered.

∞

Barbecue is clearly an art; but is it a distinctively American art? For a cultural expression to be definitively American it must embody some semblance of the range of cultures whose combination has formed American culture. Anything less than such a combination would be mere appropriation.

The roots of barbecue make clear that it evolved as a result of cultural interaction among Africans, Europeans, Mexicans, and Native Americans. Even now, this much later, this process of appropriation continues. Ingredients that were once "exotic"— from another place—are now common in barbecue sauces and marinades. Mattie Bivins Dennis, an expert barbecue cook from Hattiesburg, Mississippi, marinates her ribs in teriyaki sauce before putting them on the pit. Many recipes in the Kansas City Barbecue Society's cookbook, *The Passion of Barbecue*, call for curry powder and soy sauce, ground ginger and chili powder, ingredients that were not part of an American cook's spice cabinet even twenty-five years ago. Recipes for Jamaican jerk chicken and pork have already found their way into many barbecue cookbooks. It is only a matter of time before the influences of more recent waves of immigrants from India, Vietnam, Haiti, and other places will become similarly at home here. In this way old recipes are infused with new ingredients, and this nation's truest melting pot simmers on.

Another aspect of the United States that would argue against any sort of cultural unity is its size and its wide range of terrains and climates. Joel Garreau has all but given up on explaining this country as a coherent whole. In his remarkable book *The Nine Nations of North America* he argues that the range of people, topographies, industries, climates, and interests in effect separates the continent into distinguishable nations, nations that often cut across the boundaries

of the United States to include parts of Canada, Mexico, and the countries of the Caribbean. It seems to me that Garreau is right. Miami is certainly more Caribbean than Southern. South Texas is more Mexican than Southern. The Northwest may have more in common with the Canadian west than it does with Los Angeles or New York. But advances in transportation and communication have done much to unify this disjointed country. Those and several factors that have emerged in the period since World War II have conspired to make barbecue a truly national food.

In her meticulously researched Vassar College senior thesis, Ripley Golovin traces the development of backyard barbecue. Golovin, a New Yorker, concentrates on the emergence of barbecue in the Northeast and other parts of the country where it was not indigenous. Of course, people in the South and Southwest had been barbecuing for generations. Though Golovin is aware of what the word barbecue means in those places where it is practiced at its highest level, the definition she works with in her thesis is the one that Northeasterners are most familiar with: in essence barbecue is any meat cooked outdoors over an open fire. Steaks, hamburgers, and hot dogs all fit into Golovin's category, even though in the South and Southwest these meats are cooked only to satisfy the finicky appetites of children or the impatience of adults who can't wait until the real barbecue is ready. Golovin's is a definition that would raise eyebrows in Kansas City or the Carolinas,

Saying the Pledge AMERICAN ROYAL **KANSAS CITY, MISSOURI**

but the current popularity of barbecue could hardly have come about if the food hadn't made major inroads into the culture of the Northeast. To see how barbecue made those inroads, Golovin traces the growth of barbecue's popularity largely through articles in popular cooking and homemaking magazines.

From 1890 to 1910 America moved outdoors, Golovin writes, and picnics, bicycles, interest in nature, and the national park system all emerged. Between 1910 and 1923 the hot picnic, the precursor of barbecue, became popular; bacon and hot dogs were major items on hot picnic menus. Cheaper automobiles made it possible for more Americans to drive out to the country for these picnics. At the same time bungalows, one-story houses featuring patios, meant that outdoor cooking at home became more feasible. The 1930s saw the advent of so-called outdoor fireplaces. These brick pits, which were constructed in back yards all over the country, were often elaborate in the arrangement of their bricks, but as barbecue pits they were simple. The foundation layer of bricks would come up about waist high. The wood or charcoal would be placed in a recessed opening. Above that there was a grill on which the meat was cooked.

The World War II era was important for barbecue in several ways, Golovin writes. The rationing of gas during the war meant that people were encouraged if not forced to entertain themselves at home. In 1939 President and Mrs. Roosevelt entertained King George of England by "barbecuing" hot dogs on their outdoor fireplace. This was an important step toward making out-door cooking socially acceptable. Similarly James Beard, whose previous work included the socially acceptable *Hors d'Oeuvres and Canapés*, published *Cook It Outdoors* in 1941. That book, which went through ten printings in its first decade, was hardly a barbecue cookbook by today's standards. While it had chapters on drinks and appetizers, stews and ragouts, it contained precious little advice relevant to the preparation of a slab of pork ribs or a brisket of beef. Clearly Mr. Beard's audience was the upper-middle-class Northerner who neither knew nor cared much about barbecue as it was practiced by its experts.

Amid this increasing popularity of outdoor cooking, there was controversy regarding the definition of barbecue. Serious barbecuers were disgusted by the misuse of their word. In a 1954 *Saturday Evening Post* article, "Dixie's Most Disputed Dish," Rufus Jarman wrote:

Nowadays barbecuing, or something so called, has spread throughout the land. These days it isn't politics so much as the popularity of back-yard cookery that promotes barbecuing. Countless men in chef's caps and fancy aprons, with their eyes reddened by smoke, regale their guests with burnt and raw flesh. Many Georgia epicures insist that this is an insult to the honorable name of barbecue. They assert that, statements in various magazines to the contrary, you cannot barbecue hamburgers, roasting ears, potatoes, onions, tomatoes, wieners or salami, and it is a shame and disgrace to mention barbecuing in connection with such foolishness.

Barbecue, whatever the definition, is a central part of gatherings and celebrations throughout much of the nation. The fact that the sauces and meats and methods of preparation vary so widely is testimony to the fact that barbecue has been branded with the accent of each region in which it has found a home.

Hamburgers and hot dogs and fried chicken vary little from one coast to another. Perhaps that's because fast-food chains have so tended to homogenize our food. Perhaps it's because there is little room for constructive creativity in those foods. Although New Yorkers and Chicagoans have fierce debates over who has the best pizza, theirs is a debate that means little to people outside those spheres of influence. Pizza may be a popular food, but it is not a food that the various regions of this country have sought to stamp with their own seal. Those foods that do express the personalities and sensibilities of a given region most richly don't travel well beyond those regions. Gumbo speaks volumes about the history and culture of southern Louisiana, but it can be lethal to order the dish outside the state. The same is true with Tex-Mex.

Maurice Bessinger, the South Carolina barbecue magnate, has said he hopes to make barbecue "the hamburger of the twenty-first century." That's not apt to happen. But what has already happened is that people all across the country have adopted and adapted barbecue. In short, they've made it their own.

Ollie Gate's Stare GATE'S & SONS BAR-B-Q **KANSAS CITY, MISSOURI**

Going to Kansas City

There is the "Wild West" Kansas City, which traces its lineage from Wyatt Earp and Wild Bill Hickok and the cattle drives through Pretty Boy Floyd and the Union City Massacre, and also through the strong-arm machine politics of the Brothers Pendergast (James and Tom) and the gambling and prostitution and thwarted Prohibition that flourished during the Pendergast czarships. And there is also the promised-land Kansas City of the great black migrations, which, along with the Pendergastian laissez-faire social scene, helped make possible the Moten hot swinging Kansas City of Big Joe Turner and the all-night jazz sessions of the territory bands, the most famous progeny of which was the Red Bank, New Jersey–born count, William Basie. And then, too, there is the industrial Kansas City of railroads and packing houses and automobile manufacturing, and the royal Kansas City of baseball fame.

These Kansas Citys, all and each, share credit for the development of perhaps the most enduring Kansas City–Kansas City the barbecue capital.

Seated directly north of the South and northeast of the Southwest, Kansas City is the meeting point for the beef barbecue tradition of Texas and the pork barbecue traditions of Arkansas, Tennessee, and the rest of the former Confederacy. This marriage of traditions is made possible in no small way by the fact that in 1867 Joseph G. McCoy had the idea of driving post–Civil War surplus cattle from their Texas homes directly to Kansas City. Ultimately Kansas City became, after Chicago, the nation's second-largest meat-packing city, a crucial stopping-off point for cows and pigs en route to their final breakfast, lunch, and dinner engagements—at table. Crucial to McCoy's idea were railway lines between Kansas City and Abilene. The network of tracks grew, switched, and connected into what became one of the nation's busiest railway towns. Once in Kansas City the Texas cowboys shed their rough wear for silk vests and black sombreros, and shaved off the bristles and sweat of the trip in preparation for a richly perfumed night on the town. Invariably fools and their money are soon partying, and these men, looking for a good time, were met by women willing to sell it to them and bartenders willing to sell the oil necessary to lubricate manners and morals that might, in sober and more inhibited society, act as impediments to the smoothly simultaneous coupling of business and pleasure.

Of course, the 1870s railroads of steam and iron were second also to the foot and path Underground Railroad of reb' times that brought former slaves into Kansas as it bled, in part, on their behalf. According to one legend, it was that railroad which brought barbecue itself to the area.

Lee Green, a tall Kansan and longtime friend of my family's, moved back here recently and spent his first few months at home reading histories of his home state. Standing now on the Missouri side of the river, his back to Kansas, he tells Frank and me a legend about how Kansas and barbecue first made each other's acquaintance. It goes like this: Lawrence, Kansas, was founded largely on anti-slavery principles by a group of abolitionists from its sister city back east, Lawrence, Massachusetts. Though a few of the town's citizens did own slaves, the city's reputation for the promotion of brotherhood and goodwill was large enough to spark the anger of pro-slavery guerrillas, who burned the town almost to the ground. The reputation was also large enough to make Lawrence an important station on the Underground Railroad. One group of

slaves, who had recently stolen themselves off the asset side of their master's balance sheet, arrived in Lawrence in the fall. It was too late then for them to plant food in preparation for winter, so the citizens of Lawrence got together and donated pigs and provisions to help them survive the approaching Kansas cold.

In the eyes of these people, recently freed from bondage and long deprived of all but life's most absolute necessities, these pigs didn't look like food for the winter; they looked like celebration on the hoof. So they slaughtered the pigs, dug a pit, burned some coals, buried the pork in the pit, and a day or two later—*voilà*, barbecue!

We ask F. Neal Willis, a psychology professor at the University of Missouri at Kansas City who has written an unpublished history of Kansas City barbecue, about this story. Willis can't confirm it. But thanks to his scholarship, we do know much about the early history of commercial barbecue in Kansas City.

"First of all, there were packing houses all over town—Swift's, Armour, about seven of them in all. So we had cheap meat," he tells us. "And there's hickory all over here. (They try to act like mesquite's so wonderful out there; that's bullshit. It's 'cause they can't get hickory.) They had hickory here, they had meat here, and they had knowledge 'cause black people were moving here from the South."

As Prohibition became the law of the land after World War I, barbecue joints

became convenient covers for after-hours joints. Not only were these places dispensing barbecue and illegal liquor, they were also important centers for jazz. Thus Kansas City became the second or third most important jazz capital in the world, behind New Orleans, New York, and perhaps also Kansas City's consistent nemesis in matters of rank, Chicago.

Which brings us to Neal Willis' own theory of how Kansas City got to be renowned for its barbecue. Jazz bands from all over the country would travel to play in Kansas City. Additionally Southwest territory bands like the Blue Devils would leave their region to perform all around the country. While in Kansas City these musicians invariably tasted the barbecue and fell in love with it. In fact, Count Basie, in his autobiography, *Good Morning Blues*, all but credits "that good old Kansas City barbecue" with curing him of spinal meningitis.

"The musicians had more to do with [the reputation of Kansas City barbecue] than anybody else," Willis says. "They would eat here in Kansas City and then they would go to Chicago or New York and want barbecue and there wasn't any. So people would eventually open restaurants. In fact in New York in the 20s there were two establishments calling themselves Kansas City–style barbecue.

The railroad and barbecue traditions meet in George Gates, the patriarch of the Gates barbecue dynasty. Working as a waiter on the Rock Island Railroad he was able to save enough money to buy his own barbecue place. His son Ollie Gates—or O.G., as he is called—now presides over the most successful barbecue operation to emerge from the heyday of Kansas City barbecue. He has his own story of how the city got its reputation—a story that, since it takes place in the 1950s, years after Kansas City's prime as a music capital, may provide an explanation of Kansas City's second wind.

"Around 18th and Vine there sprouted the kinds of business that go with a segregated environment," Gates says. "There were the soul-food places, and as time went on there was a barbecue at 19th and Vine, 24th and Brooklyn, all around. Each one had a tall smokestack that went up. We surrounded the stadium. And the announcers, Harry Carry and those guys, would get on the radio and they would say, 'Man, do you smell that odor?' And we would give some barbecue to those announcers, and they would talk about it. You see that stadium was right in the black section."

Although, according to Neal Willis, all the earliest commercial barbecuers were black, there was at least one outstanding white-owned barbecue establishment in Kansas City, Kansas: Rosedale Barbecue.

"Rosedale had as many black customers as white," Willis recalls. "That's kind of the test. If black people will eat white barbecue it must be pretty good, 'cause they don't have to eat it."

According to Willis, most barbecue establishments in Kansas City, Missouri, have their roots in one of two lineages. Most of the early black establishments stem from Henry Perry, whose restaurant first appears in the Kansas City telephone directory in 1908. Many of the white establishments were founded by people who learned the art from Anthony Riecke at Rosedale, including Herbert and Earl Quick, who started Quick Barbecue, and Ron Williams, who started Wyndot Barbecue. Perhaps Perry's most celebrated disciple was Charlie Bryant, brother of Arthur. The Bryants were originally from Texas. First Charlie moved to Kansas City and began working for Henry Perry; then in 1931 Arthur joined him. Ultimately Charlie started his own place, which Arthur took over in 1946 when Charlie died. Some of the folks who've been around awhile still refer to the place as Charlie Bryant's. It was

Arthur, however, who fed President Jimmy Carter; it was Arthur whose death was written up in such faraway papers as the *Los Angeles Times* and the *Times* of London; it was Arthur who, according to the account in a *Kansas City Star* cartoon, was asked at the gates of heaven by God himself, "Did you bring the sauce?" And, perhaps most importantly, it was Arthur whose restaurant was referred to as "the single best restaurant in the world" in a now-famous Calvin Trillin essay.

The relationship between the Gates family and barbecue goes back to 1946, when George Gates, a former railroad worker, bought O'Johnny's Ol' Kentucky Bar-B-Q at 19th and Vine and proceeded to be taught the barbecue business by the pitmaster there, Arthur Pinkard. His son Ollie now owns six Gates & Sons Bar-B-Q's in Kansas City, and has eclipsed Bryant in expanse if not in mythology. Gates sauce is on supermarket shelves in places as far-flung as Houston, Texas, and his real estate and civic interests are fast becoming as synonymous with his name as his ribs.

The Galileo of Kansas City BOYD'S N SON BAR-B-Q **KANSAS CITY, MISSOURI**

The Galileo of Kansas City: Boyd's N Son Bar-B-Q

The universe of Kansas City barbecue, as mapped by popular opinion, is a co-centric one, revolving around Arthur Bryant's and Gates & Sons. There are other barbecue places—dozens of them, according to the Yellow Pages—but it doesn't matter. You ask a Kansas Citian where to get barbecue, and those two are invariably the first places, if not the only places, he or she mentions.

Considered in its own sphere, then, Otis P. Boyd's remapping of his small cosmos is no less revolutionary than Galileo Galilei's remapping of his larger one. To Boyd, the true history of this town's barbecue should speak three names, and if any should be given preeminence at this late date, it should be his. "Charlie Bryant, me (Boyd), and Gates was the ones that made Kansas City the barbecue capital of the United States," he says. "And out of them, I'm the only one who is still alive who started his own business. Hell, I go up against any guy in the United States that *thinks* he can barbecue."

Boyd is seventy-three. He walks with a hunched swagger, and gray hair peeps out beneath his ever-present yachting cap. But mention barbecue or any of the other so-called barbecue men and he sounds like a young Cassius Clay verbally painting the canvas on which his opponents are destined to fall. He doesn't say it. He doesn't have to. Ten minutes into the conversation you know this man sees in himself the greatest of all time.

His story, as he tells it, is a mingling of destiny and drive. At age ten, though hired primarily to scrub pots, he also, feet planted firmly on a box so he could see the stove, fried steaks at a restaurant in his native Iowa. When the cook at a church social fell ill, Boyd finished the meat. He was fourteen then. Those few minutes

before the cook went home were the last lesson he had in the preparation of barbecue, he says. He attended cooking school in 1939 at a now-defunct institution. "I was supposed to be there five weeks. I was there two days," he says. Then he cooked in a series of restaurants, mostly in the Midwest.

His culinary-college experience, brief though it was, separates Boyd from other barbecue men, and he is quick to make the point. He is a "cook," he says with the same sense of honor and superiority as you might employ in saying "I am the Sultan of Brunei."

"These other guys are not cooks. They just throw some meat in there and cook it till it gets done, make up a sauce and sell it. They don't know the essence of it. They don't know the depth of it. I can just stick my finger in a piece of meat and tell you how done it is. And anything I say, I can back up."

The first independent restaurant Boyd opened was a soul-food restaurant in Kansas City. When he decided to go into barbecue he approached the venture with culinary scholarship, he says, scouring libraries for information on the history of barbecue. Boyd cannot recall the titles or authors of those books read so many years ago, though he does remember the essence of what they said. "The books tell me it was in the seventeenth century when they started calling it barbecue, and it was in England," he says. "Some guys went to Australia and it kind of died out. The first thing we know about barbecue in the United States was supposedly when the slaves made it."

And there is a riveting discovery on Boyd's part: the original barbecue sauce was flavored with anise. This is a crucial fact in the mythology of Boyd's because it is from this fact that his sauce takes its name, the Old Original. "The other barbecue guys can't tell you what the flavor of the first barbecue sauce was," he says, a bit irritated, " 'cause they don't know nothing."

In the world of barbecue sauces there are very few unique conceptions. Most are some combination of ketchup, vinegar, sweetener, and spices. People's ideas of how barbecue sauce should taste tend to be so dominated by the flavors of their regional norms or the popular national sauces that when people brag about the uniqueness of their sauce they are in fact bragging only about the uniqueness of the slight variations they have made on what Kraft or Hunt's had already wrought. (There is a restaurant in Nashville that has taken the distinguishing step of serving a sauce that tastes as if it were flavored with chocolate syrup; but culinary innovations that are not first toothsome don't count.) Much in the way that Thelonious Monk's music sounded as if it had a different agenda from that of his contemporaries, Boyd's sauce tastes as if it emanates from a totally different set of priorities and aesthetic criteria from other sauces. It is mild, tending toward the sweet side, and it seems simple, lacking the encyclopedic variety of ingredients that mark attempts by other sauce makers to cover all the bases on the palate. Ingredients don't stick out in Boyd's sauce; rather, they blend. There is, of course, as with all things Boydian, a theoretical foundation for this.

"Here's another thing those other guys don't know," he says. "For every two spices you use in a barbecue sauce, there's always another you have to add to make those flavors blend. I'm the grandpa of barbecue, not no halfway. I'm a professional chef!

"I was the originator of barbecued beans in Kansas City, hickory-smoked beans right there in the pit. And I don't put no ketchup in my barbecue sauce. Everybody else puts ketchup in theirs. You can't have an authentic article if you buy anything that's prepared to go in it."

The meat at Boyd's is excellent. All of it is pink at the center, as smoked meat should be, he says, "just like ham." His sausage, which he makes from scratch, is outstanding. The barbecued lamb he serves is truly magnificent, succulent and tender. The ribs are as good as they come. And therein lies the real mystery in all this.

Though Boyd fancies himself a member of a barbecue triumvirate, a gallery of greats emeriti, the truth is that he toils at 55th and Prospect in relative obscurity. The average white Kansas Citian seems never to have heard of him, and the average black Kansas Citian, though more apt to have heard of Boyd's, will seldom suggest it as a place to eat as readily as he or she would suggest Gates or Bryant's. While those other two restaurants have a sign on the highway marking which exit leads to their doors, Boyd's has only his sign and, sunlight cooperating, the gleam of his red roof.

He has his share of writeups in regional magazines and barbecue books. He proudly displays these articles as we talk to him in his de facto office, a table in the restaurant. With its formica booths and hanging ivy plants, the place looks like most modern restaurants, which is to say that its aesthetics have been heavily influenced by McDonald's and Pizza Hut. But the combined sound of the television that the cashier is watching and the radio that the pit man is listening to give the place a noisy, disorganized feeling that a more tightly run operation might lack. There is also an ever-present cloud of smoke in Boyd's—not thick enough to make eyes water or breathing difficult, just thick enough to suggest that an indoor rainstorm lurks on the horizon.

You can come here most times of the day or night, and though the place will never be empty, neither will it be very crowded. When Boyd tells you that he was one of the three people who put Kansas City barbecue on the map, he is, to put it charitably, exaggerating his role. But when he tells you that he is far and away the best barbecue cooker alive, you taste and know that even in the forest of tall tales that is the world of barbecue, Boyd is a legitimate contender for the title he has awarded himself.

But you also know how little any of this matters. In a world where the taste of the food tends to vary inversely with the financial success of the restaurant, you suspect that he talks so much about the quality of his food because others have not said these things for him as often as they have for other places. Other places with pitmasters worthy only to wash dishes in this place.

Boyd is a funny, friendly man. His conversation is repeatedly interrupted as he greets his customers, many of them by name. He phrases his critiques of his competitors in ways clearly designed more for entertainment and rhetorical effect than for strict adherence to truth. And even amid the funniest, most extravagant appraisals of his value to world culture, contradiction and bitter irony abound.

"Gates, he has six places but they're unnecessary," Boyd says to you. "Too much overhead in six places, and people go further for good barbecue than for any other food on the market.

"And I'm number one," he tells you. "They're bigger than I am. I could have been bigger. If my son had stayed with me you wouldn't have heard of Gates 'cause I'd have shot him down long time ago."

Truth be told, the soundtrack to Boyd's career in barbecue has been composed mostly of preludes. Preludes which have led to neither finale nor fanfare. Each writeup, each book mention, portended the arrival of great, hungry hordes at 5510 Prospect Street, yet none delivered. Disaster, on the other hand, has been no stranger here.

For people who barbecue the old-fashioned way with real pits and real fire, grease fires are as common as oil spills are to their industry. Boyd's place has been badly burned twice. He stresses that these problems began when he stopped cooking and left the kitchen under the charge of pitmasters he trained. It doesn't matter who was in charge so much as it matters that after each of these tragedies he was forced

to dust himself off and give it one more try. Though the restaurant's name, like Gates & Sons, suggests the existence of a family dynasty, Boyd's two sons have never shown much interest in the business. It is a subject about which he prefers to say little.

What you hear instead are great stories like about the times when Boyd, hired as the new chef at some failing restaurant, turned the place around. Or about how in 1948 he sold his recipe for a now famous product, netting a grand total of $100. Or he will show you a battered copy of the June 1990 issue of *Midwest Living* magazine featuring "The Great Kansas City Barbecue Binge." Boyd was photographed alongside Rich Davis, the man who developed and then sold the recipe for K.C. Masterpiece. Boyd holds a special disdain for Davis' skills as a chef. He proudly displays the magazine in which he stands smiling, holding a tray of food, next to a carefully engineered blob of white space–white space where, before Boyd and his scissors went to work, stood Davis, the king of Kansas City's white barbecue entrepreneurs.

"You know Burger King at one time made me accessive to seventeen hundred Burger Kings all over the United States," he tells you. "They told me I could have them all, any way I wanted them, to start a bunch of franchise barbecue restaurants. But I'm too old," he says, "that's too much."

But this old prizefighter still has enough fire in him for one more round in fortune's ring. With the assistance from an unlikely pair consisting of his admiring assistant, Jerry Johnson, and a 900 number, Boyd

plans to market his sauce nationwide. Oh, how you see the light dance in his eyes when he mentions this! As he is winding up his pitch, Johnson produces a copy of the national telemarketing brochure, a telling document, its imperfections notwithstanding:

The Boyd's N Son Bar-B-Q Restaurant & Product Company will initiate a program to take Barbecue knowledge of sauces (dry Mixes), meat preparation, entrees & BBQ Pit building to a national market by offering a *900* telephone number, whereas the caller will be informed. In advance, the price of the call. Mr. Boyd has decided to allow for a $3.95 call, with renumeration by sending each caller a pack of BBQ sauce Dry Mix, The retail value of the sauce is approximately $4.00. This will allow all callers to feel they have been more than compensated for their efforts to gain information about the barbecue food perparation, (backyard or commercial).

"I'm getting more every day, every day I'm getting more writeups," he says. "And this 900 number is going to be something else. It's not no gimmick to this. One of these days you'll see me on all the talk programs—the Oprah Winfrey show, all them shows, when I come out with this stuff that I'm fixing to come out with now—I'm telemarketing barbecue now."

We leave Otis P. Boyd on a high note then, and that feels good. And I say a silent prayer for the success of the 900 number.

Anthony Rieke ROSEDALE BARBECUE **KANSAS CITY, MISSOURI**

Starting Small: Rosedale Barbecue

Mr. Rieke is nearly ninety. He still comes in, but only three or four days a week and only for two or three hours of those days. He walks more slowly now. But in midmorning a couple of hours before his restaurant opens, his mind is agile and able, remembering gems in the form of dates and prices and nuances. This is a polished new building. It lacks the rustic, hand-built charm his words paint of the older, smaller place, but it doesn't diminish his recollection of that place, those times, and those people.

My parents were truck gardeners, raised asparagus and tomatoes and cabbage and stuff like that. We'd take it down to the Kansas City market. It was during the Depression and we wasn't making nothing! I started truck gardening—I got married in 1930—I started truck gardening for myself in 1932. The grasshoppers come and eat up all my garden—and you couldn't sell it if you did raise it. I was selling pecks of tomatoes for ten cents a peck. And the basket cost me a nickel so I had a nickel profit, and I'd have to take 'em to the market to sell 'em.

I tried to get a job. Two of my brothers-in-law worked down at the packing house, Wilson packing house. I tried to get them to get me a job down there. And they'd say, "Well, there were three or four thousand people down here and one job that you could get." And I couldn't get that job. Best thing that ever happened to me I couldn't get no job. If I'd've found a job I was a pretty good worker and they'd've probably kept me on and kept me on until I's too old to do their work and they'd kick me out and then where'd I be? So I had to do something.

Well, there was a little building, it used to be a root beer stand. I rented it and just sold beer and hot dogs there. Then the Board of Health come—we didn't have no sewers or nothing in there, nothing but gravel and plywood. They said, "You're either going to have to put in sewers or close up." We didn't have no money then. So we just closed it.

The next spring, come like March, I went to the same outfit that owned that building, and they had already rented it to somebody else for a used car lot. And they had a vacant lot next to it, 'bout 125 foot square, but it didn't have no building on it. I rented it for twenty dollars a month. I built my own building. Twelve foot wide and sixteen foot deep. All we were selling at the other place was hot dogs and beer and soda pop. Then after we got the little building up, I built a little barbecue oven. And every so often I'd add on a little bit on that building, maybe eight feet or something like that. I'd build on pretty near every year for years.

My brother-in-law was partners with me at that time, and after I had the oven built it was four foot square and had a grate across it. You could lay fifteen slabs on there. I said, "Who's gon' cook it? I don't know nothing about barbecue." He said, "Why don't you buy a few ribs and put 'em in there. And if you burn 'em up, you'll know you're gonna pay for 'em and you'll learn not to burn 'em up." I didn't burn up very many batches of 'em. I learned how.

It didn't cost very much to start out. We was buying ribs for about ten or eleven cents a pound, and pork and beef, it was about fifteen cents a pound. We weren't making much money. It cost us about twenty cents a slab and we were selling it for thirty-five cents. Steaks at that time was around seventy-five cents a pound—sirloin or something.

At that time the theaters and shows, they was givin' away stuff to get people in—oh, like a plate or something like that, you know. So we thought we'd do the same thing. So we'd give the tickets out and we'd have a raffle. Like on Monday, we'd have a raffle and get on top of the building, little bitty ol' building, we'd get on top and raffle off the number. Whoever had the winning number on Monday they'd get a beef brisket and Tuesday they'd get a ham roll. Wednesday they'd get a case of beer. Thursday I think they'd get a slab of ribs and on Friday they'd get a keg of beer.

And that brought the people in. They just clogged that street up. But it got to be a tussle, you couldn't do that because—just like you come in and we'd give you a ticket to win something, well, you wasn't gonna come back so you'd hand it to somebody else. Well, a bunch of them gandies was hanging around here, you know, just waiting around for somebody to buy 'em a drink so they'd have a whole pack of them tickets then they'd start to win everything. So it didn't work, so we had to quit that.

Over the years we've had different people working for us. Several of 'em thought, "Well, I'm doing pretty good here; I'll start a place of my own." Well, they started a place of their own. About half of 'em made it go; half of 'em had to close it up and quit. There's still about six or seven of 'em got their own places now, but they ain't doing the business that we are. I started my son-in-law in business and I worked with him for about four years out at Marion Barbecue. But he didn't take care of the business like I did. If I seen something had to be done here, I was right here, Johnny on the spot. My wife said, "You're married to the barbecue." But my son-in-law out there running the Marion Barbecue, if he wanted to go fishing for two weeks he'd go fishing and just let some ol' [anybody] run it. They didn't watch that business like you should.

Them days I'd come down here about five-thirty or six in the morning and I'd work till about four in the afternoon. Then if I had to come back in the evening I would. And my wife would come back too and she'd help me in the daytime. Didn't pay her no wages or anything, though.

In the 30s World War II come out and you couldn't get meat unless you had points. You fellahs don't remember that. And without points, you couldn't buy no meat. Well, one of the meat companies that we did business with—the price was froze at that time at seventeen cents per pound on ribs. So this meat company called me and says, "I got a barrel of ribs." I said, "Well, I don't have no meat points." He said, "You don't need the meat points, all you need is the money." I said, "Well, how much will they cost me?" He said, "Twenty-five cents a pound." And the price was froze at seventeen cents a pound. I said, "I'll never pay twenty-five cents a pound for ribs!" Now we're paying a dollar fifty, two dollars a pound.

Then during the war we couldn't get no meat 'cause we didn't have the meat points. We just had lamb racks. That's the ribs on the lamb. So I bought 'em 'cause we didn't have no other kind of meat. Then the man that was tending bar, he told the people, "We got lamb, ram, sheep, or mutton, if you don't want that you don't get nuttin'." That was just one day, though.

I never had to close entirely. We got lunch ham one time. I remember we got lunch ham and they had to live with it. It was something to eat. And beer, beer was so short, we had enough beer to maybe last four days out the week. We'd set here, didn't have nothing to serve people, no beer, no meat. But we just set here, tried to keep it going.

For years we'd serve the black people, but they'd have to take it with them. But we didn't have room inside. We just had about nine or ten seats inside. People would just set out in their cars and eat.

Well, one time, a man that was coming in there, oh, every day or two and eating all the time and a black man come and sit down beside him and we started to serving the black man. And this man that was coming in every day, he said, "You serve him, just as well forget mine," and he walked out. We never seen him since. That was when things was changing like that. But you know, the black people were just as good customers as the white people.

You could start out little like that. When I built that building here, that little twelve-foot-wide building by sixty foot, I spent $186. Built the building, bought my first keg of beer, and what little ribs and stuff I needed for $186. That's what I started out with. Now when I opened up here two years ago, I went for about a third increase, we had a nicer place, more parking room and everything. When I built this building here, it was $125,000. The land that I put it on was another $200,000. I had about $750,000 invested here before I opened up. That's the only way you can open up a business now—big. You can't open up little. Used to be back in the 30s, these car lots, they'd have three or four cars in their showroom. Now they got three or four hundred in their lot out there. That's how you got to open up now. You can't open up little like you used to.

Hawkeyed Glances: Gates & Sons Bar-B-Q

Ollie Gates walks in and *bam!*—everything is different. Like a cop cruising the highway, he has everybody eyeing their speedometers. The manager does the quick check-double-check. Is everything neat? Is the coffee fresh?

The rank and file, already finely tuned to a high pitch, play their parts up an octave. The sing-songy "Welcome to Gates; may I help you?" with which you are invariably slapped across the ears as soon as you walk in the door, gets—if it is possible—even more high-strung.

This is the Gates & Sons at the Paseo and Swope Parkway, the one behind the corporate headquarters and the Gates training facility. Just as the Paseo is a beautiful boulevard with wide, neutral ground and grass and trees, this restaurant is a bright, shiny place of brass railings and ceiling fans. As you walk in the glass doors, you see the lighted menu on the wall right in front of you and directly behind the women working at the counter. Even if another patron stands in front of you, there is always, it seems, one extra person behind that person, yelling the Gates greeting at you, preparing to take your order far faster than you can give it.

We have told the manager what we're doing and she has told Marcus Gates and he has come to our booth. Before we have said much, his father has arrived in the restaurant—from our booth we can see the changes in tempo that have trumpeted his arrival—and Marcus has left us to see if the older man is in the mood to talk.

He is a tall man, 6'3", and light-skinned, the color of unstained oak. He stands with military erectness. He speaks at first through impersonal, hawkeyed glances and a blank, smileless face. The people who work here know what he is saying. They rewipe clean counters with friction sufficient to generate flame.

Later, when he speaks in words, they are clipped and direct. "Yes," he will have some coffee.

We stand to greet him. Hawkeyed, he looks at us, through us, as if the look itself were an interrogation capable of revealing motives and intentions that our words might not betray.

Him: braided leather braces, fine gabardine pants, oxblood string-up shoes, monogrammed shirt, graying hair.

Us: caps, sneakers.

And our purpose seems small then. I hear myself explain it, and suddenly it sounds even to me as if our New York publisher is but a high school journalism teacher, our life's work merely an adolescent diversion, our demands on Mr. Gates's time excessive and ill-considered. And standing there, shaking hand extended, Frank is but a little schoolboy who has only recently become acquainted with the advanced techniques that more expert photographers use to avoid displaying their fingers so prominently in their pictures.

Then like the passing of bad weather the interrogation is over. Gates has his answers and they satisfy him. Without warning, the gods are dispensing moments of free time like shiny new pennies and Gates has decided to spend each of his on us. Ollie Gates, the Kansas City barbecue magnate, smoking a cigarette and drinking coffee with us as if we were old friends.

My own uneasiness doesn't result entirely from Gates's shifting mood. I have spent much of the afternoon drinking free refills of iced tea. The tea, the melted ice, the lemon juice—such a gentle bargain as I was guzzling them down—are knocking on the walls of my bladder with rude insistence. They long to be on the outside, to again be one with their fellow liquids in the shoreless seas and boundless oceans. It's a dilemma. If I depart to relieve myself I might return to find that this garrulous yin is once again a reticent yang. Worse, after my brief absence I might return a stranger, unmissed, unremembered, and unexcused from another session under the bright burning lights of Gates's interrogating stare. Though I may squirm and I may wobble, yet do I sit; yet do I scribble.

And in this booth, him and Frank on one side, me on the other, Gates fills in the details of a family history in the barbecue business, the form and outline of which we already know.

"We started out because of necessity," he says. "My father was a waiter on the Rock Island Railroad. He just got tired of serving somebody else. When he left the railroad he decided he wanted to settle down to some kind of speakeasy business. In those times the state law was that you stopped selling liquor at one-thirty. But the customers could bring whiskey in. So we didn't sell liquor, but we'd sell you the set-up. We were making more money doing those things that were supplementing the product than we were selling the product itself."

Gates's father died in 1960, but before that the younger man had already opened up his own barbecue place. "My dad died an old man at fifty-two," he tells us. "He went through some harder times than I

did." Then he adds, "I was never a drinker."

We don't tarry on the question of how he got from one restaurant to six. Rather, though it doesn't come up per se, we talk indirectly about Gates's sense of mission, his belief that there is something special about barbecue, his desire to do something of lasting importance with this food.

"The advent of integration—it hit black business worse than it did anything," he begins. "You see, black business had to compete for black dollars. Well, this is one business where the white businesses had to compete with me." And then the main point. "They took the fried chicken from us, but I refused to let them take the barbecue."

Race doesn't come up again in our discussions with Ollie Gates.

Let me restate that. We mention race again neither in word nor in euphemism, in the same way that even if we were engaged in a discussion of water the word "wet" might simply not come up. We are both Americans, which is to say that race for us is so ubiquitous as to often obviate the need for any actual mention of it. But as most statements (and even some silences) are in fact counterstatements of a kind, then much of what Ollie Gates has accomplished can rightly be viewed as a counterstatement to American racial history, to American racial assumption.

Gates is a man driven. He says he was and is "married to the business." Even though we don't talk about the competition, it is clear that he is a competitor. And he dresses well and walks with a certain

dignity as affirmation and advertisement of his successes. This is the fundamental character of the man. How then does this character express itself, given its specific time and race?

Most simply it expresses itself in the desire to succeed, to run a profitable business. But on the level of counterstatement, his personality expresses itself as a refutation of the assumption that the words "black" and "Negro" are synonymous with words like "slow" and "dirty." So his staff, most of whom are of African descent, are exaggerated in their efficiency, and his brass railings shine with near-blinding brilliance. And Gates knows enough history to know that in most of the competitions between the races, certainly those involving money, the white folks have won, their collective thumb not infrequently resting on the scales. So his success is a counterstatement to the assumption that, although black people cook barbecue, it takes a white man to run a barbecue business.

The old logo for Gates's restaurant was the typical barbecue logo: an old, beat-up covered wagon. There is some old signage around that still contains that emblem, but it has been replaced now by a picture of a man in spats and cane accompanied by the old Louis Armstrong composition that serves as the new Gates theme, "Struttin' with Some Barbecue." The point, he tells us, is to polish up the image of barbecue and the places that serve it.

As Jim Wilson, Gates's second-in-command, explains it, "The image of barbecue has been changed based on the concept that he first brought into the industry. It's been elevated to the point where if you are out and have your good clothes on you don't feel that you can't eat some barbecue. I think that's been the single most significant contribution. I think it's been national to the extent that the companies around the country imitate what happens in Kansas City."

Gates's name is synonymous with barbecue in Kansas City in a way that no other name is. No doubt he takes pride in the fact that this superiority expresses itself loudly without his ever having to move his lips.

As we take our tour of the kitchen we see signs on the wall like BAR-B-QUING IS AN ART; BE AN ARTIST OR BE GONE, and BAR B Q WITH FIRE, WATER AND SMOKE, and CLEAN AS YOU GO. If you have to remind your pitmaster to include fire, water, and smoke in his barbecue recipe, you won't be in business long. Clearly, then, the signs have another purpose. It seems that their function is to serve as a reminder of the philosophy and mission of this place. Some people believe that barbecue is accomplished with smoke only and that the meat never should be touched by flames. Others, like Gates, think that fire and the flavored smoke that results when the grease hits the fire are integral parts of barbecue. "This is called closed-pit barbecue," he tells us. "There's a difference between barbecuing, smoking, and curing meat. Barbecuing to me is done over the fire. I like smoked meat, but it's not my style."

When we return to Gates on another day for a second tasting, he invites us to take a ride with him and Jim Wilson. Before we get outside the office the phone rings, and Gates and Wilson are on it talking about a golf tournament they are helping to sponsor to raise funds for the Satchel Paige Stadium. They hold the conversation over the speaker phone, perhaps for the benefit of the visiting book authors. That over, we climb into Gates's Cadillac Fleetwood Brougham, Gates driving, Wilson in the passenger seat, and us in the back. We drive along Bruce Watkins Freeway, a street named in honor of a black politician whom Gates and Wilson befriended and supported and, before his untimely death, hoped to elect mayor. We drive past some of the sites where the old barbecue places used to be. Accompanied by the sound of pop music on the radio, we pass Ella Fitzgerald Lane and the site where Kansas City, which bills itself as "the City of Fountains," plans to build a memorial fountain to its hardest-swinging native son, Charlie "Yardbird" Parker, with some financial support from Gates. We pass some vacant lots and buildings in grave disrepair.

Finally we reach our destination, Heritage Hill. Gates and Wilson are here to inspect the bricklaying work in a moderate-income housing complex they've developed. These are gray apartments with balconies and maroon trim, as clean and sharp as anything in the suburbs but with inside-the-city charm. Gates, who graduated from Lincoln University in building trades, runs his own construction company specifically and exclusively to do the building and development work associated with his restaurants and residential developments. He and Wilson speak briefly to the woman who is apparently the property manager and then we are back in the car, headed to the Commissary, the plant where the company makes its barbecue sauce.

It is in a strip of commercial development, across the street from a Gates barbecue restaurant. In this part of town, they tell us, eighty percent of the people live in subsidized housing. We see for ourselves that the Gates properties here are the newest, shiniest buildings in the area.

On the ride back we again drive along the Paseo. Gates tells us that he is the president of Kansas City's Parks and Recreation Commission, which means he is a member of the bureaucracy that manages the boulevards here. He takes pride in the fact that along some of these streets whose residents are predominantly black, there are trees and tended lawns and other amenities not generally associated with this part of town. People along these streets pay a dollar per foot each year for the upkeep of the areas between the street and the sidewalk, and in return they get well-manicured streets. "When you improve a street like this, people take pride in it," he tells us.

"When you running for mayor?" Frank asks from the back seat.

"Never in life," he says, staring straight ahead with that hawkeyed look of his. "We have bigger and better things to do with our time."

Sherman Gibbs OWEN'S BARBECUE **LAKE CITY, SOUTH CAROLINA**

CHAPTER TEN

The Carolinas

The Irrelevance of Geography

As our travels took us toward the east coast, we encountered a phenomenon much like the one that Waverley Root describes in his study *The Food of France*. France, he found, could be divided into regions of cooking based on the type of shortening used. There was the butter region, the olive oil region, and the lard region (for Root, "lard" meant goose, duck, and/or pork fat). Each of these cooking styles, Root reported, was akin to the style of other countries. Italy, Spain, and Greece championed olive oil. Germany and Austria cooked largely with animal fat. The Netherlands, Belgium, and Denmark produce and utilize large amounts of butter. Thus the political boundaries of France did not coincide with strict culinary demarcations.

Similarly, the boundary lines that divide the two Carolinas from each other and from Georgia and Tennessee have little significance in the realm of food. The people nearest the line generally have far more in common with one another than with their compatriots in the hinterlands. For example, Sconyers' Bar-B-Que in Augusta, Georgia, serves barbecue hash, a South Carolina dish, even though boundary lines would dictate that it serve Brunswick stew, which is especially popular in, if not native to, Georgia.

Charles F. Kovacik, a University of South Carolina geography professor, has mapped the boundaries of the various barbecue sauce conceptions found in that state. Along the North–South Carolina border, a tomato-based sauce is used. Along the state's western border, the sauce is ketchup-based, a variation on the tomato sauce of the northern border. In most of the state, barbecue is served with a mustard-based sauce. Along the eastern coast the sauce is made of vinegar and peppers.

While this explains a great deal about what is happening in South Carolina, it doesn't explain how the vinegar and pepper sauce got to be so popular in western Tennessee, or how a less sweet version of a mustard-based sauce became the dominant taste among the barbecue places in Phenix City, Alabama, or why, despite the border, North Carolina barbecue is so similar to that of the state just below it.

Kovacik's map is a step in the right direction, though. Perhaps what we really need is a school of cartography dedicated to mapping regions based on culinary style rather than on such irrelevant considerations as political boundaries.

The Hamburger of the Twenty-first Century

We arrive in South Carolina in the wee hours of a Tuesday morning, having rushed from Oklahoma to get here (a quick shoulder sandwich in Memphis at Hawkins Grill was our only real stop). We want to have time to find the good places and then get back to them on the weekend, when they should be in full swing. Frank's half-brother Mark, a Columbia native who knows a little about almost everything, agrees to show us the places he has heard about, but he frequents none of them, he says, and can give us little real insight.

We stop at a couple of places that next day, all-you-can-eat places in strip shopping centers, catering to the lunch crowd. On self-serve steam tables there sit mounds of chopped barbecue, long sheets of crisply fried pork skins, and that side dish distinctive to South Carolina barbecue, hash and rice. The food is not very good. The meat has dried out on the steam tables. The sauces are red, ketchupy solutions rather than the mustard-based norm we've been told to expect in this part of the state. Clearly we haven't hit the real places yet.

It's the hash that requires some getting used to. Like blood sausage and chitterlings, it's a dish that has evolved because people don't want to waste any part of the pig. Traditionally it was a stew of organ meats—lungs and hearts and livers. A few places even sell "whole-head" hash, but most make it with meat and a little liver. Of course, South Carolina is rice country, so every meal, barbecue included, has rice as a side dish.

We learn our first lesson of South Carolina barbecue when, having exhausted these self-serve places, we try to find other barbecue restaurants. But commercial barbecue here takes place almost exclusively on Friday and Saturday. The primary exception is Maurice's Piggy Park in West Columbia, just across town from Columbia itself. It's the flagship of a small chain of barbecue places. The Piggy Park itself is actually a small complex of buildings: the restaurant, the corporate offices, and the Lighthouse Mission.

Outside is not so much a parking lot as a drive-in restaurant with an old-fashioned device at each space that allows you to order from your car. Immediately to the right of the entrance is a small display with a variety of leaflets and advertisements—old reviews of the barbecue, a flyer for Ross Perot's United We Stand organization, and several religious pamphlets. Frank carefully collects these papers, then double-checks to make sure he hasn't missed any or taken two of anything.

We order a sampler plate with hash and rice, barbecued ribs, and a Little Joe barbecue sandwich. It is always a surprise to find one of these large places serving decent food, but the Piggy Park does that. Throughout the meat there is the flavor of smoke from real wood. The hash is mild here, very little if any liver in it. Maurice's sauce is yellowish brown, somewhere between peanut butter and mustard in color. The closest approximation to the taste of the sauce is a honey-mustard salad dressing. The sauce has a similar combination of sweetness and tang, though it has both in slightly greater abundance than the salad dressing.

It is this mustard barbecue sauce for which Maurice Bessinger is famous, but I think fame on those grounds does him a disservice. As far as I know, he didn't invent the concept of mustard in barbecue sauce, so to base his fame on his version of a traditional sauce rather than on his culinary innovations is rather like crediting

James Naismith with inventing the bottomless fruit basket rather than the game of basketball. Maurice's true innovation in the world of barbecue is his introduction of the word "lite" to the vocabulary. Certainly there are barbecue places all over the country that offer chicken and fish, but that's cheating, representing as it does an if-you-can't-beat-them-join-them form of surrender to current fads. The nutritionists, by insisting that we eat more whole grains and fresh produce, have made the dubious selection of the colon as the body part most qualified to run our lives at table. Maurice rejects their conclusions and has taken data from their own organs (among them the American Heart Association, the U.S. Department of Agriculture, and the South Carolina Wildlife & Marine Resources Department) to prove them wrong.

In a bright pink leaflet entitled "Lite Barbecue," Maurice compares the nutritional evaluations of fish, fowl, and beef performed by these organizations with the results Silliker Laboratories obtained in testing Maurice's Gourmet Barbecue. Granted, the barbecue is on the high end of the calorie, fat, and cholesterol counts. But Maurice's point is that it's not as far afield as the experts might have you believe. A skinless breast of chicken has only 1.5 grams of fat, while Maurice's Gourmet Barbecue has 9.0 grams. But tuna in oil has 10.2 grams, and a broiled beef rib steak has 10.9 grams. What's more, an entire sixteen-ounce bottle of Maurice's Gourmet BBQ Sauce, we learn from this same document, contains only 4.8 milligrams of cholesterol.

No parallel calculation is given for the amount of sugar or calories found in the bottle.

As Mark and I finish the ribs and drink the refills of sweet tea that the nice lady keeps pouring, he tells me what he knows of Maurice. How Maurice once ran for governor, campaigning in a white suit and on a white horse, pledging to end corruption in that accent which Mark says is low-country, from the coastal part of the state rather than Columbia. So my first picture of Maurice is somehow related to white-suited Colonel Sanders of Kentucky Fried Chicken fame.

"When we get to meet Brer Bessinger?" Frank asks enthusiastically. And the quest begins.

∽

We walk across the parking lot and into the building with the sign over the entrance that says FLYING PIG DISPATCH HEAD-QUARTERS. Inside the building we explain to the woman what we are there for. While we sit in the waiting area, she calls someone on the phone to see if our interview request will be granted. There is a sign above the door that separates the waiting area from the rest of the office. It reads PLANTATION ROOM. It is unclear to me whether we are in the Plantation Room already or just outside it. It's a question that will get no answer today. The receptionist tells us that Maurice will not be able to see us and invites us to call and make an appointment on another day.

Outside the office, Mark tells me that the problem is that we just walked in out of nowhere with no appointment, wearing jeans and jogging suits and generally looking like—"like a writer and a photographer," I say, finishing his sentence. And we expand that exchange, him telling me how these people down here in Columbia are and how they are to be approached, and me giving him my dissertation on newsroom haberdashery, a subject about which I know enough to be certain that if Maurice has been interviewed as many times as the clippings suggest, then he has been interviewed often by people far less well clad than we.

Frank, of course, sides with his brother, first yelling at me, "I told you we wasn't spruced up enough to be jawboning with Brer Bessinger. Now we ain't never gon' get to see the Plantation Room!" Then to his brother, "Where could I get me some easy walkers and a nice pair of over-hauls?"

Following the receptionist's advice I do call the next day and meet with a similar lack of fortune. And I call again the day following that, and again I am told that Mr. Bessinger is unavailable. He expects to remain so into the next week, the receptionist says. I say that I will be back in Columbia in roughly a week and would like, if possible, to pick a time when it might be convenient to see him during that coming week, assuming a time could be found that would fit into Mr. Bessinger's doubtlessly hectic schedule. And I am told then that these things are hard to predict and that I would be best advised to call back upon my return and try again.

We have been staying with Peggy Stewart, Frank's stepmother. Frank spent part of his childhood with her and his father and in so doing became "cousins" with her nieces and also the nephew of Fred and Bessie Jenkins, Peggy's sister and brother-in-law. Fred and Bessie live a few doors down from Peggy's house, and the three of them spend many of their evenings playing cards together. We join them this evening over cards and conversation and scotch, the older ones playing, the younger ones drinking. And using that abbreviated middle name by which Frank was known to them then, they talk about good times with Lee. Times when he shot BB guns and went swimming in the creek.

Before long the subject has turned to barbecue and our experiences at the Piggy Park. They tell us that Maurice Bessinger was a hero of the' segregationist South, vowing never to serve black people in his restaurant. "He put a sign out on his sidewalk that no Negroes would be allowed," Peggy says, "right on Main Street. That was his earlier place. Then he moved over on Charleston Highway. I'm not sure if he called it Piggy Park then or what."

Bessie and Fred remember there being a sit-in at Bessinger's in which their daughter, Adrienne, and her cousin Sharon participated. So we call Adrienne in St. Louis and she tells us that she remembers there being a sign in the window, but she doesn't remember there being an actual demon-stration, although Sharon was participating in demonstrations at the time. What she remembers specifically about the Piggy Park is that one day she and Sharon decided to mount their own two-woman demon-stration and that Maurice himself greeted them with steely resolve.

"Sharon was at Benedict College and I was in high school," Adrienne says. "There had been a white guy to come down from New York to help out and we used to meet in the basement of Bethel A.M.E. Church. One day me and Sharon went into Maurice's and he just came to the door with a gun and said 'No' and we decided it wasn't worth getting killed over. I just remember him coming to the door with that rifle."

"That just don't sound like Brer Bes-singer," Frank says, shaking his head in anguished defense of his unmet friend. "A hickory switch, maybe, but I can't see Brer Bessinger coming at nobody with no gun."

And Frank may be right. When we call Sharon in Atlanta she remembers the story a little differently. "We were with the NAACP and a group of us had gone to the restaurant," she recalls. "If I remember cor-rectly, we went more than once. They said if we wanted food we had to go around to the back. I remember the sign. I don't remem-ber the gun."

☙

It has become obvious to me that if I am to meet Maurice, it will require a costly expen-diture of pride. I'll have to camp out at the Piggy Park or beseech him with all the pas-sion and surrender of a scorned lover desirous of amorous reinstatement. These are not my strong suits. So I resign myself to meeting him through the written record he has left of himself.

From the handouts Frank has collected I discover that "the taste that made the South famous" was not pan-fried chicken or Jack Daniel's whiskey but Maurice's Gourmet Barbecue Sauce. I know that in the August 28, 1989, issue of *People Weekly* Bessinger's was picked as the "Best All-in-one Barbecue Restaurant: eat-in, takeout, drive-through, mail-order and Bible-study mission."

I know too that Jane and Michael Stern, the traveling syndicated food writers, had a near-orgasmic meal at Maurice's. They could hardly contain their pleasure as they recollected their experience in print:

> Dining at Maurice Bessinger's is a stirring experience. It is the kind of uniquely American meal to which we would eagerly take visitors from another country if we wanted to show them the spunk, character and quality of American gastronomy.
>
> Pardon our emotionalism, but Piggie Park inspires patriotic thoughts, and not only because the food is so darn good. The largest American flag in South Carolina waves above its parking lot.

I was pleased though not stirred by the food at Maurice's, and I envy the Sterns their experience. But I do not envy them the experience of feeding on Piggie Pocket Burgers, a delicacy for which they print the recipe in their column. It calls for two pounds of lean ground beef, eight ounces shredded American or cheddar cheese, one-half cup chopped onion, one-half cup barbecue sauce, salt, pepper, and four large pita pockets. Maurice has a mustard-colored flier with recipes for some of his own culinary creations, including Crock Pot Magic Meat Loaf, Microwave Barbecue Chicken, and Busy-Day Barbecue. This last dish consists of only three ingredients: a can of luncheon meat, some onion, and of course some his own barbecue sauce. The Sterns' Piggie Pocket Burgers is, from all indications, a cross between the Bessinger inventions Saucy Burgers and Pocketburgers, the key differences being that Maurice requires less onion and specifically calls for Maurice Bessinger's Barbecue Sauce.

From the pictures of Maurice that appear in these clippings, he doesn't look at all like Colonel Sanders or the White Knight, as Mark's description led me to imagine. Rather, he's a dark-haired, middle-aged, smiling man who sometimes wears a large hat and who as of 1986 was graying a bit at the temples.

I am disappointed that absent from the material Maurice provides on himself is any detailed biography or any mention of his activities in defense of freedom of religion and the sanctity of intrastate commerce. Sharon's and Adrienne's accounts of life in Maurice's South Carolina prior to the coming of full democracy, while contradictory on the minor points, do manage to capture the spirit of the old Maurice. But for the full details of the Maurice of this era it is necessary to look to old newspaper clippings and court documents. And it is clear from these documents why Sharon and Adrienne may not be in absolute agreement on Maurice. He is a complicated figure, a man difficult to pin down.

We know from a couple of long profiles in *The State* newspaper in Columbia that Maurice got into the restaurant business as a child, frying ham and eggs for the breakfast crowd before he went to school and serving dinner late into the evening. He was hardworking and his father had promised the business to him, but the older man died while Maurice, a senior in high school, was too young to take it over. Disgusted, he ran off to the Korean War, returning upon discharge to open his own restaurant.

And had things stayed as they were, he might have been only a restaurateur, but things changed, moved in directions counter to his and thereby gave birth to Maurice Bessinger the activist. Specifically, the United States Congress outlawed discrimination in public accommodations like restaurants. As it turns out, Sharon has been modest in discussing her role in the South Carolina civil rights movement. Along with Anne P. Newman and John Mungin, she was a plaintiff in *Newman v. Piggy Park Enterprises*, a desegregation lawsuit.

Maurice mounted a vigorous defense, admirable if only for its creativity. He didn't deny that his restaurants discriminated on the basis of race. (Black customers were served, but only on a takeout basis.) Rather, he contended that federal laws governing interstate commerce were irrelevant to his restaurant because all the food it served was processed and purchased in South Carolina. Furthermore, Maurice said he didn't serve out-of-state travelers. ("If the curb girl who serves the order notices that a customer's car bears an out-of-state license, she is instructed to inquire whether such customer is an interstate traveler or is residing in South Carolina," the court records state. But the court also found that "no effort is made by defendant to determine whether a Negro customer who purchases food on a take-out basis is an interstate traveler.")

To top it off, "defendant Bessinger further contend[ed] that the [Civil Rights Act of 1964] violate[d] his freedom of religion under the First Amendment 'since his religious beliefs compel him to oppose any integration of the races whatever.'" But the court found that most of the beef and pork and chickens and cheese and shrimp and cabbage and lettuce and tomatoes and paper products and limes that were served in the restaurant were processed or produced outside the state of South Carolina.

"Neither is the court impressed by defendant Bessinger's contention that the judicial enforcement of the public accommodations provisions of the Civil Rights Act of 1964 upon which this suit is predicated violates the free exercise of his religious beliefs in contravention of the First Amendment to the Constitution," the court wrote.

Maurice lost at trial and appeal.

He didn't give up, though. He managed George Wallace's presidential campaigns in South Carolina in 1964 and 1968, and in that way remained true to the segregationist cause. But by 1974 Bessinger had become a born-again Christian and a candidate for governor of South Carolina. He promised to return integrity to public office, recommended the death penalty for second-offense drug pushers, and vowed to "personally pull the switch" on death-row convicts. He received less than three percent of the votes cast in the Democratic primary.

If Maurice's statements are to be believed, much has changed since then. "I used to be a mean and a bad and low-down, rotten person," he told the newspaper. "I have always been sincere in everything that I've done, but you can be sincerely wrong," he said with a laugh in another interview, then added later, "When you have a truly religious conversion, you don't see black and white, you don't see rich and poor, everything is level."

And perhaps these statements reflect the Maurice that Frank and I would have met had we made it beyond the waiting area. We'll never know.

Avoiding Gas

In 1979, Allie Patricia Wall and Ron L. Layne, two Carolina writers, undertook a survey of the state's barbecue. *Hog Heaven: A Guide to South Carolina Barbecue*, they called their book. They traveled about five thousand miles and concluded among other things that "on any given Thursday over 80,000 pounds of pork hit pits, grills, ovens, and cookers around the state." That sentence sums up the irony of barbecue not only in South Carolina but to a great extent in North Carolina as well. This is certainly barbecue country, but a large portion of the meat is neither smoked nor grilled. It is baked.

"With the decline of the open pit came some new-fangled methods of cooking barbecue," Wall and Layne wrote. "Restaurant owners discovered the advantages of modern technology: faster cooking, easier cooking, less labor, cleaner food and facilities, less danger of fires. One method used in about 40% of the barbecue places visited in South Carolina is the electric cooker."

Barbecue in the Carolinas almost always takes the form of chopped meat sandwiches. By the time the meat and sometimes the fat and the skin have been minced together and smothered with sauce, the taste of the barbecue has been so masked as to make it difficult to tell how the meat was prepared. But if the meat is the main attraction and the sauce merely an enhancement, this technique defeats the entire purpose of barbecue. *Hog Heaven* is useful in part because it tells about the cooking technique used at each place. Sikes' Bar-B-Q, fourteen miles east of Columbia in Eastover, is described as "open pit - charcoal … Located in a white cement-block building connected to an Exxon station, Sikes' Bar-B-Q is a well-packed, well-worn establishment with a friendly atmosphere." So we go there.

The Exxon station is no longer, but we suspect that little else has changed, because the restaurant interior has the rustic look that comes from the accumulation of years and memorabilia. There are hornets' nests and old posters of college football schedules all around the inside of the white cement building, and when you order a barbecue sandwich they put meat to bread and then press it in an old-fashioned steamer which warms and perhaps moistens it a little. Throughout the chopped pork there is the strong flavor of mustard, but not tempered with as much sweetness as the sauce at the Piggy Park. We eat the sandwiches and taste the hash and rice, having not yet acquired a liking for them.

Allen Sikes with his black "Sikes: BBQ Capital of the World" baseball cap joins us at our table, telling us how his father started this place in 1965 as a grocery store and how after selling barbecue one Fourth of July the family gradually found itself in the barbecue business. They barbecued whole hogs then over the coals from hardwood. But his father always said that people didn't want to pay the same price for fat as they do for lean meat, so gradually they moved to barbecuing hams.

"You didn't see no fat in our barbecue, did you?" Allen asks. "You didn't see any grease in it, did you? That's the reason we cook the whole ham, 'cause of less fat and less grease."

There have been other changes. Wood got harder and harder to come by, so they use charcoal now. And they got to be so busy, Allen tells us, that they were up all night barbecuing. They had to do something, so they bought an electric pit. "Your meat ain't gon' take any smoke at all until it gets about done," he explains. So they cook the hams on the electric pit for eight and a half hours, then put them on the charcoal pit to finish them off. "You get the same identical smoke flavor," he tells us.

On the way out he introduces us to two of his regular customers, a man and wife who are connoisseurs of this state's barbecue. They tell us to go to King's Tree and find the barbecue place there that they can't remember the name of, but that is good and well known.

∞

On their advice we begin the eastward journey toward King's Tree, a town thirty-eight miles from Sumter. Along the highway there are farms and old homes, herds of cattle and some horses. But by far the most impressive buildings are the churches. The gleam of their white painted wood; the manicured fineness of their lawns; the skyward reaches of their steeples; the graveyards right beside them, white paint of tombstones and grave markers also gleaming—we are officially in the Bible Belt now. We are greeted by reminders like "Jesus died for your sins. Thank Him" and "Storm Clouds are gathering. Judgement is coming. Turn to Jesus now."

It is unclear to Frank and me which restaurant the couple meant for us to find, McKenzie's or Brown's. McKenzie's sign reads "Cooked the old fashion way. With oak wood," and there is a picture of a chef with a whole hog on the pit. But McKenzie's is closed for keeps.

By the time we reach Brown's it's late afternoon. Even if the place was very much alive at lunchtime, we are now the only customers in this huge, antiseptic building. And though she's polite enough not to actually say it, you can tell that Frank and I seem a bit strange to the sixtyish white woman behind the counter, both of us walking through the buffet line but only me putting food on my plate and Frank following as if he were just glad to have gotten out of the house and into the sunshine. I'm self-conscious because it's an all-you-can-eat deal. We're not trying to feed two people for the price of one, we're just trying to get enough food to taste it. It's difficult to explain, so Frank smiles at the woman and says in his generic accent, "He's not due to feed me again yet," which does absolutely nothing for our image.

And if we seem strange to this woman, this place seems no less strange to us, a barbecue place with a buffet that includes sweet potatoes and salted side meat and turkey leg meat and string beans in addition to the expected cracklins and hush puppies and rice and hash. There are ribs, but they look scraggly, as if they have been pulled from the sides of whole hogs rather than cooked in slabs. Adding to the strangeness, once we have gotten a little of everything the woman asks us, "Yaw'll don't need no gravy to go with your barbecue?" which is what she calls the vinegar and pepper sauce that replaces the mustard-based condiments found elsewhere in the state.

The food tastes like cafeteria food, even the barbecue. It is all inoffensively bland;

neither the pork nor the turkey has any smoke flavor. While I rearrange the food around the plate, trying to make it look eaten, Frank goes up to the counter and begins talking to the woman.

"Yaw'll barbecue the whole hog or just the shoulders?" he asks.

"Around here we do the whole hogs. Where yaw'll from?"

"I live in New York," Frank says. "They don't have nothing like this up there. Can we see the pit?"

In mild amazement the woman announces our request to her co-worker, saying, "They from up the road. They haven't ever seen it."

So we are allowed in the back to speak to the pitmaster and observe a bit of his process. And the pit area is also antiseptic, with cement floors and the shining stainless steel of range hoods and cookers. Nowhere is there the soot of burned wood or the smell of meat over fire. There are three huge pits in a row, each with a headless pink hog stretched out on it.

The pitmaster, a hollow-eyed, reticent man, tells us that they cook the hogs for six or seven hours, with all gas heat. There's not even the little stick of burning wood that some cookers use to impart flavor.

∞

We begin asking other people where there might be decent barbecue either between here and Columbia or between here and Charleston, as we would be willing to go in either direction. We find McCabe's Bar-B-Q in Manning, which boasts that its meat is

"Old Fashion Pit Cooked with Wood." And it tastes that way, a wonderful sandwich of vinegar-sauced pork that makes you regret having wasted so much stomach space on a day's worth of unworthy meats. It's a quaint, attractive place. Even before we are told, we can guess from the friendly bickering behind the counter that these old ladies are old friends if not kin.

When we ask about the place, they point us in the direction of Dave McCabe, at a corner table. He's not much for conversation. But still he tells us that his family (two brothers, a mother, and two aunts) has owned and operated this place for six years, having bought the old Haley's Barbecue. And the recipe is basically his father's old recipe, whole hogs cooked over the coals of oak and hickory and some pecan wood.

"Time, wood, temperature, and seasoning," he tells us as if this were itself the recipe. And though there may be less economy in a whole hog, they still barbecue them because "you get more variety of meat from the whole hog, and a lot of people like a different variety of meat."

The conversation ends on a chilling note. "I think you're seeing the last of the Mohicans," he says. "We're doing it the hard way and there are probably more easy ways to do it. In the long haul I think you're eventually going to see everybody going to gas or electric. If I'm around by then, we might even be forced to do that here."

The Scotts

Scotts' is a difficult place to find, even once they tell you to take a right at the fire station and that it'll be just up the road and on your left. The first problem is that the people around here talk with their teeth clenched, so the words must escape into conversation and in the process are likely to rub off a letter or two on the calcium bars that imprison them. Then too, these coastal South Carolina Americans, the black ones, talk like they were from the West Indies or somewhere, saying "mon" for "man" and "a-boat" for "about." So they keep telling us a-boat how far to go before taking a right turn, but we never see the boat, and then the next person we ask bids us turn around and tells us a-boat how far to go before making a left. All this turning, we're told, is to take place at the fire station, a building that doesn't look like a fire station even after we know it is one.

Then when we think we have found the place, the drive path is wet and muddy like a rice paddy. They do grow rice here, so we're cautious not to just drive up the path and sink. A man assures us that "itainboaggy," but that means nothing to us even when he repeats it. Frank is driving about two miles an hour, looking on both sides of the car to see where there might be solid ground, and the man is looking at us like we're idiots and saying again, "Itainboaggy!" Finally the word comes apart: it-ain't-boggy.

So we keep driving until we get to an unfinished wood frame house. We park and explain what we are doing to the man sitting there, and he directs us to a room at the back of this long, narrow building in which the "hoags" are being barbecued. In this dark, hot, smoky room there is a cinderblock pit with wire across it on which two pigs cook.

Ricky Scott does most of the work now. He puts the hogs on in the morning and his father watches them during the day until Ricky comes home from his job; then Ricky takes over. Oak coals are burning down in one corner of the room, conspiring with the sun-drenched heat of this breezeless day to make the interior of this building feel like a kiln. The heat of the coals has long ago melted Ricky's shovel into a variation on itself. He uses it to move more coals under the hog. The hog is butterflied on its stomach and the coals are put all around it so that the thick parts, the hams and shoulders, get a lot of heat while the inner sections don't get burned. Then, with help from a friend, Ricky turns the hogs skin side down and spreads the embers beneath the entire carcass. The coals are very hot now. As he puts the vinegar and red pepper sauce onto the pig, it begins boiling violently. A few minutes later the cooking is over.

In the front room of this building Mrs. Scott, Ricky's mother, is in charge. The pigs arrive on particle boards and the meat is so soft that she cuts it with a large spoon. In white styrofoam containers, the hash and rice and bread await the final addition to the orders.

The meat is absolutely wonderful. The vinegar flavor is mild, not sour or biting.

Hogs on the Pit SWEATMAN'S BARBECUE **HOLLY HILL, SOUTH CAROLINA**

The meat itself is so tender it melts. And the pit-crisped skin is infinitely better than most of what you get for cracklins either in restaurants or in cellophane bags.

Sitting outside while his mother works and his nieces and nephews play, Ricky Scott explains the origin of this operation to us. "Well, like I say, we was just doing this 'cause we used to have the place set up behind our hoase. People complain, they say, 'Mon, yaw'll ought to get yourself established, you know, where yaw'll can barbecue for the public 'cause this stuff is really good.' And we thought aboat it, family talked aboat it, and then after awhole we just put it together and we started from there. Quite naturally the crode was steady coming, you know. Every Thursday we have it jam up, they travel around late to get that barbecue, just before dark."

Sherman Gibbs

Wall and Layne are apparently polite, genteel people. As a result their book, while helpful in many ways, is far too generous in its descriptions of restaurants. It doesn't bother me that they elect not to damn restaurants for mediocre barbecue. Bad food, while unfortunate, is not criminal. Excessively negative reviews serve no useful purpose; they lower a chef's spirits without having an inverse impact on his abilities.

But the writers' description of Owen's Bar-B-Q in Lake City ("almost too moist with a strong spicey-hot flavor") only vaguely distinguishes this place from other restaurants the book discusses, and thus both the pitmaster and the potential diner are done a sizable disservice. Owen's serves some of the best barbecue in the state. It's a shame that the guide fails to make that point more emphatically.

With its pictures of Jesus on the wall and the Toastmaster in which they steam the sandwiches, Owen's looks like a diner straight out of the Mayberry R.F.D. television show. We order our usual sandwich to split, and it reminds me of no other experience we have had in our travels as much as the shoulder sandwiches at Hawkins in Memphis. There is the same thoroughness of smoke flavor, a similar thin, sweet, tomato-based sauce, and of course the same plain white hamburger bun.

Sherman Gibbs, the pitmaster here, is a light brown man with light brown eyes. He is the adopted son of Chessie Owens and the late Mellon Owens. Mrs. Owens is not feeling well today, so before we can say much to her, she retires for the afternoon. But it's late and the other customers have left, so Mr. Gibbs talks freely. He sketches for us the story of how he, a black child, came to be adopted by a white family.

"My mother left me when I was small, left me with my grandmother," he says. "His brother—the old man's brother—I went to working with him. Then he took sick and so he told the old man to take me and raise me. I was twelve years old and I been here ever since. As far as mother, the only mother I really actually knew was her and the old man, her husband, was my daddy, see.

"Well, you see what color I was. My daddy—they better not say nothing about me, or they would get a fist right in the mouth. He didn't play around no way. If they said my hide was black I'd tell him who said it and he would go and talk with them the next day.

"We used to use oak wood, but the people got so tight on that oak wood we use charcoal now. We don't use no gas. The old man didn't like gas and neither do I. I can't stand that gas. It don't give the meat no taste—you start adding artificial stuff to it and all of that. You get a pretty good flavor with charcoal, but you don't get as good a flavor as you do with oak wood."

Sweatman's

Sweatman's is open only on Friday and Saturday. You can't even call them on other days. But theirs is supposed to be some of the best barbecue in the state, so we drive over to Holly Hill this Thursday evening under the assumption that if they intend to serve on Friday, someone has to be cooking on Thursday.

That someone is Chalmon Smalls. Behind the renovated house that serves as the dining room, Mr. Smalls is lying in a wheelbarrow cushioned by a cardboard box and a piece of red cloth. Danny Jenkins, a younger man who shares the cooking duties, is similarly relaxed.

Mr. Smalls, in his baseball cap and full-length blue apron, is neither impressed nor unimpressed by our presence. We've interrupted his nap. That doesn't make him happy.

Danny, on the other hand, goes out of his way to let us know he's unimpressed. "Who yaw'll say yaw'll was?" he asks, his tone one of interrogation more than curiosity. After we have answered his questions, he says the same thing that everybody says to people who do what we do—"Yaw'll gon' send me a free copy of the book?" Neither of them wants to say much about what they are doing until we get clearance from Mr. Sweatman.

At six-thirty the next morning we drive back out to meet Mr. Sweatman. He's a shy, gentle man with watery blue eyes. Once he gives the word that it's okay to talk to us, things improve a bit in the smokehouse. Mr. Smalls shows us around the cookers, the place at the corner of the L-shaped building at which they burn the oak wood down to coals, the cinderblock pits, the elaborate pulley system that they use to lift the metal tops off the pits when it is time to turn or sauce the meat. "Six and six," he explains. "Turn 'em on they belly first for six hours, then turn 'em over for six. I don't have to guess at them hogs. When I put up the cover, I know it's time to turn 'em." On a cart Mr. Smalls has a pail of golden barbecue sauce. With a dipper he puts sauce over the meat. Then, as if to prove to us that he really does know what he's doing, he pulls off a little of the meat, still hot, juice dripping, and hands it to us.

It's wonderful. The sauce is neither too sweet nor too heavy, so it does not blot out the smoke flavor. Mr. Smalls watches us as we smile in appreciation. He tries not to blush at his own perfection.

The cooked hogs are brought inside an air-conditioned room and placed on a stain- less steel table. Here two men and two women scrape off the fat, cut the meat into lean chunks, and put the skin on the side to be returned to the pit to make cracklins. Every so often the fat is scraped off the table with a dustpan and put into a bin.

The women talk a little. The men are silent.

Sweatman's dining area is an old converted house. I sit at one of the tables there with Mr. Sweatman. He's a kind man, and you get the impression he'd tell you anything you'd want to know. But he's shy and our conversation flows erratically. I ask him why he opens only two days a week. "It takes me just about all week to get ready," he says. "I farm too. I still farm like a fool. Besides, I wouldn't want to do it every day. In fact I couldn't, not at my age now. I'll be seventy next month."

Sweatman's is buffet style, all you can eat, like most places around here. The meat that we had seen taken off the pit and trimmed is now on a steam table along with hash and rice and cracklins and ribs. Sitting down amid lunchtime discussions of Atlanta Braves baseball, I get a chance to taste what has happened to this meat since Mr. Smalls let us sample it several hours ago. It has not fared well. The process of losing its skin and fat and then being placed on the steam table has sapped its essence. It's moist still, but mostly because of the sauce. That's what puzzles me: Is there a reason not to leave the meat intact and let the diners or the servers carve it up as it is to be eaten?

It isn't until we stop at Shealy's Bar-B-Q Buffet Style in Leesville that I begin to understand the workings of commercial barbecue in this state. Shealy's is in a large building, undecorated both inside and out. We walk through the buffet past the usual barbecue and hash and all the boiled and fried vegetables that you find on any other cafeteria buffet line. The tables here are in long rows; if it's crowded you will be literally rubbing elbows with a stranger. The dessert buffet, of which green Jell-O is the star, is in the middle of the restaurant, placed away from the entree buffet as if to minimize crowding.

Most of the people working here are older women, retirees perhaps, happy to have some extra money or simply a good reason to get out of the house. These old ladies dote on you, especially if you happen to be a man unaccompanied and thus uncared for by a female companion. The women remind you to get yourself some more, it being buffet style and all and you being a growing young man with no one to look after you. And we smile broadly as they bring tea and more tea, but even good manners cannot bring me to accept these dear ladies' suggestion that I have some Jell-O.

And I understand then why South Carolina barbecue places are set up this way. This place resembles nothing so much as a church social. There are no private booths or small tables in these places because, as in church, there are only the friends that you've met and those that you haven't. In either case the thought of not sitting with your Christian neighbors is unheard of. And it's buffet style because, as at church, part of the point of serving the food is to encourage fellowship and perhaps to allow the cooks to bask in the warm feeling all cooks get when diners ask for seconds or thirds. In the Baptist Church there are the ushers in their white uniforms who seat you and serve you and dote on you at the suppers. And though not all of these places have older women working, McCabe's and Brown's and Shealy's do.

Which is not to say that this is a conscious or intentional replication. Rather, the point is that the tradition of barbecue is one of fellowship and celebration in a way that is not true of other food traditions. You might very well have fried chicken or pot roast at home and not invite other people. But if you are going through the trouble of barbecuing, especially the trouble of barbecuing a whole hog, it is likely to be an event for the extended family and a large number of friends as well. So when barbecue became institutionalized and commercialized in South Carolina, it apparently sought to retain some of that feeling of fellowship, a feeling that is best exemplified by perhaps the greatest of South Carolina institutions, the church.

Maurice Bessinger is just one man whose personal relationship with God does not necessarily say much about the religion in his home state. Yet even at an establishment like his, which is unabashedly commercial, there is something of that church social gentility. Since it was not crowded when we were there, the waitress remem-

bered us and brought our food directly to our table without the use of whatever system they use to match customer and order when it is more crowded. That initial point of contact between us and our waitress carried over to the other bit of personal service we received, the refills of iced tea. They don't just refill your glass. They ask you if you want more, and in so doing they comment on something else—the nice cap you're wearing or how much Frank and Mark look like brothers. With his mix of religion, barbecue, political conservatism, and a segregationist past, Maurice Bessinger is indeed a fitting emblem for South Carolina barbecue. In fact, he may be its most fitting emblem.

Smokey Joe's Bar-B-Q, Spartanburg

∾

We have gotten into the habit of calling places around South Carolina and asking them if by "barbecue" they mean meat smoked over wood or charcoal or merely baked or broiled in an electric or gas oven. Sometimes we forget, but we don't forget this time because we've just eaten at the Beacon, Spartanburg's culinary landmark. We have stood in a long line of natives and tourists, all excited to be eating here. But we can't finish the sandwich we order. It is that bad.

It's strange to have to ask for a definition of barbecue in South Carolina, of all places. But it's necessary. We wish we'd remembered to ask the people at the Beacon. Thumbing through the Yellow Pages as we are driving through Spartanburg,

I see Smokey Joe's. I call and ask the standard question.

"Sir, I don't know any other way to cook barbecue," comes the reply. I get directions.

This place isn't on one of the big streets like the Beacon and the Spartanburg location of Maurice's Piggy Park. A tourist won't happen upon it. But the food is good. The sauce is tomatoey-sweet and a nice accompaniment to the tender St. Louis–cut ribs and the sizzling hush puppies.

Joe Wynn grew up eating barbecue in Birmingham, Alabama. When he speaks of the barbecue in his adopted state he colors his tone with the excruciating combination of disgust and loathing that children express when asked to eat something they don't like. He pronounces hash "harsh," with a mocking formality that highlights the British overtones of the accents in this part of the country. Mustard-based sauces look like "baby shit," he says. "My taste buds rejected it."

He had been a district sales manager with General Motors, a job he had promised himself he wouldn't keep for more than ten years. He'd been there nine years, eleven months, and fifteen days when he was fired. He opened up Smokey Joe's Bar-B-Q ("Delightfully different") because of how bad he found the barbecue in his adopted state.

In the end we find he has tricked us. There is no conventional pit, only an electric cooker with a strip of pecan wood, the electricity for heat, the wood for flavor. Somehow he has made it work.

Gathering Wood SWEATMAN'S HOLLY HILL, SOUTH CAROLINA

I went to every place here trying to get barbecue, and I got this bun with this soupy stuff on it. Have you ever heard of pints and quarts of barbecue? Those are liquid terms! My reaction was always, "Good Lord, where have I landed? What is this I keep getting when I ask for barbecue?" I barbecued for the first time in my life when I got here. I figured, "If I can't buy it, I'll cook it."

They all told me that to make barbecue you take this stew-beef-type meat and put it in a wash pot. Put in one third of the weight in onions and start boiling and stirring all night on the third of July. Then you pour in your barbecue—meaning your sauce. Black or white, it didn't matter. They told me the same thing. They call it "harsh," barbecue harsh. The end result was pretty much guaranteed heartburn or indigestion. I started this business because of harsh; I'm trying to bring some sanity and respect to the word "barbecue."

Prior to having my barbecue experience here with this barbecue harsh junk, I had promised myself I was going to open me a barbecue place in Spartanburg. I had never dreamed before of being in a restaurant business. The way it happened it just seemed as if it was all destined.

Being with GM in sales, I learned the four most important things in business are location, location, location, and location. But God, in his infinite wisdom, didn't give me enough money to get where I thought I needed to be. Had I opened downtown and paid downtown prices I wouldn't have lasted six months. No kind of way.

This has been the toughest thing I ever faced in trying to bring barbecue into this town. The Beacon is a Spartanburg tradition; there are people here who will frequent the Beacon two or three times a week. I will eventually become a Spartanburg tradition. People will forget that I'm from out of town. My feeling is, once these people taste real barbecue, this is going to be my town.

Joe Wynn SMOKEY JOE'S **SPARTANBURG, SOUTH CAROLINA**

North Carolina

Before we started this book, back when we were traveling the world with the Wynton Marsalis band, Frank kept asking everybody where he could get good barbecue. When we got to the eastern part of North Carolina, we kept hearing about the barbecue in Wilson, one of this state's many barbecue capitals. "Your best place for barbecue is Beal's," a young woman told us. "B-e-a-l-s?" I asked so I could write it down. "No," she said, "B-i-l-l-s. Beal's."

The gig in Wilson was real cool. The band played at Barton College in the gymnasium. The band members always seem to play their best in these small places. It is as if they feel especially good to be asked to play their music in a place where they assume jazz is not often heard.

The dressing room was a classroom down the hall from the gym. After sound check there was a meal there for us, pecan pie and iced tea and maybe even some greens. But the highlight was Bill's barbecue. Frank beamed.

The ribs were huge, funny-looking bones that were no longer in slabs but already separated from each other. The sauce accompanying them was a thin, almost clear, vinegary liquid. Since then we have seen a lot of barbecue like this, but back then it struck us as odd.

When people ask us about barbecue at the large chain restaurants and nonbarbecue establishments, we always make a distinction between good food and good barbecue. It is possible to make great spare ribs or brisket in an oven without benefit of smoke or fire. But that's not barbecue. The meat from Bill's fit into that category for us. It was okay, but we tasted no smoke. We feared for the quality of North Carolina barbecue.

Outside Meat

Barbecue in North Carolina exists primarily in the towns and smaller cities. Checking the phone book in Charlotte, for example, we see very few listings for barbecue, whereas in other Southern cities of similar size there are dozens. Since we are passing through Charlotte, we decide to stop at one of these places. We choose Bar-B-Q King Drive-Inn Restaurant. We sit in the Legend eating a barbecue sandwich with a red, tangy vinegar-based solution that we like. But overall the meat on this bun leaves us unsatisfied. It lacks the deep smoked richness that we're looking for.

We stop next in Lexington, which is nationally famous in part because it has seventeen barbecue places for a population of only seventeen thousand. Though not the oldest, the most famous of these places is Lexington Barbecue. And something about it feels rustic and classic—the way the counter sits right in front of the doors to the kitchen, perhaps, or the look of the limited menu, or the waitresses in their smocks. Again we get a barbecue sandwich, and it comes with a red vinegar coleslaw. It's pretty bland fare. I argue with Frank that you can taste some smoke flavor, and every few bites I hit a morsel that makes my case. He counters that he doesn't taste what I taste and that even if I were right the flavor is too faint to warrant further consideration.

We try three other places in Lexington, but with even less satisfaction. There is little difference between them. Each has the look of a 1950s-era restaurant, most of them are drive-ins,

Wayne Monk LEXINGTON NUMBER 1 **LEXINGTON, NORTH CAROLINA**

and all of them serve pork, chopped or sliced, with vinegar coleslaw on a hamburger bun.

So when we arrive back in the Winston-Salem suburb that Frank's friend Diane Caesar lives in, we are looking forward to her expert advice on where to get good barbecue. She is a native of this state and is a bit surprised that we have been having such trouble finding what we are looking for. She recommends a place near her father's house, which they know only as the barbecue on 158th. It looks like an old filling station. We see no smoke or fire, and when we order the barbecue, a woman goes to the refrigerator and removes the amount of meat that we have ordered. We don't think to stop her because Diane has recommended this place and she knows about good food. Frank tries some cold. I heat mine. We nonetheless agree: this isn't good even by the standards of leftover barbecue.

But Diane has also seen a feature segment on the local TV show entitled *Roy's Folks*. Roy Acklin, the host of the show, traveled the state and profiled some of its most interesting barbecue restaurateurs. We call Acklin and he immediately invites us to come up to High Point to talk with him and his producer, David Weatherly, about their findings.

As in South Carolina, North Carolina has developed more than one style of barbecue: Down East, as the eastern part of the state is known, and Piedmont or Lexington style. "I'll be real honest with you, and I think David will agree," Roy says. "We went looking for this difference and we never

really found it. There is as much difference between Lexington and High Point as there is between eastern and western North Carolina—which is not much."

David lists several differences for us in rapid succession as if to suggest that they combine to make only a small differential in taste. "The two biggest things you'll find is the slaw and the hush puppies. They make a yellow slaw Down East and here we make a red slaw. They all use a vinegar base in their sauce; in Lexington they put ketchup in it. Down East they make cornbread sticks; they bake them, then they fry them. Here they just fry them. Down East, not only do they use the whole hog, but they cook over gas. Here everybody uses wood. In the east, when they grind it up, they fry the skin and then mix it in with the chopped barbecue.

"It's funny, we went through very objectively and we just couldn't tell that much difference between east and west," David says. "But I swear to you there are people in this TV station that are from the eastern part of the state that say you can't get good barbecue here. And there are people from this part of the state that say you can't get good barbecue down there."

In the production room we watch some of the segments that Roy and David have done. They are short, upbeat features. The one detail of the shows that attracts my interest comes in a segment they did on the barbecue at Lexington Number 1. While they are tasting the meat, Roy suggests to viewers that they ask for the outside meat, that darker, drier meat that comes in great-

est contact with the seasoning and the fire. We tell them that we've already been to Lexington and were unimpressed. They tell us to go back and put their advice to use.

So we return to Lexington Barbecue and order one barbecue sandwich, this time specifying outside meat. Bingo! This is some of the best barbecue we've had all summer. What arrives is a small bun enclosing the brown, salty, crusty outside meat steeped in smoke and the flavor of the pit. The barbecue sauce—or "dip," as they call it—tastes like a version of Worcestershire sauce. Serving as the perfect counterpoint to the hot meat is the cool, finely chopped vinegar coleslaw.

Wayne Monk owns Lexington Barbecue. Before he started it he did a lot of other things, cleaning machines at a textile mill, packing shirts at a shirt factory, while still working weekends at barbecue places.

Many of the other barbecue restaurant owners in the area used to work here. After seeing enough young men come to work, learn the business, and then open up on their own, Wayne decided that he would set up a formal training program.

"Of course when you're successful everybody wants to copy. They think there's not a whole lot to what you're doing. The fact is any employee who has been here any length of time, especially a cook, can leave and take that knowledge with him. He knows what I'm cooking and how I'm cooking it. So why not sell that same thing? You're already giving it away. And as big as I am, as many cooks as I have, I can't keep secrets.

Smokestack Lightning

"So we set it up and said, 'All right, you can come here on the day shift all week long, six days. We charge you a thousand dollars. We'll give you most of our recipes. We'll give you our percentages—how much yield you can expect out of a shoulder, how much meat you should put on a sandwich, how much meat you should put on a plate and at what price—we give you all that basic information where you don't start off having to guess at anything. I don't show 'em how much money I make, and I don't give 'em the recipe for my sauce—I paid five thousand dollars for that and I just never give it away. I'm the only one that knows it. My son don't even know that. It's in my safety deposit box. If I kick the bucket they'll find it. But basically anything that I can teach you in eight or nine or ten hours a day for six days, you're welcome to it."

The Piedmont or Lexington style of barbecue, Wayne tells us, is pork shoulder cooked over hickory and/or oak coals and then chopped or sliced and topped off with dip and coleslaw. Behind the kitchen there are five huge pits which Wayne's brother Tommy, the main cook now, shovels hot coals into. The shoulders cook for about eight hours. But environmental concerns are conspiring to change that. The Carolina Department of Natural Resources has been pressuring them to stop cooking this way, Wayne says.

"Really, nobody knows who's supposed to enforce all these laws," he tells us. "Like when they holler at me, I holler back, 'Hell, if you gonna get me, let's get 'em all.' I'm talking about Burger King. They're charcoaling.

"One of these days they'll get me," he says. "They'll make me change my way of cooking, and when they do, that'll hurt my product. The style of barbecue we have in Lexington is very unique. I think it will start to fade away.

"One of these days everybody will either be using some kind of a gas or electric smoker type thing. But you don't get the same product. We have brought in cookers back here and put them outside and let them demonstrate. And the food comes out tasting more like a baked ham instead of our type of barbecue. Same cut of meat, same temperature, same length of time. But without the coals in there, or the smoke, without the grease actually burning itself—in other words, that grease that drops out of the shoulder and hits the coals, it burns; it puts flavor back in that meat—you can't get our type of barbecue. They even talk about maybe if I could channel that grease away from each shoulder, catch it in little pots, that way it wouldn't burn and you wouldn't have the pollution going up. But it's gonna change the flavor and that's not what I want, see. I'm resisting that.

"I got all this pride, see. I'm doing it the way it's supposed to be done. That's my reputation. But I really think within three generations in this barbecue—see, most of these guys in business are my age. I just don't know if the next generation is going to do this. They're probably going to try to get their kids out of college and make doctors out of 'em."

The Inventor: Back Country Barbecue, Linwood

∞

Doug Cook doesn't worry about the increasing intrusion of environmental regulators. He has invented a pit that he says can produce Lexington-style barbecue, but with half the wood and pollution. Hearing him explain this machine or just about anything else he's done is like hearing a carnival hawker in slow motion. Doug isn't trying to sell anything, but he exudes a salesman's confidence and it permeates much of what he says. We have already come here one afternoon and eaten an excellent sandwich. But after a couple of hours of talking to him, hearing about how he grinds his own hamburger meat and makes the best steaks in North Carolina, we're longing to come back and taste these things.

We meet him early in the morning at his restaurant in Linwood, a town neighboring Lexington. He looks younger than his forty-eight years; he's tanned, with gray-green eyes, and wearing a pair of Reebok sneakers. We follow him to the back of the restaurant, to the concrete floors of the cooking area. There we see three of his prototype pits, one stainless steel, one black metal, and one brick. The stainless steel one has a peaked top like a pyramid and drawers so that meat can be put into it easily.

Doug worked for Wayne Monk for about seven or eight years, so he knows how traditional Lexington barbecue is made. The brick pit is the most like a traditional Lexington pit, but he says he's going to dismantle it. Air leaks in and so it's too hard to control. His latest invention is the stainless steel pit, lined with soapstone. It is this pit and its computer attachment that he says will take the guesswork out of Lexington-style barbecue.

Wayne's the greatest. I can't say enough good things about Wayne. But the old-fashioned way, like Wayne cooks now? You 'bout got to work as an apprentice. If you don't you'll 'bout fail. It's hard, the way Wayne does, that's hard. It does a terrific job. It cooks great barbecue. But it's hard to clean and there's a fire hazard.

With our pit, the meat just goes on, we got electric coils in there that heat this box hooked to this computer. We just shovel coals under there, we just use the coals for flavor.

The old way, you throw your coals in, your temperature starts to rise. Then when it starts down that slope, that's when you start to lose control. But this pit has electric coils, six of them, 2,400 watts apiece. This computer, when you select your program, it takes over the temperature in that box. It has nothing to do with the smoke and the coals. Then the timer buzzes every forty-five minutes and you put fresh coals in there. We've cut our cooking time by a couple of hours. It takes us six hours now to cook a shoulder and we've cut our wood consumption by fifty or sixty percent. And we've just about eliminated the fire hazard.

Heavy Grant HEAVY'S BAR-B-Q **CRAWFORDVILLE, GEORGIA**

Other People, Other Places

Although on some days it didn't seem that way, there are a lot of great barbecue restaurants in this country. For instance, we didn't spend enough time in Oklahoma to say much about that state's barbecue, but we did make it to Mike McMillan's place, Mac's B-B-Q, in Skiatook. Mike came up in the competition circuit and has won and placed at some of the biggest competitions in the country. He has designed his own strange-looking cooker, but it works quite well. And up the road in Tulsa at Little Joe's, the quality of the food is echoed, though the surroundings are rougher.

Barbecue is a sideline at Olan Murray's Restaurant in De Vall's Bluff, Arkansas; they also sell fried catfish, frogs' legs, and fried quail. But the barbecue sideline there is better than the main dishes at most barbecue places. And not far from Murray's is Miss Mary Thomas' pie shop, which is not to be missed.

We had hush puppies at scores of places around the country. Almost all of them tasted the same. But at Home Folks Corner near Jackson, Georgia, the hush puppies are light and fluffy and made even more wonderful by the addition of the honey that they suggest you put on them. And the barbecue was good, but after a few servings of hush puppies, who has room?

JR's Restaurant, outside Atlanta, is in the suburbs and doesn't look like it would have good barbecue. You just automatically assume that if they have vegetable lasagna on the menu the barbecue won't be good. But the ribs and Brunswick stew there are some of the best in the state.

The Curator: Heavy's Bar-B-Q, Crawfordville, Georgia

"Now just turn around and go 1 mile to Heavy's Bar-B-Q Restaurant and Antique Dining Room"

We had ignored the first placard, seventeen miles before this one, and then drove by its echo without really thinking about it. But Heavy Grant, in person or in print, is not easily bypassed; he has begun to haunt us. After we've gone a mile or two without seeing a third advertisement, we are worried that we have missed our last chance. Heavy does not disappoint, however. He sends another sign, this one advertising not just the restaurant and the antique dining room but also a "unique museum."

Heavy's is an indoor/outdoor museum and starts on the fringes of the restaurant. There are old-fashioned Coca-Cola trucks painted yellow and still holding cases of empty Coke bottles. There are toy animals of all descriptions—dogs, pigs, horses, and even reindeer, which accompany the Santa Claus in a small Christmas scene that Heavy exhibits, despite its being September.

But the highlight of the outdoor collection is the "1st in GA Heavy's Bar-B-Q Kicking Machine HWY 22." The machine is a bicycle-based contraption that allows the pedaler to be kicked in the ass by the wheel of old boots connected to where the tire should be. The harder you pedal, the harder you're kicked. Heavy is in possession of a pair of them. Two other themes with their accompanying variations are visible in the outdoor division of Heavy's permanent collection. The words "Heavy's Bar-B-Q" appear about a dozen times around the place on all different kinds of signs including one of granite in which the words have been meticulously carved alongside a silhouette of their owner.

Heavy's is an old wood building with wood floors and walls and a brick hearth and pine board tables. "Antique dining room structure built in the 1800s, moved to present site by Heavy Grant in 1979," another sign informs us. In fact, the building encompasses not one but three "antique dining rooms" filled with antiques and *objets d'art* literally from the floor to the ceiling. There's the collection of baseball caps and the old scale used to weigh sacks of cotton, an old Bull Durham tobacco sign and an old-fashioned saw "used by Heavy Grant in 1949." Like the outdoor collection, the indoor exhibit consists largely of animals, though these are furry, mounted, and stuffed rather than plastic, painted, and weatherproof. There are deer and a bobcat, a red fox, white-faced bears, the front parts of a bear, the hind parts of a bear, sharks, catfish, swordfish, and bass. Most of the exhibits are identified with a sign detailing the approximate date and location of their deaths; "wood duck killed on Ogeechee River," one sign says. A couple stand out as genuine curiosities, like the doe who was lucky enough to attain her seventh point but not her eighth, and a menacing beast with its tongue hanging out, below which the sign reads, "Ugliest deer in Georgia killed by Heavy Grant 1979." In one of the rooms there is a big jar with some coins and dollars and a handwritten red sign: "Antique donation Here. Thank you."

By the time we meet William F. "Heavy" Grant himself, we have already ordered and eaten our chopped pork sandwiches, which are mildly seasoned Georgia barbecue with a light, slightly sweet sauce. Heavy is aptly nicknamed, a sixtyish man, large, though not huge. His belt is an inch or two smaller than his belly, and he has a laugh that erupts loudly and unexpectedly, then dies down just as it began.

Heavy assures us that his barbecue is the best money can buy; his hams and pork shoulders are smoked over oak wood. "That sandwich thar, every bit on thar is eatin' meat," he says. "No bone in it, no gristle in it, no fat in it. People cain't eat all that fat like they used to. Used to be people couldn' get enough fat to suit 'em." Heavy's Brunswick stew, though, is the star of the menu. It's well-seasoned but not spicy, and there is no liver or entrails in it. Just meat and seasonings. "In south Georgia they have English peas and ar'sh potatoes and onions in the Brunswick stew," he explains to us. "In north Georgia they have bell pepper in it and that roons it."

Heavy has found that most people like what he likes, he says, so his recipes must first and foremost please him. Similarly, the museum is a reflection of his own experiences and preferences in restaurants. "If I go to a café, if it's something I like to look at, I go back," he says. "So I fixed it so

Charlie Vergos THE RENDEZVOUS **MEMPHIS, TENNESSEE**

there'd be something to look at. Most of the stuff is donated. Most of 'em, they keep the stuff at home and nobody see it but them. They give it to me and everybody see it."

As we are walking out, our Georgia tour guide, Jordan Dayan, asks Heavy, "Who was the most famous person to eat your barbecue?"

"Heavy Grant, number one," Heavy says, erupting in a quick spurt of heavy laughter. "Then Kenny Rogers and Bobby Cox. Kenny Rogers say he been all around the world and he ain't never seen a place like this."

The Rendezvous, Memphis, Tennessee

The most legendary Memphis barbecue place these days is doubtless the Rendezvous. Ironically, it's an American barbecue restaurant with a French name, owned by Charlie Vergos, the son of Greek immigrants. It's downtown, right near the Peabody Hotel, so the tourists flock here. And it bills its food not as barbecued but as charbroiled, the meat being cooked with more fire than smoke. But despite the faux folk decor and the abundance of tourists, this place has its own authenticity, owing in large measure to the fact that Charlie Vergos is real and has his own fast-talking, grown-from-Memphis-soil authenticity.

First of all, I was raised in the Pinch down here where it was nothing but Jewish people, black folks, and all them kind of people, all them back alleys and everything where we was raised at. My family's been in the restaurant business since the 1920s. I was raised in the restaurant business. My dad's first restaurant was on Beale Street right there at Beale and Second. It was named Joe's Place back in those days. He was in there with his uncle, his relatives. Restaurants was all I ever knew all my life. I got to the army in World War II and I'm still in the kitchens in the mess halls and everything.

When I come back, I went to my dad's. There wasn't enough there for all of us so I went into business for myself and in doing so we opened up a little place in the basement. All we had was ham and cheese sandwiches. I needed a place to cook and I looked over there and they had a chimney and I said, "I believe I can put a pit there." So I blocked it off and made doors for it and everything and that's where the pit come in. And we cooked our hams, and in cooking our hams the fellow said, "Why can't we cook something else in there?" so I started cooking ribs for us to eat, not to sell.

So we got into the rib business by cooking ham, using just plain seasoning like the normal Greek people do, with salt and pepper and garlic and all that. Guy said, "Man, I want barbecue ribs, I don't want no regular ribs." So I figured, "How in the hell I'm gon' solve this problem?" So I went and got me a bunch of paprika, which has no flavoring at all. And I dumped it in there with it, and then I was basting with the pickle vinegar that we had then. And when I would baste it and throw this seasoning on top of it, this seasoning would get crusty and then the people said, "My God, we got dry ribs." That's how the dry ribs started. Now they call it dry rub and they call it all these different things and all, and that's where it got started. Really all we done was maybe cook a few ribs on the weekend. Then we got to cooking ribs and it got to be a standing thing. It's not what you call a really true old-fashioned barbecue, if you want to know the truth. But people have gotten to where they like it because it's not as messy and it's easier to eat.

Why is Memphis known for barbecue? We are in the tristate area of Arkansas, Mississippi, and the foothills of Missouri and we have such a large group of black people down here. That's where it originally started was the black people. You know, working out on the big plantations out in the country and back in them days before I even got into it, there were people on Beale Street and they sold ribs, but they sold spareribs, not loin ribs like we sell. The black people were just down-to-earth cookers, just like we were. And they cooked in our homes and all that.

We were very close, we grew up together, we played together. In those days, I mean today, it's a complete different world. We depended on one another. We had to play games, wasn't enough of us there, we'd all play together.

I've stopped many a time—they would get that old washtub and put a grill on it and go to cooking. I'd leave my restaurant. I didn't cook ribs then. Take a six-pack. I had a place down there I'd eat with the old boy. The old man, you know. Take my beer along and he'd slice me off a sandwich up there. I'd sit till two or three o'clock in the morning and talk and I'd watch him and learn from him too.

The first generation [of Greeks], they done three things: they either was shoe repair people, or they were in the cleaning business, and the rest of them went in the restaurant business. That was all. Now the second generation, they're all doctors; they're lawyers; they got the hell out of the restaurant business. I suppose they got tired. Their daddies, they were working eighteen, twenty hours a day, seven days a week in those days. They never saw 'em. I think they got into it, they said, "Well, we don't want to go through that with our families." They've become more sophisticated, professional. I got both sons and a daughter here. But I don't think they'll ever do what I accomplished. For them it's sitting here. It's not like creating something yourself. It's a different feeling when you walk into it and find it ready. But they're great kids and they'll do a great job; don't misunderstand me.

I still come down here and work some. I do all the buying. I got me a little office upstairs. I don't do much. I don't stay at night much anymore. But I been coming here lately 'cause I miss it. When you been in it so long, hell, you miss the action and the flow of the traffic. You get where you love to be around people.

The Idealist:
Remus Powers, Ph.B.

☜☞

I do solemnly swear to objectively evaluate each barbecue meat that is presented to my eyes, my nose and my palate. I accept my duty to be a cooking judge, so that truth, justice, excellence in barbecue and the American way of life may be strengthened and preserved forever.

A caricaturist would need only a bowler hat, a pair of wire-rimmed glasses, and a plain white apron to capture him. The folks at the competitions would recognize him from that. And like his fictitious namesake, he is responsible for much of the lore of the barbecue circuit. The legend says he penned the official Kansas City Barbecue Society judges' oath on a scrap of butcher paper from Arthur Bryant's restaurant. He started the Diddy-Wa-Diddy National Barbecue Sauce Contest and is still its tastemaster, though since it has become part of the American Royal International Barbecue Sauce Contest it has abandoned the original name. And he is the founder and dean of the College of Barbecue for Greasehouse University, in which capacity he administers the Doctor of Barbecue Philosophy degree on those who have made outstanding contributions in the field.

He came up with the idea of the sauce contest because he wanted to try all the barbecue restaurants listed in Jane and Michael Stern's book *Road Food*, but he couldn't afford to travel to all those places. So he started sending off for their sauces and eventually decided to enter them in a small competition to be judged by him and some friends. That contest grew up and became the Diddy-Wa-Diddy.

It's a silly, whimsical name for a contest (it was named for a Blind Blake tune), and Ardie has his silly, whimsical side. But he is also shy and reflective and soft-spoken and in many ways at odds not only with his garrulous alter ego but also with the loud-talking, hard-drinking atmosphere that pervades the barbecue competition circuit. Amid the comings and goings of volunteer sauce judges he tells us that he came to be Remus Powers in college originally. Remus was his nom d'amour when he was writing "silly love poems" to the woman who would become his wife. When he got into barbecue, somehow "Ardie Davis" didn't strike him as a good barbecue name, so he resurrected his Remus persona, this time complete with costume.

"When people see me they think, 'He's either a teacher or a preacher,' and they're sort of afraid to relate sometimes," he says. "But when I get in barbecue and I put this costume on, we have something to talk about; we share the passion for that, and I look like such a clown that people aren't going to get too serious with me. It's my way of overcoming my shyness too."

And Ardie tells us he takes much of his inspiration from another shy man, Joel Chandler Harris, creator of the Uncle Remus character and collector of Negro folklore. "There's a lot of misunderstanding today of Joel Chandler Harris and the Uncle Remus character," he tells us. "Harris was a very shy man. At the time he created the Uncle Remus character, the South was in the Reconstruction period and there was a lot of fear from former slaves and former slave owners about how this was going to work. Harris created Uncle Remus as a bridge between the former slave and the white culture trying to live together there.

"And he communicated those priceless stories that belong to everyone, not just to the Africans that brought them over. They're universal. Brer Rabbit appeals to everyone. And by telling these stories his goal was to help soften that fear and build some bridges. Now obviously we have a long way to go on that. Dr. King said time is neutral; we have to work at it. It doesn't just happen over time. That's why I chose the Remus character because as a white per-

Pappy MOONLITE BAR-B-Q INN **OWENSBORO, KENTUCKY**

Gil Bosley MOONLITE BAR-B-Q INN **OWENSBORO, KENTUCKY**

son I can do what I can to bridge those gaps. I'm sounding too much like an idealist or something. I don't want to come across as sentimental."

And he does come across as sentimental and idealistic and shy and academic. And it's not fake or affected or the least bit unbecoming.

Lamb, Ram, Sheep, and Mutton: Owensboro, Kentucky

They allow Protestants to barbecue in Owensboro, but they don't encourage it. The first recorded barbecue here was in 1834 at a gathering of Baptists. But in this century the Catholics have taken over and people are disinclined to wait for the Protestants to catch up. For the Protestants barbecue is a secular undertaking, but for the papists it is a calling of a higher order. Catholic churches raise much of their money from barbecues, so they have good reason to do it well. Patti Lolley, a Protestant and the office manager of the Owensboro-Daviess County Tourist Commission, has observed that Protestants have been increasing in number here, but "they still can't cook the barbecue."

In Owensboro barbecue means mutton, those sheep that outlived the lamb chop stage. The menus of Owensboro barbecue restaurants have expanded to include pork and beef and chicken, but that's largely a concession to the people who have moved here from other places.

Frank doesn't like mutton. He knows this because he doesn't like lamb, and

someone has told him that mutton *is* just like lamb, only worse. I try to tell him that it might be different, but he won't listen. He doesn't even think that a book on barbecue need include a section on barbecued sheep. "I don't like muttons. I didn't grow up around no muttons, and I don't see why we need to be encouraging the muttons by writing about them," he says.

When I order the ribs at Old Hickory B-B-Q and they look like T-bone steaks in miniature, he laughs at the cuteness of them and eats the absolute minimum required for him to confirm his distaste. And mutton *is* like lamb, only stronger. The same gamy flavor that makes the taste of lamb more akin to the taste of wild game than to that of domesticated meat is present in great abundance. But that's part of this meat's richness, a richness compounded by the thin, Worcestershire sauce–like "dip" that is served in squeeze bottles at each table.

Burgoo, a rich soup/stew of mutton (sometimes beef and/or chicken), tomatoes, potatoes, onions, carrots, and corn, is the primary accompaniment to barbecue in Kentucky. It's a lot like Brunswick stew. The meat in it is from the neck and other parts of the animal that are less desirable; it is not barbecued. Burgoo is a wonderful dish, hot and well-seasoned, but it seems like it should be served on its own and not as a side dish to so consuming a main course as barbecued mutton. It's hard to have an appetite for large amounts of both.

The most famous place for mutton in Owensboro is Moonlite Bar-B-Q Inn, a

thirty-year-old restaurant that has never been an inn as far as any of its current owners can remember. But it's a catchy name; it somehow conjures up the image of an old guesthouse where the proprietor's wife serves home-cooked meals to weary travelers. And there is a stone mantel and a cozy feeling here that would suggest that this is a small, old-fashioned business, which it isn't. Pappy, the Bosley family patriarch, bought the place in 1963. Nearly eighty, he doesn't come in much anymore, so we are lucky to catch him here one morning. He takes us on a walking tour of the parking lot, the best place to see the hickory wood they use and the very best place to discuss the cornfields that have given way to the vast expansion of this place. Pappy in overalls, a Moonlite baseball cap, and a Rolex watch big enough to choke a mule, keeps one cigar in his mouth and one in his front pocket, the latter being unlighted. His voice is pitched in the same octave as the upper register of a fiddle, so you have to strain to hear it. And even if you strain, you may have difficulty understanding what he says because his sentences are sometimes interrupted by coughing.

"When I bought this place, hell, I didn't know what a restaurant was," he says. "The place just had twenty-three seats and my wife claims she lost $10,000 the first year. There was two guys that we kept here for a month after we got it, but they didn't want to teach me how to make dip or nothing."

Moonlite is now a huge restaurant. In the front there is a retail area where they sell jellies, Moonlite dip, "Thick and Spicy" Moonlite barbecue sauce, Moonlite country ham, frozen mutton, bean soup mix, and a long list of caps and buttons and paraphernalia with the Moonlite logo on it. The all-you-can-eat buffet is responsible for the drastic improvement in Moonlite's fortunes, Pappy says. Most of the locals order it and apparently order it often.

Moonlite cooks its barbecue in a set of pits totaling twenty feet by six feet in area. They are three or four feet deep, so the pit man has to use a pitchfork to turn the meat at the back. The sheep that Moonlite uses tend to weigh about a hundred pounds, but by the time they are cooked and deboned there's only about twenty-five pounds of edible mutton from each. They sell ten thousand pounds of it a week.

Gil Bosley, one of the grandsons who work here, takes us on a tour of the pits and the meat lockers and the packaging area. Frank is taking pictures and making observations, and then, before I can stop him, he says something to Gil along the lines of "Yeah, but do you really like this stuff?" It's clear from Gil's answer that he realizes the taste of mutton is not one that sits easily on the palate of outsiders. "It's good if you cook it right," he says. "If you cook it wrong it's tough as leather." (Here they cook it eleven to twelve hours over hickory coals versus the eight to ten hours they cook Boston butts.)

A little later Janet Howard, Pappy's daughter, asks us if we like mutton, and I say yes, because I do. Frank again blurts out his opinion, somehow infusing his tone

with the exact sound that my mother got in her voice when she used to read that passage in Dr. Seuss that went, "I do not like them, Sam-I-am. I do not like green eggs and ham." But Janet is polite. She explains that a lot of men don't like mutton because they ate so much of it in the service during World War II. Mutton remains popular here, she continues, because years ago this was sheep-ranching territory, so it evolved as part of the regional culture. "It's not like mutton's the best thing you ever ate," she says, "but you crave it. We don't eat lamb chops, we don't eat lamb ribs, just barbecued mutton."

Owensboro bills itself as the "Bar-B-Que Capital of the world," and each year during the second week of May the town has a huge barbecue festival. We arrive much too late in the year for the big event, but each of the Catholic parishes has its own combination barbecue-and-county-fair fundraising event. The Bosleys tell us about one that will fit into our schedule. It is being held this weekend as a fundraiser for the retired nuns.

Sunday morning we drive past the fields of tobacco, some stalks growing, others hanging stem up, leaf down, to dry. We are following a long line of cars with license plates from various Kentucky counties and also from nearby states. The site of the barbecue is a huge outdoor grounds with grass and trees all around. It's a family affair with the usual fair games and prizes. Everywhere underfoot are small children and candidates for public office.

Each of the parishes in the diocese has contributed members to the three or four hundred people needed to put on this event. The burgoo parish is engulfed in the smell of fresh onions, vinegar, and smoke as the parishioners constantly stir eight huge metal pots, rusted and blackened and perched over burning wood.

In another area the mutton and the chickens are being cooked over open cinderblock pits. Men with hoses stand by to douse the flames. St. Mary Magdalene Parish is in charge of the chicken, and men in yellow T-shirts with green lettering take turns twisting the legs of the chickens to see if they're done. The mutton, on a different set of pits, has bones sticking out of it in a way that indicates that it was boiled before being put on the grill. At the competitions and in other serious quarters they will tell you that parboiling is not traditional and in fact ruins the meat. But even though most of the restaurants don't boil their meat before putting it on the grill, most of the churches and many of the backyard cooks do.

Houston Warren is seventy-two. "I was in St. Alphonso Parish," he says, "but I'm not anymore 'cause we got a holy-roller preacher down there and I ain't no holy roller! I'm a Catholic! I've been cooking barbecue all my life and I never cooked a piece of meat without parboiling. You boil it till it's tender, then you put it on the pit.

"I've got a son lives in South Carolina and them people down there think they know what barbecue is. I never et any of it. I went down there and cooked some for 'em and they kept asking me when I was going to put my mustard in. I said, 'Ain't no damn mustard going in this dip!'"

Warren's dip recipe calls for Worcestershire sauce, vinegar, lemon juice, ketchup, lard or butter, brown sugar, a little nutmeg, Red Hot sauce, black pepper, and salt. What strikes me about it is that in both name and recipe it is similar to the barbecue sauce of the Lexington area in North Carolina. The term "dip" as the name of the sauce that accompanies barbecue seems to have evolved from the word "dipney." In her senior thesis Ripley Golovin cites an old recipe for dipney which is not unlike the Worcestershire sauce dips of Kentucky and North Carolina: country lard, red pepper, black pepper, and strong vinegar.

I am anxious to taste the barbecue here. I ask Frank to buy us some while I finish taking notes on what's going on. I find him under a tree with a soda in hand, breath reeking of chicken. He can see by my expression that I'm expecting a good explanation for why he has spent our research money on a food that is not the specialty. Before I can say a word, he offers me what remains of his dinner. "They told me this was a two-foot mutton," he says, "but it tastes just like chicken."

We visit a few more barbecue places in Owensboro. My favorite is Pogue's, which in its seventh year is one of the newer restaurants. It looks like a hunting lodge with its mounted animal heads and rough wood decor. The mutton arrives dripping in a spicier version of Kentucky dip and accompanied by rye bread. But perhaps the main attraction is Darryl Pogue, the owner's son, and the spirit with which he approaches the business.

He has been working at barbecue places for nearly half his life, starting out thirteen years ago at Ol' Hickory, where his father was a manager. "Our recipe is totally different from theirs," he assures us.

"I just love barbecuing," he says. "The most thing I like about it is the people. You get to meet new people every day. Most of the people, they're friendly, and that's worth more to me than money. Then around Christmas all the ladies call up for advice on cooking hams and turkeys. That makes you feel important."

Dreamland, Tuscaloosa, Alabama

I

I dreamt about it. See, my knees got bad. I say, "Lord, I got to find me something to do." So I dreamt about this. That's the reason I named it Dreamland. In fact I was walking along out there, the guy was laying the blocks. It was nothing out there but trees then. One of the guys asked me, "Mr. Bishop, what you gon' name it?" I say, "I don't know. What you think I oughta name it?" He said, "Name it Dew Drop Inn." I never will forget that. I walked right through here. Something walked behind me and whispered, "Dreamland." Then I walked back around there and told him, "I tell you what I'm gon' name it. I'm gon' name it Dreamland." That was in '57, I believe.

I coulda put it in town, but people go where they want to go anyway. Ain't nothin' in town but trouble. I'm just strictly a country boy, see, regardless to what. I was reared up in the country. I just like it out here. It look more like a Dreamland in these woods out here.

II

His is a lawn chair throne, a huge piece from a department store's maroon-brown set of tables, chairs, and recliners meant to be relaxed on outdoors at barbecues and such, its girth sufficient to accommodate a king of generous proportions, its armrests of similar size, and its stiff wooden back and seat softened by padded cushions now thin and well used. A foot away from his head is a fan, suspended there by old electrical cords, the white plastic of its grille now black with grease and soot from the smoke of the pit. And there are flies here, big Southern summer ones that buzz around; visitors swat at them in wild frustration, yet they seem not to disturb his regal countenance even when they land on his exposed neck or arms. All of this, throne, fan, and flies, shares space under the carport with a 1975 Ford Country Squire station wagon, which, Mr. Bishop says, still runs.

We have arrived on the appointed day but at an unannounced time, so we catch him a bit unaware. Mr. Bishop out of costume. His head, usually covered by a baseball cap, especially for the benefit of visiting photographers, is bare and bald. His trademark pipe, usually held stiffly in place by a gold tooth and the stumped remains of its fallen neighbors, is out of sight, replaced by a filter-tipped Marlboro cigarette.

Out of costume, but never out of character.

As we talk, two white men exit from the restaurant and end up at the back where Mr. Bishop holds forth.

"We want to get a picture with the man that cooked the ribs," one says.

"You Mr. Bishop?" the other says.

"This him."

"I'm Joe Christian. I came all the way from Texas to try some of these ribs."

" 'Preciate it."

"I want to get a picture of you. Yaw'll ready?"

"Wait a minute, I ain't got my thing. I got to have my stuff."

Beside his right armrest is a plastic bag like they give you at supermarkets. The pipe and the Dreamland cap are in the bag. He dons the cap and puts the pipe in his mouth, then poses, giving the thumbs-up sign. Snapshot.

"Thank you," Mr. Bishop says. "Yaw'll come back, hear?"

Frank takes pictures too. Whenever Mr. Bishop knows that Frank is about to shoot, he gives the thumbs-up sign. "I got that shot already," Frank says. "Let me just get one of you sitting there."

Mr. Bishop puts his thumb down and says nothing. But each time he thinks Frank is about to shoot, he gives the thumbs-up sign. Frank shoots. "I got that one already," Frank says, and they begin the dance again.

III

I started in 1958. Hadn't ever cooked a rib in my life. I had a man come here and cook for me. Called him Frog. But I didn't like the way he cooked 'em, though. He was burning 'em up. Well then, I say, "God give a person five talents; it's up to him to develop 'em." That's what I said. My wife, she come up there, she start to cooking. And I said, "Well, I hate to get my wife up every morning early"—see, I gets up out the bed, I can't help that. Well, Frog, he got sick—the man that cook for me? He got sick. And I say, "Well, I ain't gon' get my wife out the bed. I'm gon' go and make a fire and try to cook my own self.

You got the talent, all you got to do is develop it. 'Zat right? Main thing I wanted was to work on that sauce. You know, people be sitting down over there eating, I'm watching them and they be frowning. They be just shaking their head. I say, "Something's wrong with that shit." Word get round to me, say it's hot, too hot. He was half drunk anyhow—Frog. I just stopped messing with him. He died, though—'58 or '59, one. I think he died the same year I opened up. No, it was the second year I opened up, I believe, 'cause he stayed sick long time.

IV

We enter the barroom darkness of this dreamland-cum-restaurant from the bright sunlight of an Alabama afternoon, having made our way to Tuscaloosa and found the "light market" and the McDonald's the lady told us to look for, which, just as she indicated, helped us also find Jug Factory Road and the folks in the trailer home that were able to tell us when we were getting close to the barbecue. And entering this darkness we hear mostly the talk of loud white voices but also the fizzing sounds of cold drinks and beers being opened and poured into plastic cups and the ringing of the phone and the voices answering it. To our left behind the bar is a wall of potato chips and such and at the other end of this concrete floor is a stack of wood and the wall into which one of the pits has been built. Between the pit and the door are rows of tables and chairs and people and ribs.

"Sit anywhere you want," says a waiter, moving quickly in front of us. Like all the others, our table is brown and covered with advertisements for various local companies. I face the door, which means that I can watch the same soap opera either on the television to the right of the entrance, behind the bar, or on the television to the left of the door, above a table. Frank can only watch the game show that is playing on the television at the other end of the bar.

Ray Robinson from Cozy Corner in Memphis had already told us that they don't sell anything but ribs, chips, and drinks here, so there's no real need to read a long menu. "Give us an order," we say, just as Ray told us to do. What arrives is a paper plate with several ribs bathing in a tomato sauce. Before we start, the waiter also hands us a plastic Dreamland bib with the logo on it: a sketch of Mr. Bishop, chef's cap on his head, pipe in his mouth.

The meat is firm, though not tough. It tastes as if it has been cooked quickly and directly over the fire rather than slowly smoked. The outside is slightly charred and crisp; the inside is succulent and good. The sauce is a lot like Chicago sauce, only not as sweet. Thin, mostly tomatoes, but a lot more vinegar than up there. The first bite is slightly tart.

V

Jeannette, she the head of it now. I'm just here sitting down trying to cool. I don't cook no more. I trained a man. He take care of it. I live right up back there. I be up here every morning about seven-thirty. Stay here till about nine. I was trained to get up like that. I been working since I was nine or ten years old.

My daddy, he lost his mind, see. He lost his mind. What it was, white man called him a black son of a bitch. He shoulda never did it. My daddy knocked all his teeth out. They sunt him to the penitentiary for a year and a day, and while he was in there he got into it with a guard. He was off; he was way off. Guard hit him upside the head. Hit him up in the temple. Lost a lot of blood out of there. He lost a lot of blood out his temple. Made him lose his mind then. I got two brothers and a sister up under me. I had to help take care of them.

Yeah man, I been on the road a long time, I ain't just now started. It's been pretty rough with me. I ain't gon' to tell you no lie.

VI

Dreamland is an icon of the barbecue circuit. It has been featured in national publications and has come to be synonymous with the other national icon with which it shares this city, Alabama Crimson Tide football. It is on our list of places not to be missed even before Frank's friend from elementary school, Linda, tells us that her friend from college, Jeannette, has returned home to run her father's barbecue business. We have called Jeannette to make arrangements to talk to Big Daddy, as Mr. Bishop is also known.

We find her at the house that her father has built for her, behind the restaurant and up a slight hill from it. She has a space in her teeth just like her father's, and she speaks freely as he does, though more quickly. They have opened a franchise operation in Birmingham and she has just come back from checking things out over there. We sit on her porch, laughing, talking, and exchanging information mostly about the new place and her decision to return to Tuscaloosa after college and time away.

But before meeting her we had already gotten a sense of her and her influence. The Dreamland logo, the plastic bibs, the well-designed, well-executed flyer advertising Dreamland's availability for rental, are touches that the barbecue entrepreneurs of Mr. Bishop's generation usually haven't thought of. It would be neither surprising nor impressive for a newer, flashier place to incorporate these little touches of sophistication. But in an old barbecue place, these basic advancements have generally been unknown. Jeannette has worked them in without changing the feel of the place too much. There is still more graffiti than wall in the men's room. They haven't added wine or low-calorie specials to the menu to attract a broader clientele. They sell only ribs, confident in the power of their slogan, "There Ain't Nothing Like 'em No Where."

VII

Well, a few white was already coming. But they wasn't laying around like they is now. When they integrated, that capped it off. I said, "I ought to go and kiss Martin Luther King!" They come in here then, boy!

I didn't know how to take it when the white folks start commencing to sitting down. It took a long time for me to get used to it. When the white folks started coming, the niggers started saying, "You can't get waited on out there." Niggers are a mess—some of 'em. You know how it is. People always gon' talk, you know. "Man, don't go out there. Bishop wait on the white folks." I'm waiting on the dollar. It don't make me no difference. I don't pay it no mind. You listen to folks talk, you go crazy, man. I couldn't stay in business, if I depended on the Negro.

VIII

The people who know this place know that Big Daddy is always in the back under the carport. You walk all the way to the back of the restaurant, and just before you get to the pit you turn left, pass the room with the other pit in it on your right, and exit.

Jesse Pevear lives in Birmingham but is a regular here. As I am talking to Mr. Bishop, he comes to the back and helps fill in the details of Dreamland history.

Then one of the pit men comes by asking to borrow ten dollars, but Mr. Bishop swears he doesn't have it. Then the potato chip man comes by and kids him about burying money in the back yard and stuffing it in the mattress. Mr. Bishop tells him to stop lying like that.

Then Jesse comes back with his son and the kidding about money continues.

"I decided to stop here and drop a bunch of money," Jesse says.

"Man, *please* dump some here," Mr. Bishop says, imploring. "I need it worse than old folks need soft shoes!"

"We bringing two or three slabs back with us."

Big Daddy DREAMLAND DRIVE-INN BARBECUE **TUSCALOOSA, ALABAMA**

"I love you that much harder."

"Every year at homecoming we come down on Friday," Jesse says to me. "I usually try to come down in the early afternoon because ain't nobody here. By Friday night, the line's three hours long. One homecoming Jeannette said the line was so long, they went ahead and opened up at nine o'clock. There were already people here lined up out in the street. I've been here many a time when there was a long line. Two or three hours' wait. The good part about those long lines is they sell three million dollars' worth of beer."

"Man, stop! You know one thing, I'm gon' tell you something. The Lord has wonderful blessed me. That's all I have to say about it. Man, if I was open on Sunday, I bet they'd be a line all the way over yonder. But I don't believe in that, opening on Sundays."

"No question about it. But he's already making all he can spend."

"Man, knock it off! Talk right! Man, I tell you the truth. I just don't like that Sunday stuff. People be driving with beer all in they car. They come in here drinking. I don't like that."

"I've been here when they've run out of ribs."

"Yeah, I have run out."

"Many times."

"Yeah, that made me sick, too!"

"How many slabs you average in a day?" I ask.

"I don't know."

"It's a secret," Jesse says.

"It ain't many. It's a few, though."

"Three or four maybe?" I suggest.

"Three or four, about that."

"I bet Jeannette knows within one penny how much this place makes every day," Jesse says. "She's sharp."

"You got to be sharp to count that high," I say.

"Aw, man, cut it out!"

Mr. Bishop seems a little uncomfortable about his success. The obvious explanation is that in the late 1980s he ran into some problems with the tax collector. Part of the settlement was that he cook ribs for the William D. Partlow Developmental Center, a school for mentally retarded children. Although that was not the most severe penance you could imagine, the whole experience has probably left him wary of detailed discussions of financial matters.

X

The Lord have blessed me and I appreciate it. Everywhere I went in my travels, I joined a church. I believe in that. I was brought up in the church. I can't help that, see. I love the church, boy. My mother dead and gone. I missed one Sunday going to church. I never forget these words she told me, she say, "Son, don't forget the church. Regardless, come to your church."

The Lord done brought me, boy. I swear he did. And I know it. I know it. I don't have no doubt about it. Lot of people too easy forget where they came from. Don't ever forget where you came from, man. Don't ever do that. I'm just Bishop anywhere you see me. Anywhere, anytime. I believe in that.

1993 HAWKINS GRILL **MEMPHIS, TENNESSEE**

CHAPTER
TWELVE

Tradition and Transition: A Dinosaur Without a Mate

When I returned to Paris in the fall of 1939, after an absence of twelve years, I noticed a decline in the serious quality of restaurants that could not be blamed on a war then one month old. The decline, I later learned, had been going on even in the twenties, when I made my first studies in eating, but I had had no standard of comparison then; what I had taken for a Golden Age was in fact Late Silver…"After the First [World] War, everything had already changed," Mirande wrote in 1952, when he was 77. "The mentality of today began to show the tip of its ear."

A. J. Liebling, *Between Meals: An Appetite for Paris*

The dogs may bark, but the caravan moves on.

Moorish proverb

We make our final stop a stop at Hawkins Grill in Memphis because Frank's mother, who is in town from New York, has agreed to meet us there, and because it has come to symbolize something of the old order to us, and because we know that since it was the first place we went, ending up at Hawkins will lend a poetic symmetry to our travels.

Frank's mother doesn't usually go to Hawkins even when she's in town, she tells us. Meeting at Hawkins is sort of a favor to Frank.

"I can't blame her," says Frank's buddy Halvern as he declines to join us. "I only go there when Frank comes to town."

Mrs. Johnson, Halvern's mother, is a real estate broker. She's been trying to sell the place on behalf of the Hawkins family for years, but no one will buy it. I ask her how much she is trying to get for it.

"It's not worth anything right now," she explains to us. "That corner down there is just a bad corner. I'm scared to go to that Big Star. I go in there to buy neck bones and stuff like that. They have the pork dressed up

for black people and you can't get it like that in the white neighborhoods. But people have gotten robbed over there, and some people have had their cars stolen, and somebody was shot in there. This neighborhood is really going down. Also with so many fast-food places around there—McDonald's, Pirtle's, Dairy Queen—with all those places people don't go into little places like Hawkins."

The rumors about someone getting shot *in* Hawkins turn out not to be true. The way it is explained to us by the regulars is that a guy was shot and died in front of the place next door. But setting the record straight is not apt to reinvigorate business.

When we arrive in the late afternoon hardly anyone is here. J.C. Hardaway, in whom the shoulder sandwich has discovered its Stradivarius, is wiping down the counter and putting away a few dishes, but there is apparently little work to do. Two women walk in, sit at the bar, and order beer and sandwiches.

"How's your daddy doing?" J.C. asks one of them in his expansive drawl.

"You know they held him up the other day?"

"No!"

She nods and sips her beer.

"No. You know sometimes he flashed his money and I don't li'e to see nobody flashing no damn money," J.C. says.

"You know they hit us again last week," the woman adds.

"I saw you all had a bolted-up door."

"They knocked the door down."

The pay phone near the entrance rings. "Hawkins," J.C. answers. "One mild shoulder? Okay. Be 'bout five minutes." As he begins preparing the sandwiches J.C. turns back toward the women. "I didn't know you all had got robbed again. There was another woman over there got robbed and whipped."

"Yeah, they put a gun to her head...I want mine kinda hot."

"Spicy, huh?"

"They robbed and killed my son on the fifth," says the second woman, breaking her silence.

"You gotta be kidding. You just had the one?"

"The Saturday before Labor Day they found him out in the field stabbed and shot. He was going to buy him a car that day." She reaches into her purse and hands J.C. a program from the funeral.

"Nineteen years old," he reads aloud through the lower section of his bifocals. "This is real nice. I saw a program the other day and they had pictures ever since the boy was a baby."

She takes the program back, puts it into her purse, and takes another sip of her beer.

∞

Unlike the many places we've seen with the artificial vintage advertisements that attempt to fake authenticity, Hawkins has a treasury of classic signs, all authentic and utilitarian. I walk over to the jukebox, behind which is a cluttered bulletin board, and begin reading. Beneath the out-of-date sign advertising a bus trip to New Orleans, I see NO DANCING. When I ask J.C. about it he explains that in Memphis you need a separate license to allow dancing in your establishment. "You can't stop 'em, though," he says.

Another separate license, which Hawkins also does not have, is required to serve hard liquor. But it is okay to allow customers to bring in bottles of their own hard liquor and consume it on the premises, so there are one or two brown bags in each of the booths. Of course you can't charge people for their own liquor. But you can charge them for the chasers, the set-up. There is a sign listing those prices:

Bowl of ice	$1.65
empty glass	.30
glass of water	.40
pitcher of water	.55
glass of ice	.55
orange juice	.65
grapefruit juice	.65
all taxes included	

Frank and I sit and drink beer until bit by bit the after-work crowd begins arriving

at Hawkins. Still we sit, and by eight o'clock the place is almost full. There are a couple of seats at the bar but no room in the booths. By nine, "Let Me Love You" by Willie Clayton has been put on the jukebox and the man who had been dancing by himself finds a partner and the two of them are joined by two other couples, one of whom is only a few feet from the NO DANCING sign. "Can't hold 'em steel," J.C. says matter-of-factly.

The dance they dance harks back to the days when the act of dancing was the formation of a partnership and what one partner did mattered to the other. Connected by one hand, each of the partners gets a few measures of music in which to do his or her own thing before pulling close again. The man in one of the couples dances down to his knees and back up again and then begins stepping suggestively toward his partner.

"Work with it!" someone calls from a booth. "Come on now, boy! Look out! Come on up to it."

"Oh, all up to it with your tongue out!" J.C. says with uncharacteristic excitement.

Hawkins closes at ten on Friday and Saturday, which means that at that hour J.C. turns on the lights and locks the door. Frank's mother walks in just then. She joins us at our booth in the back and looks around. "I haven't been in this place in forty-five years," she says.

"How much has it changed?" I ask.

"Not much."

People continue coming in long after ten. They knock on the door and usually someone gets up and unlocks it. By ten-thirty the party is still going on. Each time "Southern Girl" by Maze is played the dance floor fills up. I get the impression that J.C., who is washing dishes and cleaning up in between making shoulder sandwiches, is grateful to have the company in the loneliest part of his night. Suddenly, as he is scooping up glasses from the bar, one slips and breaks. For the first time I see J.C. befuddled and clumsy; at that moment he looks all of his sixty-eight years. The long days and late nights are probably not easy anymore. He continues working, but he seems shaken a bit by the misfortune.

"Who is Hawkins?" I ask him, once he has recovered.

"Emmett L. Hawkins, Sr., he's the owner."

"What about Emmett L. Hawkins, Jr.?" I ask. "Does he ever come around?"

"He doesn't help me. He just waiting for me to give it up so he can sell it. They don't want it; you have to be in it to want to do it."

∞

It's a theme we've heard often. Up near Blue Goose, Tennessee, Arthur Gray, Chinaman Hutch's eighteen-year-old grand-nephew, is counting the days before the McDonald's opens. That's where he really wants to work. Frank had asked him if he'd even consider doing what his great-uncle does for a living. "If it come to that," he had said, his tone full of the hope that it doesn't. Despite what its name implies, Boyd's N Son in Kansas City is a sole proprietorship

unlikely to survive the retirement of its founder. Edgar Black has recommended that his sons not return to the barbecue business. Too much work; too little return. In much of North and South Carolina, the restaurant owners have elected to replace barbecue pits with gas and electric ovens as a means of reducing the work.

Which is not to say that none of the good places we've visited seem likely to survive the retirement of their founders. Ray Robinson at Cozy Corner in Memphis and Ollie Gates up in Kansas City and the Hinze family in Wharton, Texas, and Wayne Monk in Lexington, North Carolina, are creating dynasties of a sort at their restaurants. You can get great food at these places and in some of the other places we've been to, but you can't get the feeling of being in Hawkins Grill or on the front porch of B.E. Anderson's barbecue. Even more tragic, among the newer, better capitalized, more viable businesses, the art of cooking is often not of primary concern. It is as if modern and mediocre are synonyms.

Of course it's difficult to tell the extent to which the world has declined in the culinary arts. In music there are recordings and scores to compare. In literature there are the texts. In painting and sculpture the works survive. But in food the earliest masterpieces were consumed long before we arrived at table, and even rejudging those delights of our youth is difficult. We are left with old memories and a palate that is no longer youthful. If we are to say on prima facie evidence that our grandmother's chocolate chip cookies were the best ever made (as was

clearly true in the case of my paternal grandmother, Mama Lizzie), we must also admit that we were once avid consumers of cotton candy and bubble gum and a host of other things the mere thought of which is enough to make our teeth ache now.

So tastes and palates change; there is also the clouding effect of simple nostalgia. It's not just coincidence that the Golden Age of Barbecue was the 1950s, the same era that the nation as a whole longs for through movies like *American Graffiti* and television shows like *Happy Days* and *Laverne and Shirley*. That's also the era when Ollie Gates remembers Kansas City barbecue coming into its own, with the help of major league baseball. That's when Jim Quessenberry remembers those great Fourth of July goat barbecues in Birdeye, Arkansas, and roughly when all the old Memphis places like Leonard's and Brady and Lil's were in their heyday. That's the period when Lyndon Baines Johnson was perfecting his political skills and their culinary accompaniments, the combination of which he would bring to the White House. It doesn't even matter so much that Ray Robinson, when asked about some of those old Memphis rib shacks, recalls that they were "filthy" by today's standards. In *Yearning for Yesterday*, Fred Davis refers to this as second-order nostalgia, nostalgia combined with, though not necessarily diminished by, the questioning of whether things were ever really as perfect as we like to think they were.

Nostalgia also contains within it a mythology of a stagnant past, a previous

Free Barbecue Line XIT RODEO AND REUNION **DALHART, TEXAS**

world in which today's fast-paced changes did not occur. And while it is clear that change occurs more rapidly now than before, it is also true that many of the things we view now as being classic or traditional are relatively recent in the history of civilization. What we think of as classic Italian food, for example, doesn't date back to the Golden Age of Rome. Rather it results in large part from the importation of tomatoes from America in the wake of Columbus' voyages. Similarly, the chili peppers so important in the Szechuan cuisine of China were originally imported from the colonial Americas.

But when we see the changes occurring in front of us we don't trust them, and often for good reason. We know what the Chinese and the Italians of a few centuries ago probably knew: that spicy cooking and tomato sauces were not mere additions to, but often replacements for, some styles of cooking that were worthy of preservation. As those same factors—improved technology in communications, transportation, and food preparation, alter the way we prepare barbecue, we wonder about the ratio of steps forward to steps backward.

And perhaps it's a matter of evolution. In the 1940s during the jazz revival period, the world began to rediscover traditional New Orleans jazz. Louis Armstrong, that most worthy master, was popular throughout the world. But in comparing his work during that period with music being played in New Orleans at the same time, it is clear that, whatever the enduring merits of his music, it had distanced itself from many of the elements it had evolved from. So people like Bunk Johnson and George Lewis were sought out and presented as authentic examples of traditional New Orleans jazz. By the 1950s, however, neither these men nor any of their contemporaries could be said to be playing authentic New Orleans jazz. They had heard the orchestras of Duke Ellington and Count Basie and Don Redmon in concert and on records. Their music, though still firmly rooted in the New Orleans tradition of riffs, breaks, polyphony and blues, was influenced and enriched by its contact with other musics. The resulting mixture was not "authentic."

It is unlikely that any young entrepreneur would open up a place like Hawkins Grill or Kreutz or Dreamland or any of the other places that derive much of their classic image from rustic, inelegant trappings. A place like Rudy's in San Antonio, which seems to have franchise ambitions, though they wouldn't talk about that or anything else with us, has tried to replicate the feeling of an old country gas station/barbecue joint combination. You can see the stacks of wood used to barbecue the meat and you can also read about Rudy, the mythic owner of the place, and the pickup truck that he has for sale and those other aspects of his personality that mark him as the type of country boy who should know about barbecue. The place is newer and shinier and less natural than those places whose atmosphere it seeks to replicate, but it has chosen a worthy goal, the replication of both the food and the feel of the old barbecue places.

It's nearing eleven o'clock, but when we see someone else ordering a shoulder sandwich and J.C. beginning to prepare it without saying anything about the kitchen being closed, Frank and I decide to order one for ourselves. It arrives as always on the old-time plate and with a toothpick sticking out. And it tastes the same; the meat is well seasoned, well prepared, and well worthy of being served without any sauce, though the thin, sweet sauce with the vinegar and pepper is an appropriately wonderful accompaniment. Music is still playing and glasses are still clinking.

The songs that we have picked out on the jukebox have finally come on. The dance floor fills up when Marvin Gaye begins to sing, and it remains full when Howlin' Wolf begins, "Smokestack Lightning, shining just like gold." Even J.C. seems to be cleaning up in rhythm.

"You know," Frank says, looking around, "what we have here is a dinosaur without a mate."*

*Since this was written, Hawkins has been sold. The new owners, a couple, do their own cooking and thus gave J.C. his leave. The good news is that J.C. is working at Big Sam's Grill on Dunnivant Street. On the weekends the menu also includes chitterlings and ribs and fish. He assures us that his shoulder sandwiches are as good as ever, though we've yet to have the pleasure.

Epilogue: Nostalgic Impressions

And when it has been over that many months and when you know that you cannot possibly go back to everywhere, you know too that even going back it could never be the same, and it's just nostalgia then. Two men babbling like *absolute* idiots about outside meat and small ends and hickory getting bitter on you if you don't mix it up with a little oak or better still wild cherry—if you can get it. And the people looking at you as if you were crazy to speak of such foolishness in a serious tone of voice.

Not to overstate the point, but don't you yourself sometimes forget that long hot summer of broken car days and cheap hotel weeks and "I don't have even one minute to talk to you" people and remember only those certain places? And you know you'll never get back to all of them, but still it's nice to think of them and imagine that there will be some occasion that will allow you to go back. There are other good ones, even great ones, but somehow these are special and you think most often of them. You secret them like hot-fun-in-the-summertime memories of public swimming pools and pretty legs and snowballs.

You think of Black's Barbecue in Lockhart, Texas, because of the pork loin, but mostly because of that straight-backed dignity of Edgar Black's which is echoed and subverted by his huge signs and souvenir sale items. Kirby's Barbecue on Highway 14 in Mexia, Texas, where you were too full to really eat, but where the brisket sandwich was the best and the cinnamon-nutmeg sweetness of the peach cobbler was so good Toni Joseph even liked it. But in Texas you think most often of Hinze's, either location, because nowhere else were there so many good things on the menu, all of them first rate.

And after all that has been said about Kansas City, you know that it's the oldest of the old standbys there that really are the best. And you wonder how old Boyd is doing because, like you, he likes him some barbecued lamb. And because, like the best of us, perhaps even you at your best, he's undaunted.

And what about Cozy Corner in Memphis and how the people treated you there?

That place had been the national standard for good barbecue until you found other places, not better places, but different places that were just as good. They were glad to see you and hear about where you had been, even invited you to join in on the board meetings held at the table in the front of the place where special friends were served special things like the poundcakes that were auditioning to replace those made by the old woman who had got sick and couldn't make them anymore. And each time you were glad to get back to a place with good conversation and air-conditioning and of course that good jazz playing all day long.

One of you even started calling the man Cozy, and it fit. So if you were ever going anywhere near Memphis, traveling from New York to Texas, say, one of you would ask if the other wanted to stop off and see Cozy.

"Ol' Cozy?"

"Yeah."

"Our main man Cozy who have them barbecued Cornish game hens and that dry sauce he came up with?"

"That's him!"

"Shee-it! Let's go ahead and see our boy!"

And wasn't it Cozy himself who told you about the fried peach and apple pies at A&R in Memphis, or did you discover those yourself? He was certainly the one who told you about the pie lady in De Vall's Bluff, Arkansas, and he was right in the pocket and dead on the money about the delicately browned art of her confections. But also don't forget Ace Bar-B-Q in Atlanta, where the barbecue's not bad but those fried pies are so good that when you call about them they tell you to hurry up and get there before they're sold out and they're not just saying that.

You know without a follow-up call that the Quain hasn't changed. (The last time you saw her she was wearing that button: "A hard man is good to find.")

Alan Cheuse may have just thrown this phrase in among the many other beautiful phrases he crafted to conjure up Fishka and old Russia and the immigrant's son Oll-an for you, people you spent time among as you read while you were supposed to be writing. But you feel the force of these words in motion now, rising at the back of your throat. You feel it in the hollow churning energy of your stomach. Your stomach which seems suddenly empty even though you just ate. Which is to say it is empty of barbecue and all that goes with it.

That which was mystery to Cheuse is fact and substance to you now, this ironic longing for something that has passed. This longing occasioned in part by that very passing. This realization that whatever it was, whatever it can and must now be, it will never be the same.

As Cheuse put it, *the physics of nostalgia.*

Final Courses

—

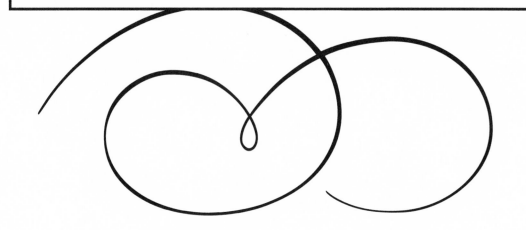

The Recipes

The range and variety of the following recipes mirror the range and variety of what we saw and ate on our barbecue safari. Because cooking techniques vary so widely across the country, you will no doubt have to adjust the recipes to accommodate your own style of barbecuing.

There are two basic schools of barbecue cooking: direct and indirect. Direct cookers prefer to cook the meat directly over the wood, coals, or charcoal. That way, the juices from the meat drip down onto the coals. The burning of these juices imparts added flavor to the meat—flavor that is crucial to good barbecue, the direct cookers claim. The disadvantage of direct cooking is that the grease dripping from the meat often causes grease fires, and thus you have to be extra-vigilant to insure that the meat isn't cooked too quickly. Direct cooking is usually hotter and faster than indirect cooking; it relies more on heat than on smoke, and cooking temperatures range from about 300 to 350 degrees F.

Proponents of indirect cooking, citing the fire hazard and the preference for a deeper smoked taste in their barbecue, cook almost exclusively with hard wood (oak, hickory, pecan) as opposed to the charcoal or mixture of wood and charcoal that a lot of direct cookers prefer. Many modern pits are built with two separate chambers, a firebox and a cooking chamber in order to separate the meat from the fire. Smoke goes through a passageway between them, and thus the meat never touches a flame. Even if you don't have a specially constructed barbecue pit, you can cook indirectly by stacking your wood or charcoal on one side of the pit and putting your meat on the other side. Putting a drip pan underneath the meat also helps keep the grease from making its way down to the burning wood or charcoal.

Although the seasonings in these recipes should taste good regardless of which technique or temperature you use, those barbecue recipes with lower temperatures and longer cooking times generally indicate that the meat should be smoked over indirect heat. The temperature for these recipes ranges from 225 to 275 degrees F. Other recipes are intended to be cooked at temperatures ranging from 275 to 375 degrees F.

The word "rub" refers to a combination of dry seasonings that is either sprinkled on or rubbed into the meat before cooking. There are several commercial rubs and barbecue spices on the market. In each of the meat recipes that calls for a rub, you can use a commercial rub, seasoned salt, a rub of your own design, or one of the many rubs for which recipes appear here.

MEATS

Baron of Barbecue Ribs

(serves 6–8)

3   slabs of racks, 3½ and down, pork spareribs
     (3½ down means each slab weighs
     3½ pounds or less)
1   cup barbecue rub

To prepare the meat, remove the membrane from the back of the ribs. Work your fingers under it and pull it off. (The membrane is tough, and smoke and seasonings will not penetrate it very well.) Remove any excess fat. Season with barbecue rub and cook using an indirect method at 225 degrees for 6 to 8 hours.

Oklahoma Joe's Brew-B-Q Ribs

(serves 2–3)

1   slab pork spareribs
12 ounces beer
1   12-ounce jar Oklahoma Joe's Sweet Rub
1   12-ounce jar Oklahoma Joe's BBQ Sauce

Before grilling, sprinkle Sweet Rub on the ribs. Prepare Brew-B-Q sauce by mixing the beer with a cup of the BBQ Sauce. Put ribs on grill and cook for 2 hours, basting with Brew-B-Q sauce every 20 minutes. After 2 hours the ribs will be a reddish brown color and will be about half done. Now spread out a large piece of heavy-duty foil. Fold up the edges of the foil so it will hold liquids like a pan. Pour about 1 cup of the Brew-B-Q mixture onto the ribs. This mixture will run off the ribs and onto the foil. Wrap foil over ribs and seal as tightly as possible. Cook for 2 more hours, maintaining a temperature of 225 degrees in the pit.

Mattie Bivens Dennis' Hattiesburg Mississippi Ribs

(serves 6–8)

3   slabs pork ribs
⅓   cup salt
⅓   cup mixture of black and red pepper
⅓   cup seasoned salt
3   tablespoons meat tenderizer
12   ounces teriyaki sauce
6   ounces Worcestershire sauce

Have your butcher crack each rib bone at the rib tip so that it will then be possible to separate the ribs without having to cut through bone. Trim excess fat. Rinse ribs. Dry. Sprinkle them with meat tenderizer, salt, pepper, and seasoned salt. Place the ribs in a deep pan and marinate them in Worcestershire sauce and teriyaki sauce for at least 12 hours but preferably overnight. Cut the slabs into thirds. Cook the ribs on a hot grill at about 350 degrees. The large ends of the slabs should be put on the pit first, the center-cut ribs five minutes later, and the short ends five minutes after that. The ribs should cook 45 minutes to 1 hour.

Remove the ribs from the pit and separate them with a knife. Mop them with barbecue sauce and wrap them in heavy-duty foil until you are ready to serve them.

Ray Robinson's Ribs in Ashes

(serves 2–3)

This is an old recipe, Ray says, and he does not take credit for inventing it. The secret is that the biscuit dough traps all the flavor inside. The same cooking method can be used to cook potatoes.

1   slab of pork ribs
     Salt and pepper, barbecue rub,
       or seasoned salt
     Enough biscuit dough to cover the entire
       slab of ribs 1½ inches on all sides

Season the ribs. Cover them entirely with biscuit dough, 1 1/2 inches thick on all sides. Place the ribs into the coals and ashes of a fireplace or barbecue pit. Cook approximately 12 hours. Remove from the pit; peel off and discard the biscuit dough. Serve the ribs.

J.C. Hardaway's Pork Shoulder

(serves 12–18)

1   7-to-8-pound Boston butt, untrimmed
     Salt

Put the shoulder on the pit fat side down, directly over the coals. Let it brown for about 1 hour. Salt the lean side of the shoulder, turn it, and salt the fat side. Cook the meat for 6 or 7 more hours, turning it every 15 to 20 minutes. If the coals flame, use plain water to dampen them.

Recommended woods: hickory, red or white oak.

KCass World-Class Combination Pork Shoulder
(serves 12–18)

1 7-to-8-pound pork shoulder
   Barbecue rub

Trim excess fat off shoulder. Work in the rub. Place in smoker at 250 to 275 degrees, adding hickory every 3 or 4 hours. Smoke for 6 to 10 hours, depending on your temperature and your smoker.

Wrap in aluminum foil and let cook another 3 hours. When the bone pulls out of the shoulder, take it out of the foil and place it back on the smoker. Baste with barbecue sauce. Do not add more wood at this point, as it will impart a bitter flavor to the sauce.

The Scott Family's South Carolina Whole Hog

1 hog, 80 to 130 pounds, dressed and
   butterflied
   Vinegar and water
   Salt, black pepper, and red pepper

Mrs. Scott declines to give her exact recipe for barbecue sauce, but her son Ricky says that the ingredients are vinegar, water, salt, black pepper, and red pepper. Make a sauce to your own taste out of these ingredients. Set aside.

Burn oak or another hard wood down to coals. Shovel the coals into the pit in such a way as to form a square roughly the size of the butterflied hog. Put the hog on the grill. Cook it skin side up, adding coals to the pit approximately every 25 to 30 minutes and adding wood to the coal fire as needed. Cook skin side up for approximately 4 to 6 hours. When the skin has begun to curl, it's time to turn the hog over. Once the hog is on the pit skin side down, spread coals under the entire body, rather than in a square. Pour sauce into the body of the hog as the skin is crisping. Once the skin is crisp, remove the hog from the fire and serve.

The Vienna Volunteer Fire Department Whole Hog

1   whole hog, dressed weight 125 to
    150 pounds
1/2 gallon to 1 gallon basting sauce
    Olive oil
    Salt
    Black and red pepper
    Garlic powder
    Onion powder
    Oregano
    Butter

Rub the hog's skin well with olive oil. Rub the inside of the hog. Sprinkle inside cavity with salt, red and black pepper, garlic powder, onion powder, and oregano.

Place the hog on the grill, skin side down. Cook about 4 hours at 275 to 300 degrees. Then pour about 1/2 gallon of basting sauce into the hog's cavity and continue to baste with the sauce in the cavity throughout the cooking process, adding more sauce if needed. Cook another 10 to 12 hours or until done at 225 to 250 degrees.

Recommended wood: red oak. Use an indirect method of cooking. Charcoal may be used, but also use wood chips to increase smoke flavor.

Oklahoma Joe's Barbecue Brisket

1   10-to-12-pound beef brisket
    Oklahoma Joe's Sweet Rub
    Oklahoma Joe's Steak Maker
1/3 cup lemon juice
1/3 cup water

Trim the excess fat from the brisket, which will then weigh 6 to 8 pounds. Season both sides of the brisket with Sweet Rub and Steak Maker and place in a pan. Mix the lemon juice and water, and pour the mixture over the brisket. Let stand overnight in the refrigerator.

Remove the brisket from the pan, reserving the marinade. Smoke the brisket at 250 degrees, 1 hour per pound. Baste with marinade and cover. Continue to smoke the brisket at 250 degrees for another 1 1/2 hours or until tender.

Recommended wood: pecan, hickory.

World-Champion Arkansas Trav'ler Prime Rib

(serves 10–12)

1 10-to-12-pound prime rib, butchered into its three component parts (see below)
½ to 1 cup olive oil
   Ground red pepper
   Garlic powder
   Salt
   About 3 ounces fresh-cracked black pepper

The standing rib roast has three main parts: the bone or rack, the fat or lip, and the lean beef commonly known as the ribeye or prime rib. Have your butcher separate the three parts. Then after sprinkling the ribeye lightly with ground red pepper and not quite so lightly with garlic powder, reassemble the roast and bind tightly with butcher's twine. Tie at each joint or between ribs.

Rub the outside of the roast with salt. Next bathe the outside of the roast liberally with olive oil. Then rub all surfaces thoroughly with fresh-cracked black pepper. (For best results, blend peppercorns in a kitchen blender until the pepper is cracked to varying degrees.)

Insert a meat thermometer into the center of the largest part of the roast. Be careful not to touch the thermometer to the bone, as that will cause inaccurate readings. Cook the roast over an indirect medium-hot charcoal fire until the thermometer reads 140 degrees for rare. (Approximate cooking time is 20 to 25 minutes per pound.)

Take roast up and immediately wrap tightly in heavy-duty foil. Let stand for 10 to 15 minutes before carving. Separate meat from bone and fat and slice the meat into portions 1/2 inch thick. Serve with Quessenberry's Heavenly Horseradish (recipe below). For a real treat, make a meal out of the leftover ribs.

To make Quessenberry's Heavenly Horseradish, combine:

1 pint sour cream
1 5¼-ounce jar of prepared horseradish
   Juice of 1 lemon
1 tablespoon salt

Mix well and refrigerate. This sauce is best made a day ahead.

Arkansas Trav'ler Beef Kabobs

(serves 12–16)

4   pounds sirloin tip roast, cut into 2-inch cubes
12 small new potatoes, cut into quarters or 4 medium red potatoes cut into 2-inch cubes
2   medium yellow onions, cut into quarters
1   red onion, cut into quarters
3   medium bell peppers, cut into 2-inch squares
4   ears of fresh corn, cut into 2-inch lengths
4   large carrots, cut into 2- to 3-inch lengths
4   small apples, cored and quartered
2   medium zucchini, cut into 12 chunks
12 large fresh mushrooms
12 cherry tomatoes
¼   cup peanut oil
¼   cup wine vinegar, either red or white
1   tablespoon salt
1   tablespoon black pepper

Toss all ingredients. Cover and refrigerate overnight, or 4 hours at the very least.

In an open barbecue pit, build a hot broiling fire. Charcoal works best, as it is easiest to control. Start by broiling the longest-cooking pieces first (beef); as they begin to get done, add the other ingredients based on the amount of time they require to cook. Add potatoes first, then carrots and onions, then corn, then apples, then squash, then mushrooms, then peppers, then tomatoes.

When everything is skewer-ready, thread all pieces alternately onto bamboo skewers. Paint the kabobs with your favorite finishing sauce and return them to the fire for 2 or 3 minutes to glaze.

Wood Brothers' Lamb and Irish Smoked Potatoes

(serves 12–18)

1   6-pound boneless leg of lamb
3   tablespoons minced fresh garlic
4   tablespoons of dried rosemary
1   tablespoon salt
2   tablespoons ground black pepper
    Butcher's twine
20 red potatoes, sliced
1   cup diced red onion
⅓   cup diced yellow bell pepper
⅓   cup diced green bell pepper
⅓   cup diced red bell pepper
¼   cup diced scallion
1   tablespoon minced fresh garlic
½   cup minced fresh rosemary
1   tablespoon black pepper
1   teaspoon salt

Slice the leg of lamb lengthwise and butterfly it open. Mix the next 4 ingredients together, and rub the inside and the outside of the lamb with the mixture. Tie the lamb with butcher's twine. With a meat hook or hanging hook, hang the leg of lamb in the barbecue pit, or place the lamb on the top shelf of the pit so that its juices will fall into the pan of potatoes on the shelf below. Cook the lamb 3 to 4 hours at 225 degrees.

Place potatoes, vegetables, and seasonings in a pan. Mix thoroughly. After the lamb has cooked 1 hour, place the pan in the pit beneath the lamb. Smoke potatoes for about 2 hours or until tender, stirring occasionally.

Lamb Chops à la Donna McClure

(serves 4)

8   loin lamb chops, cut 1 inch or thicker
1/4   cup olive oil
2   tablespoons honey
2   tablespoons soy sacue
2   tablespoons apple cider vinegar
2   tablespoons minced onion
1   small clove garlic, minced
1/2   teaspoon salt
1/2   teaspoon black pepper
1/4   teaspoon ground ginger
1/4   teaspoon dry mustard

Place the lamb chops in a glass dish. Mix the remaining ingredients and pour the mixture over the meat. Marinate 1 hour.

Grill chops 7 to 8 inches from hot coals for 10 to 12 minutes per side, brushing frequently with sauce. If using a meat thermometer, lamb will be rare at 140 degrees. Serve with the remaining sauce.

Tip: I throw sprigs of dampened rosemary on the coals while cooking. Smells wonderful and imparts a special flavor.—D.M.

P.D.T. Spicy B-B-Q Chicken

(serves 4)

3   pounds chicken quarters
2   tablespoons vegetable oil
1/4   cup chopped onion
1/4   cup chopped green pepper
1   clove garlic, minced
3/4   cup ketchup or your favorite barbecue sauce
1/3   cup vinegar
1   tablespoon Worcestershire sauce
1   tablespoon brown sugar
1   teaspoon celery seed
1   teaspoon dry mustard
1/2   teaspoon salt
1/2   teaspoon black pepper
1   teaspoon hot pepper sauce

Heat oil in pan. Cook onion, pepper, and garlic until tender. Add ketchup, stir, and add all ingredients except chicken. Bring to a boil, then reduce heat and simmer uncovered for 10 minutes, stirring occasionally. Set sauce aside.

Season chicken pieces with additional salt if desired. Place chicken bone side down over medium-hot coals. Grill 25 minutes (until bone side is well browned, then turn pieces over. Grill another 25 minutes or until chicken is tender. Brush chicken frequently with sauce during last few minutes of grilling. Use all the sauce.

Kansas City Barbecue Factory Chicken Baste

3 to 5 split frying chickens
1   cup barbecue rub or seasoned salt
1   gallon apple cider vinegar
1   cup of black pepper
1/4   cup cayenne pepper
    Garlic salt to taste

Sprinkle chickens lightly with rub or seasoned salt. Place chicken, bone side down, directly over the coals in a pit. Cook the chicken 2 1/2 to 3 hours at 225 to 250 degrees, turning after 1 1/2 hours and basting continuously with a mixture of the other ingredients. (The vinegar will seal the skin, keeping the juices inside.)

This baste is also good for smoking a whole hog.

Back Country Barbecue Chicken Dip

(serves 24)

12   chickens, cut in half
1 1/2   pints 40-grain vinegar
1   ounce iodized salt
1/2   teaspoon ground black pepper
1/2   pound light brown sugar
1   quart ketchup
1   quart water
1/2   pound margarine
1   lemon, squeezed (use both juice and rind)

In a large pot combine the vinegar, salt, black pepper, and sugar. Stir until sugar is dissolved. Add the remaining ingredients and bring the mixture to a light boil.

Put the chickens on the grill skin side down for 1 1/2 to 2 hours or until brown. Immerse them in the dip and then return them to the grill bone side down until done.

Ray Robinson's Sauerkraut-Stuffed Smoked Turkey

Although the main seasoning in this recipe is sauerkraut, the turkey somehow doesn't end up tasting like sauerkraut, Ray says.

1   10-to-12-pound turkey
    Sauerkraut to fill the cavity of the turkey
    Salt, pepper, and/or seasoned salt

Wash the turkey inside and out. Fill the cavity with sauerkraut and sew up the cavity, front and back. Sprinkle the outside of the turkey with salt, pepper, or seasoned salt. Place the turkey on the pit. Cook for approximately 8 hours, turning it every 20 to 30 minutes.

Ed and Corda Tuttle's Turkey Smoked in a Kettle Cooker

1   10-to-12-pound turkey
1   apple, cored and quartered
1   medium onion, peeled and quartered
1   teaspoon lemon pepper or other salt-free seasoning
1   cup orange juice

Wash turkey inside and out, and dry with paper towel. Sprinkle cavity well with lemon pepper; put in quartered apple and onion. Place drip pan in center of charcoal grate and pour in 1 cup of orange juice.

Smoke turkey in covered kettle cooker by the indirect method, using charcoal and alder wood, for about 3 hours.

Otis P. Boyd's Famous Hot Link Sausage

(yields 5 pounds)

2½ pounds ground pork (shoulder cut)
2½ pounds ground beef (brisket, round, or sirloin)
2   teaspoons dried sage
2   teaspoons crushed red pepper
2   teaspoons paprika
2   teaspoons ground cumin
2   teaspoons dried sweet basil
2   teaspoons anise seed
2   teaspoons dried oregano
    Dash salt and ground black pepper

Mix the meats with the spices. For sausage links, attach 2 1/4-inch sausage casings to the stuffer nozzle on a hand meat grinder. Stuff the casings to the desired length, cut the links, and secure the ends with string. Barbecue at 225 degrees for 2 hours, or slow-smoke at 185 degrees for 4 hours. For sausage patties, form the meat mixture into a roll and cover with wax paper. Slice the roll into patties and peel off the wax paper. Patties can be fried or grilled.

SAUCES AND RUBS

Julius Robinson's Father's Barbecue Sauce

This is the recipe for the first barbecue sauce Frank ever tasted.

10 ounces Worcestershire sauce
10 ounces chili sauce
2 to 4 large cloves garlic
¼   cup sugar
1½ level teaspoons salt
¼   cup flour
¼   teaspoon black pepper
¼   cup vinegar
2½ cups water

Mix the dry ingredients. Add Worcestershire sauce and chili sauce, then vinegar and water. Stir over low heat. Chip garlic and add to mixture. Cook until slightly thickened, stirring constantly.

Chuck's Smoke House BBQ Sauce

(yields 1 1/2 gallons)

2   pounds brown sugar
1   cup vinegar
½   cup Worcestershire sauce
1   cup mustard
¼   cup hot sauce
1   gallon tomato sauce

Mix ingredients well so that sugar is dissolved.

Ray Robinson's Coffee-Laced Barbecue Sauce

1   cup ketchup
⅓   cup hot sauce
⅓   cup Worcestershire sauce
⅓   cup brown sugar, honey, or molasses
¼   stick margarine (optional)
2   tablespoons lemon juice
1   teaspoon instant coffee
1   tablespoon cider vinegar

Mix all ingredients in saucepan. Simmer for 30 to 40 minutes.

Jason Levine's Kansas City Barbecue Factory Sauce

(yields 1 gallon)

- 2   32-ounce bottles ketchup
- 1   box brown sugar
  (or a little less if you prefer)
- 15   tablespoons vinegar
- 5   teaspoons salt
- 5   teaspoons pepper
- 1¼ teaspoons cayenne pepper
- 1¼ teaspoons garlic salt
- 10   tablespoons celery seed
- 5   teaspoons Worcestershire sauce
- 3   cups water
- 3½ teaspoons horseradish
- 5   tablespoons liquid smoke

Mix all ingredients except horseradish and liquid smoke in a saucepan. Simmer for 15 minutes. Cool. Add horseradish and liquid smoke.

J.C. Hardaway's Barbecue Sauce

- 2   18-ounce bottles Kraft Hickory Smoked Barbecue Sauce
- 2   3.5-ounce bottles liquid smoke
- 3   pounds granulated sugar
- 64   ounces vinegar, white or red
- 1   32-ounce bottle Hunt's ketchup

Mix all ingredients; no cooking necessary.

Mac's Pork Basting Sauce

(yields 1 quart)

- 1   cup apple juice
- 1   cup apple cider vinegar
- ½ bottle hot sauce
- 3   tablespoons lemon juice
- 1   cup Mac's BBQ sauce or any sweet tomato-based barbecue sauce
- 3   tablespoons lemon pepper
- 2   tablespoons seasoned salt
- 2   tablespoons brown sugar

Mix ingredients well. Sprinkle over pulled or chopped pork just before serving. This sauce will give your pork a unique flavor while keeping the meat moist. It is also excellent as a baste or marinade, and is especially good on pork shoulder and fresh ham.

Vienna Volunteer Fire Department Basting Sauce

- 1   cup salt
- 1   gallon vinegar
- 1   lemon
- ¼ stick butter
- 3   small cans red pepper
- 1   small can black pepper
- 1 to 2 bottles of ketchup

Mix all ingredients, adding as much ketchup as is desired for color. Bring to a boil for 5 minutes. This basting sauce may be thickened with flour or cornstarch and used as a barbecue sauce.

Kansas City Barbecue Factory Beef Marinade

- 1   cup vegetable oil
- ¾ cup soy sauce
- ½ cup lemon juice
- ¼ cup Lea & Perrins Worcestershire sauce
- ¼ cup prepared mustard
- 1   tablespoon coarse pepper
- 1   tablespoon seasoned salt
- 2   cloves minced garlic

Blend all ingredients well in blender. Place meat and marinade in plastic bag. Marinate for 24 hours, turning meat occasionally. Rinse meat under cold water and pat dry with towel. Marinade can be refrigerated and used once more without loss of flavor.

Wood Brothers' BBQ Sauce

- 1   pound smoked beef or pork, coarsely chopped
- 4   chicken necks, coarsely chopped
- 1   onion, chopped
- 1   green bell pepper, chopped
- 1   carrot, chopped
- 1   stalk celery, chopped
- 1   #10 can ketchup
- 2½ cups white vinegar
- ½ cup Worcestershire sauce
- 4   tablespoons liquid smoke
- ½ cup chicken stock
- 1   pint Louisiana Hot Sauce
- 2   cups brown sugar
- ½ teaspoon onion powder
- 2   tablespoons granulated garlic
- 2   tablespoons chili powder

4 teaspoons black pepper
2 teaspoons salt
2 teaspoons allspice
2 teaspoons ginger
2 tablespoons coriander
4 tablespoons dry mustard
2 bay leaves
2 teaspoons cayenne pepper
1/4 cup olive oil
1/2 pound barbecued brisket trimmings, chopped fine

Heat olive oil in a large stockpot. Brown the chicken necks, barbecued beef or pork, and all vegetables in the oil. Add all liquids and mix well. Sift all spices and mix them with other dry ingredients, then add to the liquids. Simmer for 45 minutes, stirring occasionally. Strain sauce through a food mill or strainer. Add brisket trimmings to sauce and serve.

Charlie Mac's Barbecue Sauce {NO. 1}

3 quarts ketchup
2 quarts white vinegar
1 16-ounce bottle Heinz 57 sauce
1 small jar French's mustard
1 small bottle lemon juice (real lemon concentrate)
1 small bottle Red Hot Sauce (not Tabasco)
1 ounce black pepper
1 ounce red pepper
8 teaspoons salt

Mix all ingredients well.

Charlie Mac's Barbecue Sauce {NO. 2}

(yields 3 cups)

1 tablespoon margarine
1 clove garlic, chopped fine
1 teaspoon dry mustard
1 tablespoon brown sugar or honey
1 small onion, chopped fine
1 teaspoon celery seed
1/2 cup water
2 cups ketchup

Mix and heat sauce gently to dissolve the ingredients. Simmer below the boiling point for 20 or 30 minutes, taking care not to scorch.

Charlie Mac's Cure for Cornish Game Hen and Turkey

(yields 2 cups, enough for 6 Cornish game hens or other small birds, or 1 10-to-12-pound turkey)

1 1/4 cups *non*-iodized salt
3/4 cup brown sugar
1 teaspoon saltpeter

Small birds—Cornish game hens, quail, doves—should be soaked in the cure and refrigerated for 2 to 3 days, then soaked for 2 hours in clear water, then cooked about 4 hours over charcoal and hickory chips. Turkeys should be soaked in the cure for 5 or 6 days, soaked in clear water for 3 to 4 hours, and cooked 4 to 6 hours.

Paul Kirk's Basic Kansas City Barbecue Seasoning or All-Purpose Rub

(yields 3 cups)

1 cup cane sugar
1/2 cup garlic salt
1/3 cup paprika
1/4 cup seasoned salt
1/4 cup BBQ Spice
2 tablespoons onion salt
2 tablespoons celery salt
2 tablespoons chili seasoning
2 tablespoons black pepper
1 tablespoon ground ginger
1 tablespoon lemon pepper
2 tablespoons dry mustard
1/2 teaspoon thyme
1/2 teaspoon cayenne pepper

Sift all ingredients together. Store in an airtight container away from sunlight. To use, sprinkle ribs, brisket, or chicken as if you were putting on heavy salt and pepper.

Kansas City Barbecue Factory Rub

(yields 1 gallon)

2 cups salt
3 cups garlic powder
3 cups black pepper
3/4 cup cayenne pepper
1 cup cumin
2 cups paprika
2 cups tenderizer with no salt or seasoning
1 cup lemon pepper
2 cups granulated or brown sugar

Mix ingredients well.

Dousing the Flames CHICKEN COMER'S BAR-B-Q **PHENIX CITY, ALABAMA**

Moonlite Mutton Dip

(yields 1 gallon)

This is an original recipe that is no longer in use at the Moonlite Bar-B-Q Inn.

1   gallon water
1⅔ cups Worcestershire sauce
2½ tablespoons black pepper
⅓   cup brown sugar
1   teaspoon allspice
1   teaspoon onion salt
1   teaspoon garlic
2   tablespoons salt
2   tablespoons lemon juice
1⅔ cups vinegar

Mix all ingredients and bring to a boil.

Carolyn and Gary Wells's Dry Rub

(yields 1/2 cup)

4   tablespoons sea salt
3   tablespoons chili powder
2   tablespoons black pepper

Combine ingredients. Store in a glass jar with tight-fitting lid. Rub onto meat before cooking. Rub can be made into a marinade and basting sauce by adding a pint of vinegar.

Wood Brothers' Dry Rub

(yields 1 1/2 quarts)

2   cups sugar
½   cup seasoned salt
½   cup celery salt
½   cup garlic salt
½   cup onion salt
½   cup paprika
¼   cup chili seasoning
6   tablespoons ground black pepper
4   tablespoons ground white pepper
4   tablespoons cayenne pepper
2   teaspoons ground cloves
½   teaspoon ground cumin
½   teaspoon marjoram
½   teaspoon nutmeg
½   teaspoon dry mustard
½   teaspoon ground coriander

Sift all ingredients together.

SIDE DISHES AND DESSERTS

Baron of Barbecue's Barbecued Baked Beans

3   16-ounce cans pork and beans
½   cup diced onion
¼   cup molasses
1   cup barbecue sauce or ketchup
¼   barbecued beef brisket, bacon, or other barbecued meat
2   tablespoons oil or bacon grease
2   tablespoons liquid smoke
1   teaspoon barbecue seasoning or seasoned salt

Preheat oven to 350 degrees. Drain the beans in a colander and rinse off the tomato sauce. Heat the oil in a skillet and sauté the onions and peppers until soft. Mix all ingredients well and adjust seasoning to taste. Put into a baking dish and bake uncovered for 45 minutes. Serve hot or cold.

"People that I cater for rave about these baked beans and I just smile and thank them," Paul says. "The reason that I smile is, how could anyone think these were great baked beans? I grew up on homemade baked beans—made from scratch. In fact, my mother had some of my baked beans and I got into trouble for putting in green peppers. I just told her that people liked them so much I keep making them that way. Anyway, here is her recipe." (See next recipe.)

The Baron's Mother's (Mrs. Mary Kirk's) From-Scratch Baked Beans

1   pound navy beans or Great Northern pea beans
½   cup dark brown sugar
½   medium onion, diced
⅓   cup sorghum
¼   pound bacon square (smoked hog jowls), diced
1   tablespoon soy sauce
1   teaspoon Worcestershire sauce
½   teaspoon dry mustard
½   teaspoon salt

Wash and clean the beans, then place them in a bowl and cover with water. Let soak overnight, adding more water if necessary.

Drain the beans and wash again. Put beans in a saucepan, cover with fresh water, and bring to a boil. Boil until the beans are soft, then drain, reserving the broth. Preheat oven to 275 degrees. Layer the beans, onions, diced bacon square, and seasoning in a bean pot or ovenproof dish, adding bean broth to bring beans to the desired consistency. Bake uncovered for 5 to 8 hours, stirring occasionally. If beans seem to be getting too brown, put on cover while baking.

Arkansas Trav'ler Barbequed Beans

2   pounds dried Great Northern beans
1   pound dried pinto beans
1   pound dried small kidney beans
3   small bell peppers
2   large yellow peppers
2   large red peppers
2   large white onions
1   Boston butt, barbecued
    Optional: garlic, bay leaves, basil, oregano, sage, hot peppers, sorghum or maple syrup

Take the butt (already barbecued) and boil it for 30 minutes. Discard the water. Chop the onions and peppers coarsely. In a large pot bring 3 or 4 gallons of water to a boil. Add the butt along with the peppers and onions. Boil for 1 hour. Remove meat and peppers. Pour the beans into the pot and cover. Let the beans soak for 2 hours. Meanwhile, bone and chop the butt, saving any juice. When beans are well soaked (fully swelled), combine all ingredients and simmer for at least 4 hours or until tender. Thirty minutes before serving, add salt and black pepper to taste.

Kenny Calhoun's Brunswick Stew

(yields about 6 quarts)

4   pounds chicken
4   pounds pork shoulder
2   quarts tomatoes
3   medium onions, peeled and diced
5   pounds potatoes, peeled and diced
1   can cream-style corn (yellow)
1   can whole-kernel corn (yellow or white)
1   26-ounce bottle ketchup
1   cup apple cider vinegar
1   5-ounce bottle Worcestershire sauce
1   10-ounce bottle Heinz 57 sauce
1   teaspoon hot sauce
1   tablespoon black pepper
1   teaspoon crushed red pepper

Sprinkle pork and chicken with salt and pepper to taste. Boil the meat until it is tender and falls off the bone. Pull meat from the bones; discard skin and bones but save the broth. Grind, chop, or pull meat into small pieces. You may use a food processor or sausage mill. If using whole tomatoes, run them through as well. Cook diced onions and potatoes in salted water until about half done. Mix all ingredients together in a large pot. Mixture will be thick; add reserved broth to the desired thickness. Simmer for 1 hour, stirring frequently to prevent sticking. Served with saltines or cornbread, Brunswick stew makes a meal; also goes well with barbecue.

Tips: Turkey can be substituted for chicken. Leftover barbecued pork can be substituted for boiled pork or can be the only meat in the stew. Spray the pot with a nonstick coating to prevent sticking.

Moonlite Bar-B-Q Inn Burgoo

4   pounds mutton, on the bone
1 to 3 pounds chicken
$3/4$ pound cabbage, ground or chopped fine
$3/4$ pound onion, ground or chopped fine
5   pounds potatoes, peeled and diced
2   17-ounce cans corn
$3/4$ cup ketchup
3   $10^{3}/4$-ounce cans tomato puree
    Juice of 1 lemon
$3/4$ cup distilled vinegar
$1/2$ cup Worcestershire sauce
$2^{1}/2$ tablespoons salt, or to taste
2   tablespoons black pepper
1   teaspoon cayenne pepper, or to taste

Boil mutton in enough water to cover. Cook until tender, about 2 or 3 hours. Remove the meat from the bones. Throw out broth and bones. Chop meat fine; set aside. Boil chicken in 2 gallons of water in large kettle until tender. Remove chicken; add potatoes, cabbage, onion, corn, ketchup, and 1 gallon of water to chicken broth. Bring to a boil. Meanwhile, chop chicken meat; discard bones and skin. When potatoes are tender, add chicken, mutton, lemon, salt, pepper, Worcestershire sauce, vinegar, and puree. Let simmer 2 hours or longer, stirring occasionally as it thickens.

Boys of Barbecue and Patty's Barbecued Vidalia Onions

(serves 12–16)

4 to 6 large onions, quartered
8   ounces fresh mushrooms, sliced
1   stick unsalted butter, sliced
3   strips bacon
2 to 3 tablespoons Cajun spice

Put onions, mushrooms, and butter in a 9-inch aluminum pan. Sprinkle with spices, then top with bacon and cover with foil. Put on grill for 1 to 1 1/2 hours or until onions are very tender.

Carolyn and Gary Wells's Grilled Corn on the Cob

Fresh corn in husks
Margarine or butter
Salt and pepper

Pull husks down 3 to 4 inches and remove the corn silks. Pull husks back up. Soak corn in icewater for 30 minutes. Place on the back of a grill (not directly over the coals). Grill over medium-hot grill 25 to 35 minutes, turning frequently. Serve corn hot either without the husks, or with husks peeled back to form a handle. Add salt, pepper, and butter to taste.

Lady Causey's Overnight Cabbage Slaw

(serves 8–10)

1   medium cabbage, shredded
1   small onion, grated
1   medium bell pepper, chopped
2   carrots, grated
$3/4$ cup sugar
$3/4$ cup vinegar
$1/2$ cup vegetable oil
1   teaspoon celery seed
1   teaspoon dry mustard
1   teaspoon salt
$1/8$ teaspoon black pepper

Combine cabbage, onion, green pepper, and carrots in a large bowl and sprinkle with sugar. Set aside. Combine remaining ingredients in a pot and boil 3 minutes. Pour over vegetables, stirring well. Chill overnight.

Gerri Elie's (Lolis' Mother's) Potato Salad

(serves 12)

8   medium-sized red potatoes
6   eggs
2   tablespoons finely minced onion
5   tablespoons finely minced green onion (tops and bottoms)
$1/4$ cup chopped green bell pepper
$1/4$ cup yellow Creole mustard
$1/2$ teaspoon cayenne pepper
$1 1/2$ teaspoons seasoned salt
1   teaspoon finely ground black or white pepper
1   cup mayonnaise
3   tablespoons lemon juice
2   tablespoons chopped fresh parsley
1   teaspoon paprika
12 large lettuce leaves

Peel potatoes and cut into quarters. Boil over medium heat until soft but not mushy. In a separate pot, hard-boil the eggs, starting in cool water to prevent breakage. Drain potatoes in a colander for about 2 minutes until all excess water has been removed, then place potatoes in a deep mixing bowl. Add mustard and cayenne pepper. Mix with a large fork, taking care not to mash. Refrigerate potatoes for about 20 minutes or until thoroughly cooled.

In a separate bowl, place chopped onion, bell pepper, 2 tablespoons of green onion, 2/3 cup mayonnaise, and half of the lemon juice. Peel and chop 5 of the hard-boiled eggs. Remove the potatoes from the refrigerator and chop with a knife into small cubes, then gradually stir in the mayonnaise mixture until thoroughly mixed. Add seasoned salt, pepper, and chopped eggs. Continue to stir, adding the remaining 1/3 cup mayonnaise and lemon juice.

Smooth the top of the salad with a spoon or spatula. Then slice the remaining egg and place as a garnish on top, along with chopped parsley and paprika. Serve on lettuce leaves.

Otis P. Boyd's Sweet Slaw

(serves 6–8)

1   large head cabbage, cored and shredded
2   medium carrots, shredded
1   medium green pepper, chopped
$1 1/2$ cups mayonnaise or salad dressing
3   tablespoons sugar
1   tablespoon vinegar

In a large bowl, toss together the cabbage, carrots, and green pepper. In another bowl, stir together the mayonnaise, sugar, and vinegar. Spoon the dressing over the cabbage mixture; toss. Store, covered, in the refrigerator.

Wood Brothers' Special Poppyseed Coleslaw

(serves 12–16)

2   heads green cabbage, cored and
    shredded fine
1   cup apple cider vinegar
½   cup granulated sugar
1   large carrot, peeled and shredded
½   cup poppyseeds
2   cups raw broccoli, coarsely chopped
2   cups raw cauliflower, coarsely chopped
1   cup cooked garbanzo beans
2   cups commercial coleslaw dressing
    Salt and ground white pepper to taste

Combine all ingredients and chill.

Lady Causey's Cornbread

1   cup yellow corn meal
½   cup vegetable oil
2   eggs, slightly beaten
3   teaspoons baking powder
½   teaspoon salt
1   tablespoon sugar
8   ounces sour cream
1   10-ounce package frozen cream-style
    corn, thawed

Preheat oven to 375 degrees. Mix all ingredients. Bake in a greased 9-inch-square pan at 375 degrees for 35 minutes.

Ray Robinson's Barbecued Cabbage

(serves 6–8)

1   large cabbage
    Salt, pepper, and/or seasoned salt
1   ¼-inch slice onion, diced
2   slices bacon or 1 tablespoon margarine

Core the cabbage, leaving a 3- or 4-inch cavity. Sprinkle the cavity with the salt and pepper or seasoned salt. Fill the cavity with onion. If using bacon, cut it into 1-inch pieces and place on top of the onion; otherwise place the margarine in the cavity. Double-wrap the cabbage in heavy-duty foil. Place it on the pit, being careful that the cabbage sits flat so that the ingredients will not spill out. Cook the cabbage over indirect heat for 2 or 3 hours or until soft.

Oklahoma Joe's Smoked Cabbage

(serves 6–8)

1   whole cabbage
    About 1 stick butter
2 or 3 chicken or beef bouillon cubes

Cut out the cavity of the cabbage until a hole 2 or 3 inches deep has been formed. Pack cavity with bouillon cubes and butter. Wrap cabbage in heavy-duty foil except for the top. Add butter as needed and cook for 4 to 5 hours at 225 degrees.

Kansas City Barbecue Factory Grilled Cabbage

(serves 6–8)

1   head cabbage
    Cream cheese
    Butter
    Garlic salt or a minced fresh clove of garlic
    Salt and pepper
    Grated romano and parmesan cheese

Core the cabbage, but not all the way through. Take cream cheese, butter, garlic salt or fresh garlic, salt and pepper, any favorite spices, and romano and parmesan cheese, and pack them into the cavity core of cabbage: layer of cream cheese, layer of butter, romano and parmesan, more cream cheese. (Can't mess it up.) Pack it in as tightly as possible. Wrap it in foil. Put it core side up, either directly on the coals in the pit, or on the grill. Sometimes the outside few layers scorch. Quarter the cabbage and serve.

Guy's Spuds

(serves 6–8)

6   medium russet potatoes (3 pounds)
3   tablespoons seasoned salt
¼   cup olive oil
    Buttermilk dressing

Rub potatoes and cut lengthwise into 1/2-inch-thick wedges. Place wedges in a large pan and sprinkle with oil and seasoned salt. Toss to coat well.

When a full bed of charcoal is white, put potatoes directly on the grill or on a perforated metal sheet that will keep them from falling through. Set about 4 to 6 inches above coals. (Put hood down quickly, as coals will spurt and possibly flame when hit by oil.) Cook about 40 minutes, turning with broad, long-handled spatula every 10 minutes until potatoes are browned and tender. Serve with buttermilk dressing for dipping.

Lady Causey's Pickled Pineapple

2   20-ounce cans unsweetened
      pineapple chunks
3/4 cup sugar
3/4 cup white vinegar
15   whole cloves
1   cinnamon stick, broken in half
      (more if desired)
1/8 teaspoon salt

Drain the pineapple chunks, reserving 1/2 cup plus 2 tablespoons of the juice. Place the chunks in a 1-quart jar. In a medium saucepan combine pineapple juice with remaining ingredients. Simmer 10 to 12 minutes, then pour over the pineapple chunks. When cool, cap jar and refrigerate 3 to 4 days. Keeps up to 8 weeks.

Mac's Sweet Potato Pie

(serves 6–8)

1   unbaked 9-inch deep-dish pie shell
2   eggs
2 to 4 sweet potatoes, peeled, boiled,
      and mashed to yield 2 cups
3/4 cup sugar
1/2 teaspoon salt
1   teaspoon cinnamon
1/2 teaspoon ginger
1   12-ounce can evaporated milk

Preheat oven to 425 degrees. Beat eggs lightly in a large bowl. Stir in remaining ingredients in order given. Pour into pie shell. Bake for 15 minutes at 425 degrees, then reduce temperature to 350 degrees. Bake for 40 to 50 minutes or until knife inserted in center comes out clean. Cool and serve.

Burrer's Peach Cobbler

(serves 8)

4 to 5 cups tree-ripened peaches
1/4 pound melted butter
1   cup flour
1 1/2 cups sugar
2   teaspoons baking powder
1/4 teaspoon salt
1   cup milk
      Cinnamon
      Ground nutmeg

Preheat oven to 350 degrees. Butter and flour a 9-by-13-inch glass casserole dish. Pour melted butter into the dish. In a saucepan, slowly cook the peaches with 1/2 cup sugar until soft. Add cinnamon and nutmeg to taste. Combine flour with remaining sugar, baking powder, and salt. Whisk in milk and pour mixture into pan over butter. Gently pour cooked peaches evenly over batter. Cook for 45 minutes or until golden brown.

Chuck's Smoke House Sweet Potato Pie

1   pound sweet potatoes (2 to 3 potatoes)
1   ounce lemon juice
2   tablespoons vanilla
1/2 pound butter
      Pinch of nutmeg
2   eggs
1   teaspon baking powder
1   cup sugar
4   ounces evaporated milk
1   tablespoon flour
1   9-inch pie shell

Preheat oven to 425 degrees. Peel the sweet potatoes, boil them until soft, and mash them. Add the other ingredients, mix well, and place in the pie crust. Bake for 10 minutes at 425 degrees and an additional 30 or 40 minutes at 350 degrees.

Mattie Bivens Dennis' Pecan Pie

1   9-inch unbaked pie shell (not deep dish)
3   eggs
1   cup light corn syrup
2   tablespoons margarine or butter
1   teaspoon vanilla
1   cup pecan halves broken in half
1/2 cup sugar

Preheat oven to 425 degrees. Beat eggs until light. Add sugar gradually. Add corn syrup, melted margarine or butter, vanilla, and pecans. Pour mixture into pie shell. Bake at 425 degrees for 10 minutes, then reduce heat to 325 degrees and continue cooking for 30 minutes or until tip of an inserted steak knife comes out clean.

Dancers 19TH OF JUNE CELEBRATION **MEXIA, TEXAS**

The Places

Alabama

**Dreamland Drive-Inn
Barbeque Inc.**
5535 15th Avenue East
(Jug Factory Road)
Tuscaloosa, AL 35405
(205) 758-8135
MON–FRI 10 A.M.–10 P.M.
SAT 10 A.M.–Midnight
SUN 11A.M.–9 P.M.

Arkansas

Walker's Bar-B-Que Company
5107 Warden Road
North Little Rock, AR 72116
(501) 758-3145
MON–SAT 11 A.M.–9 P.M.
Closed SUN

Illinois

The Rib Joint
432 East 87th Street
Chicago, IL 60619
(773) 651-4108
MON–THU 12–2 P.M.
FRI & SAT 11 A.M.–3 P.M.
SUN 2:30 P.M.–Midnight

Lem's BBQ House
311 East 75th Street
Chicago, IL 60619
(773) 994-2428
FRI & SAT 2 P.M.–4 A.M.
SUN–THU 2 P.M.–2 A.M.
Closed TUES

Kenny's Ribs and Pizza
8601 South Stoney Island
Chicago, IL 60617
(773) 221-6466
MON–THU 11–Midnight
FRI & SAT 11–2 A.M.
SUN 1–10 P.M.

Kansas/Missouri

Arthur Bryant's Barbeque
1727 Brooklyn Avenue
Kansas City, MO 64127
(816) 231-1123
MON–THU 10 A.M.–9:30 P.M.
FRI & SAT 10 A.M.–10 P.M.
SUN 11 A.M.–8:30 P.M.
(When the Chiefs are in town,
10 A.M.–8:30 P.M.)

Gates & Son's Bar-B-Q
4621 Paseo
Kansas City, MO 64110
(816) 923-0900
MON–FRI 8:30 A.M.–5:30 P.M.
Hours vary at other locations

Rosedale Barbeque
600 Southwest Boulevard
Kansas City, KS 64152
(913) 262-0343
MON–THU 10 A.M.–9 P.M.
FRI & SAT 10 A.M.–10 P.M.
SUN 11A.M.–8 P.M.

Kentucky

Moonlite Bar-B-Q Inn
2840 West Parrish Avenue
Owensboro, KY 42301
(270) 684-8143
MON–THU 9 A.M.–9 P.M.
FRI & SAT 9 A.M.–9:30 P.M.
SUN 10 A.M.–2:30 P.M.
Call for buffet times
www.moonlite.com

Oklahoma

Mac's B-B-Q
1030 West Rogers Boulevard
Skiatook, OK 74070
(918) 396-4165
MON–SAT 11 A.M.–8 P.M.
Closed SUN

Tennessee

Cozy Corner
Raymond Robinson, Sr.
745 North Parkway
Memphis, TN 38105
(901) 527-9158
TUE–SAT 10:30 A.M.–5 P.M.
Closed SUN & MON

The Rendezvous
Chalie Vergos
52 South Second Street
(General Washburn Alley)
Memphis, TN 38103
(901) 523-2746
TUE–THU 4:30 P.M.–11:30 P.M.
FRI 11:30 A.M.–11:30 P.M.
SAT 11 A.M.–Midnight
Closed SUN & MON

Texas

Bob's Smokehouse
Bob and Billie Wells
3306 Roland Road
San Antonio, TX 78210
(210) 333-9611
DAILY 10:30 A.M.–8 P.M.

Black's Barbeque
Edgar Black
215 N. Main
Two Blocks Off Highway 183
P.O. Box 509
Lockhart, TX 78644
(512) 398-2712
DAILY 10 A.M.–8 P.M.
www.blacksbbq.com

Sonny Bryan's Smokehouse
Charlie Riddle, Manager
2202 Inwood
Dallas, TX 75235
(214) 357-7120
MON–FRI 10 A.M.–4 P.M.
SAT 10 A.M.–3 P.M.
Closed SUN
www.sonnybryansbbq.com

City Market
633 E. Davis Street
Luling, TX 78648
(830) 875-9019
MON–SAT 7 A.M.–6 P.M.
Closed SUN

Cooper's Old Time Pit Bar-B-Que Restaurant
604 West Young
(Highway 29 West)
Llano, TX 78643
(325) 247-5713
MON–THU 10:30 A.M.–7 P.M.
FRI–SUN 10:30 A.M.–8 P.M.
www.coopersbbq.com

Ken Hall's Barbeque Place
87 E E Highway
St. Fredricksburg, TX 78624
(830) 997-2353
MON–THU 11 A.M.–4 P.M.
FRI & SAT 11 A.M.–7:30 P.M.
SUN 11 A.M.–3 P.M.

Hinze's Bar-B-Que
3940 Highway 59 Loop N
Wharton, TX 77488
(979) 532-2710
DAILY 10 A.M.–10 P.M.

Hinze's Bar-B-Que
2101 Highway 36 South
Sealy, TX 77474
(979) 885.7808
SUN–THU Breakfast 5 A.M.–
    11 a.m.
Barbecue 10:30 A.M.–9 P.M.
FRI & SAT Barbeque 10:30 A.M.–
    10 P.M.

Kirby's Barbeque
216 N. Highway 14
Mexia, TX 76667
(254) 562-5076
TUE–SAT 10 A.M.–6 P.M.
Closed SUN & MON

Kreutz Market
619 N. Colorado
Lockhart, TX 78644
(512) 398-2361
MON–FRI 9 A.M.–6 P.M.
SAT 9 A.M.–6:30 P.M.
Closed SUN

Luling Bar-B-Q
709 East Davis Street
Luling, TX 78648
(830) 875-3848
MON 9:30 A.M.–6 P.M.
Closed TUE
WED & THU 9:30 A.M.–6 P.M.
FRI–SUN 9:30 A.M.–7 P.M.

New Zion Missionary Baptist Church
2601 Montgomery Road
Huntsville, TX 77340
(936) 295-2349
TUE 10:30 A.M.–5 P.M.
WED–SAT 10:30 A.M.–7 P.M.
Closed SUN & MON

Pardi's at Brick's
504 East Main
Fredericksburg, TX 78624
(830) 997-4301
DAILY 5 A.M.–2 P.M.

Southside Market & BBQ Inc.
1212 Highway 290 East
Elgin, TX 78621
(512) 285-3407
(877) 487-8015
MON–THU 8 A.M.–8 P.M.
FRI & SAT 8 A.M.–10 P.M.
SUN 9 A.M.–7 P.M.
www.sausage.cc

Vera's Backyard Bar-B-Que
2404 Southmost Road
Brownsville, TX 78520
(956) 546-4159
MON–SAT 11 A.M.–11 P.M.
SUN 5:30 A.M.–12 P.M.

Pit Boss NEW ZION MISSIONARY BAPTIST CHURCH HUNTSVILLE, TEXAS

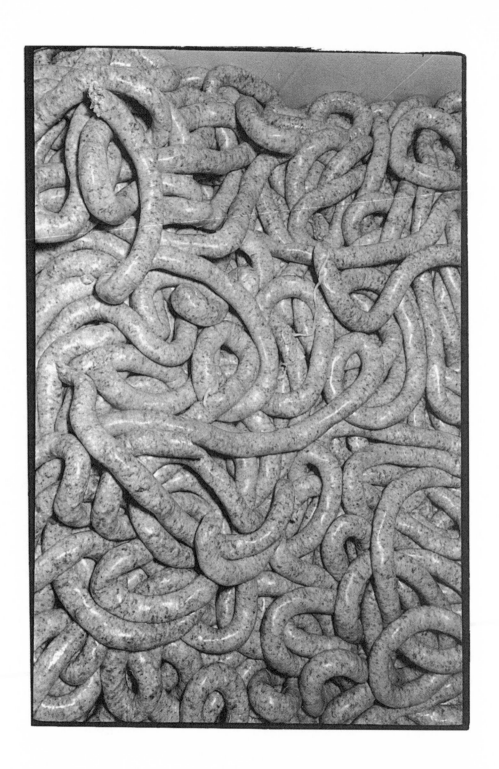

The Sources

The Guides

As we were traveling, we relied on several guidebooks for starting points in deciding where to go and what to eat. The most outstanding of these is Greg Johnson and Vince Staten's *Real Barbecue* (New York: Harper & Row, 1988). It's national and, as its cover indicates, is "a guide to the best joints, the best sauces, the best cookers—and much more." There are also some more local guidebooks: James W. Latimer's *The Pits of Middle Texas* (Lubbock, TX: L'Adrienne Press, 1993); Remus Powers' *Kansas City BBQ Pocket Guide* (Kansas City, MO: Pig Out Publications, 1992); and Allie Patricia Wall and Ron L. Layne's *Hog Heaven: A Guide to South Carolina Barbecue* (Lexington, SC: Sandlapper Store, 1979). And finally there are two videos on barbecue places done by Great Chefs Television and Publishing (New Orleans).

The Scholarly Works

Food culture is an increasingly popular area for scholarly research, and the study of barbecue has grown accordingly. I discovered enough papers written on the subject to become convinced that there are many others available. The ones I found most helpful are the following:

Adler, Thomas A. "Making Pancakes on Sunday: The Male Cook in Family Tradition." *Western Folklore*, vol. 40 (1981). California Folklore Society, Los Angeles.

Brandau, Rosemary. "Early Fair Foods and Barbecuing." August 1984. Colonial Williamsburg files, Williamsburg, VA.

Ezell, Johanna. "The Joys of Cooking: Sex Stereotyping Among the Pots and Pans." *Studies in Popular Culture*, vol. 8, no. 1 (1985). Popular Culture Association of the South, Tallahasee, FL.

Golovin, Ripley. "In Xanadu Did Barbecue ...: A Historical Examination of the Evolution of an American Institution, the Backyard Barbecue, a Product of Our Changing Culture." Senior Project, Vassar College, February 1981.

Hall, Robert L. "Savoring Africa in the New World." In Herman J. Viola and Carolyn Margolis, eds., *Seeds of Change: 500 Years Since Columbus*. Washington, DC: Smithsonian Institution, 1991.

Montano, Mario. "The History of Mexican Folk Foodways of South Texas: Street Vendors, Offal Foods, and Barbacoa de Cabeza." Ph.D. dissertation, University of Pennsylvania, Folklore and Folklife Department, 1992.

Shweder, Richard A. *"Why Do Men Barbecue?" and Other Postmodern Ironies of Growing Up in the Decade of Ethnicity*. Cambridge, MA: Dædelus, 1993.

Smith, Steve. "The Rhetoric of Barbecue: A Southern Rite and Ritual." Studies in Popular Culture, vol. 8, no. 1 (1985). Popular Culture Association of the South, Tallahasee, FL.

The Newsletters

Many barbecue societies have sprung up in this country. Their newsletters are good guides to competitions and good sources of other information on barbecue trends.

Barbecue Today, official publication of the National Barbecue Association (P.O. Box 29051, Charlotte, NC 28229)

Drippings from the Pit, published quarterly by the Pacific Northwest Barbecue Association (4244 134th Ave. S.E., Bellevue, WA 98006)

The K.C. Bullsheet, published by the Kansas City Barbecue Society (11514 Hickman Mill Dr., Kansas City, MO 64134)

National Barbecue News (P.O. Box 981, Douglas, GA 3133)

The Pits (7714 Hillard, Dallas, TX 75217)

General Books

Baker, T. Lindsay. *The First Polish Americans: Silesian Settlements in Texas*. College Station, TX: Texas A&M University Press, 1979.

Beard, James. *Cook It Outdoors*. New York: M. Barrows, 1941.

Bolt, Richard. *Forty Years Behind the Lid: Chuck Wagon Grub*. Guthrie, TX: Richard Bolt, 1974.

Davis, Fred. *Yearning for Yesterday*. New York: Free Press, 1979.

Duke, Cordia Sloan, and Joe B. Frantz. *6,000 Miles of Fence: Life on the XIT Ranch of Texas*. Austin, TX: University of Texas Press, 1961.

Garreau, Joel. *The Nine Nations of North America*. New York: Avon, 1992.

Haley, J. Evetts. *The XIT Ranch of Texas and the Early Days of the Llano Estacado*. Norman, OK: University of Oklahoma Press, 1977.

Hess, Karen and John L. *The Taste of America*. New York: Grossman, 1977.

Jordan, Terry G. *Trails to Texas: Southern Roots of Western Cattle Ranching*. Lincoln, NE: University of Nebraska Press, 1981.

The Kansas City Barbecue Society. *The Passion of Barbecue*. Kansas City, MO: Pig Out Publications, 1989.

Linck, Ernestine Sewell, and Joyce Gibson Roach. *Eats: A Folk History of Texas Foods*. Fort Worth, TX: Texas Christian University Press, 1989.

Morgan, Ted. *On Becoming American*. New York: Tesoro Books, 1988.

Murray, Albert. *Stomping Blues*. New York: Da Capo Press, 1989.

——. *The Omni-Americans: Black Experience & American Culture*. New York: Da Capo Press, 1990.

Reeves, Dona B., and Glen E. Lich, eds. *German Culture in Texas*. New York: Twayne, 1980.

Senderens, Alain. *The Table Beckons: Thoughts and Recipes from the Kitchen of Alain Senderens*. New York: Farrar, Straus and Giroux, 1993.

Skrabanek, R. L. *We're Czechs*. College Station, TX: Texas A&M University Press, 1988.

Sokolov, Raymond. *Why We Eat What We Eat: How the Encounter Between the New World and the Old Changed the Way Everyone on the Planet Eats*. New York: Summit Books, 1991.

Stein, Shifra, and Rich Davis. *All About Bar-B-Q Kansas City Style*. Kansas City, MO: Barbacoa Press, 1985.

Wells, Carolyn. *Barbecue Greats Memphis Style: Great Restaurants, Great Recipes, Great Personalities*. Kansas City, MO: Pig Out Publications, 1989.

Chellis with Frogs **MARINGOUIN, LOUISIANA**

Acknowledgments

A lot of people helped make this book possible. Some let us sleep on their floors. Others read the manuscript. Some sent research materials. Some fed us vegetables. Others were just generally helpful. For all these things, we'd like to thank them.

Roy Acklin, John Baeder, Billy Banks, Nelson Breen, Diane Caesar, Margaret M. Charles, Carol Clarke, Stanley Crouch, Charles Crump, Chellis Crump, Eloris Crump, Deborah and Curtis Davenport, Jeffrey Day, Jordan and Terri Dayan, Tom Dent, Elie, Jones & Gray, Max Feaman, Rob Gibson, David Goldberg, Jeffrey Goldberg, Mike Goodwin, Lee Green, Lisa Green, Sally Helgesen, Charles M. Henderson, Jr., the Hills family, Hilary Hinzmann, Murray Horwitz, Toni Irving, Halvern and Catherine Johnson, Mary Allen Johnson, Rodney Johnson, Marvin and Marcus Jones, the Kansas City Barbecue Society (Gary, Carolyn, Bunny, Sonia), Richard Kaplan, Eugene Kidd, David Kindig, Halili Knox, Ed and Yvette Lewis, Rudy Lombard, the Management Ark (Ed, Vernon, Leslie, Larry), Wynton Marsalis, Valerie Matthews, Charles Mazique, Jr. and Sr., Ed McDonald, Colleen McMillar, Mario Montano, Albert Murray, Bettina Owens, Michael Pagan, Adrian and Hasmukh and Pratima Patel, Donald Payton, Edwin "Beau" and Darryl Phillips, Jennifer Reed, Langton D. Reed, Cynthia Reilly, Robert D. Richardson, John W. Roberts, John Robertson, David Robinson, Robert Sengstacke, Don Shanche, Johnny Simmons, Allan Smith, Marcus and Marvin Smith, Michael Smith, Dorothy Stewart, Mark and Peggy Stewart, Susanne and Michael Thais, Major Thomas, Viola Tucker, Carl Vigeland, Perry and Mary Moon Walker, Jerry Ward, Orson Watson, David Weatherly, Joseph and Louie West, Tom Whalen, Vincent and Dottie Wilburn, Neal Willis, Lisa Wrice.

We'd like to extend special thanks to Richard Derus, Elisabeth Kallick Dyssegaard, Joan Mathieu, Claudia Menza, and Denise Oswald.

This book was designed by Jilly Simons and David Shields at Concrete, Chicago. The primary text was set in Berthold Clarendon BQ (light, heavy, bold and black) and Berthold Caslon Buch BQ (regular, italic) on an Apple Power Macintosh 7100/66. This book was printed in the United States of America.